Paths Less Traveled

In the Great Smoky Mountains

By Greg Hoover

ISBN-13: 978-1540483621

ISBN-10: 1540483622

He talked to me about all sorts of things: fitting in, and getting lost, and how to find peace in a world so filled with chaos, and whether it's okay to keep magic places secret when so many people need magic.

From "The Last Best Place" by Eddie Oglander
Backpacker Magazine, November, 2010

I took the one less traveled by,
and that has made all the difference.

From "The Road Not Taken"
by Robert Frost

Somebody left the gate open....

From the song "Into the Wild" by LP

Contents

Preface: Bearways   1

Another Preface: The 900 Mile Club   3

Introduction: In the Beginning 5

Chapter 1: Keepers of the Secret.   17

Chapter 2: The Saddest Spot in the Smokies   .   .   . 36

Chapter 3: Don't Do It! 46

Chapter 4: The Hunt for Drinkwater Pool   .   .   . 61

Chapter 5: Place of the Balsams 81

Chapter 6: A Gorge, A Ranger, and Raven Fork .   .   . 95

Chapter 7: Friends in High Places   109

Chapter 8: The Land of Sharp Edges   124

Chapter 9: Cat Stairs, Falcon Cliffs, and Snake Dens   .   . 141

Chapter 10: The Three Sisters   159

Chapter 11: A Road Runs Through It   185

Chapter 12: Alone on the Chimneys   198

Chapter 13: The Simple Gifts of Styx Branch   .   .   . 211

Epilogue: More Stuff You Might Want to Know .   .   . 223

vi

Preface

Bearways

The title of this book is a bit of an exaggeration, if not an outright lie. Most of the places described in these chapters don't have trails, they don't have paths, and they don't even have "manways." At most, they have "bearways" — scant traces that have been created by animals, not people. Maybe coyotes, but I prefer to believe bears because they have a certain romance that coyotes lack. While a single bear can create a traffic jam of urban proportions, some folks will swerve to hit a coyote.

In another book, I've written about trails and hikes and fishing trips. To be sure, there have been some long, hard hikes and some exciting moments, but there's something I've been keeping quiet about – off-trail hiking (or, "bushwhacking" – but we get whacked by the bushes more than they get whacked by us). These off-trail trips have taken us to some lonely, wild, beautiful places. These are places that only about a dozen people visit in a typical year. There are a few places that no one visits – let that sink in: *no one* – except the two or three of us that have "discovered" them and return to them annually, places like The Best Lunch Spot or the Roman Column or the Fern Garden. Every group of off-trailers has its own, obscure spots with unique names that only they know, because they are the ones who named them. Sometimes these names catch on and persist for years; others die with their authors.

There are just a few avid off-trailers in the Smokies, and I think I've crossed paths with most of them at one time or another; although, we do tend to form our own little cliques and to avoid each other, so there may be more out there than I realize. There was a time when I saw these others as competitors who had no right to explore "my" rivers and ridges, and they probably felt the same way about us, but I've lightened up since then, mainly because there are so few of us that it's simply not worth getting indignant over, but also because I've met many of them, and they are good, easy-going folks who love the same things I do. So I

1

now see these other cliques as kindred spirits who have discovered the same wilderness wonderland that my friends and I have. We're just one big, happy family, but an extended family that rarely sees each other.

These chapters describe my favorite places in the park – places where you are more likely to see falcons and bears (and snakes) than humans. These stories provide enough information to enable the motivated hiker to figure out where we were and how we got there, but I haven't provided excessive details about elevations and GPS coordinates, so there will, I hope, be an element of mystery as you read these stories. If you are so inclined, you could replicate most of these trips simply by paying attention while you read. Or, there's always Google or GoSmokies.

Of course, to keep the lawyers at bay, here's the disclaimer: some of these trips can be dangerous. Don't overestimate your own capabilities, and never do these trips by yourself. In the beginning, go with someone who's done these kinds of off-trail trips before; the Smoky Mountains Hiking Club would be a good start. Learn how to read a topo map and to use a compass. A GPS is a good Plan B when Plan A fails. In other words, do your homework before you ever try an off-trail trip, no matter how easy it may appear. The best way to handle an emergency is to not have one, and the best way to not have one is to be well prepared. By the way, unlike many disclaimers, all that stuff is true. By the way again, you probably won't ever see this book in an official NPS bookstore because they don't want you to know about these places and to venture out to look for them. Search & Rescues can be annoying for everyone concerned. I imagine they are also expensive.

Even if you never try any of these off-trail trips, I hope you can enjoy them with me vicariously, in the quiet and comfort of your favorite reading chair or perhaps sitting on a rock by a musical river. The chapters which follow are, after all, stories to be read and enjoyed more than they are detailed descriptions of hikes to be taken.

No matter how you choose to use this book – as a source of information for your own adventures or as a way to pass the time during those long, dark months of winter – I hope and pray that you'll gain some joy and insight from our time together.

Another Preface
The 900 Mile Club

In the Smoky Mountains there are over 800 miles of officially designated trails, so if you ever encounter someone who is in the *900 Mile Club*, they've hiked all of these trails plus the extra miles involved in the various loops and backtracking required to get to them. I'm not a member and don't expect to ever become one because I'm just not a goal-oriented type of person. If a trail appeals to me for some reason (history, vistas, convenience, adventure), then I'll hike it. Otherwise, I might never get around to it. (I'll probably never hike the trail from Gatlinburg to the Sugarlands Visitor Center. It's not my type.) On the other hand, I might hike all 800 miles simply because I have a congenital case of wanderlust. So if I ever finish all 800 miles, it will be more by accident than intent; which, now that I think about it, is how much of my life has unfolded. People like me were put on the earth to balance out those Type A folks who live and die by goals and deadlines. They are the ones who get things done, but they die young from heart attacks. People like me probably live longer but accomplish less. (Having entered my 60s, it's now mathematically impossible for me to die young, which is the silver lining on the cloud of old age.) Our obituaries will be short and easy to write because when we pass on, there's just not much to say except "good bye."

These 800+ miles of trails are well-documented and easy to follow. There are maps and books that describe them in meticulous detail. There are almost always other people on the trails, so you can ask for directions when necessary. There are even quaint, wooden signs at all the trail intersections to make sure you don't make a wrong turn. I'm tempted to say it's impossible to get lost on these well-worn trails, but people occasionally do, so apparently it is possible – mostly, I suppose, by folks who don' t bother with maps and books and planning.

3

I don't recall ever having committed any significant acts of theft, but if I ever do, it will be one of those wooden trail signs. I've seen some of these signs so often that I've formed an emotional attachment to them. I've spoken with other folks who have similar feelings, so I think the NPS could make some money by auctioning off these old, wooden trail signs to the highest bidder. If I had the money, I'd bid recklessly on a well-weathered sign from Mount Le Conte or the AT.

I won't go so far as to say that setting hiking goals contradicts the zeitgeist of hiking, but I do wonder...

I once heard a guy who was chasing that 900 mile goal say that he'd done all the trails up to Le Conte except the Boulevard. He was a bit miffed because to hike the Boulevard, he'd have to re-hike about three miles of the AT from Newfound Gap to the Boulevard. That struck me as sad, and it also reconfirmed my commitment to a goal-free lifestyle. It's the kind of philosophy of life that pretty much guarantees I'll never get rich, but it also means that I'll never be bummed out about having to hike an "extra" three miles on the most famous, hallowed trail in the US. Granted, those particular three miles can be a bit crowded at times and are very well-worn, but it's the AT for cryin' out loud! How can you possibly be frustrated with "having to" hike on the AT, no matter how many times you've already done it? That's the danger with setting goals, especially about something you love. The goals can take on a life of their own and can drain the joy out of an otherwise pleasant experience.

By the way, the guy ended his comments about hiking to Le Conte by saying that once he did the Boulevard he'd be – and I quote – "finished with Le Conte." He probably didn't mean it the way it sounded, but I still think there was some sort of dark, twisted truth lurking beneath the surface. A true lover of the Smokies can never be "finished with Le Conte," and that guy should have known better than to say it. Or, as soon as he uttered those words, he should have immediately back-peddled and tried to explain himself. But he didn't apologize, blush, or try to explain. In fact, he didn't even realize the blasphemy he had spoken. I now think of him as another lost soul who's toiling under the burden of the Law instead of basking in the Grace and Freedom of hiking because you *want* to, not because you *have* to.

4

Introduction

In the Beginning

For my little group of off-trailing partners, it all began with a passing reference about Mill Creek Cascade by Carlos Campbell. There apparently used to be a trail to it, but not now and not in 1967 when he wrote about it in *Memories of Old Smoky*. Although I am pretty well acquainted with the Great Smoky Mountains National Park, I'd never heard of this waterfall before. In fact, I'm embarrassed to say that I'd never given much thought to the fact that there might be some decent waterfalls and peaks around the park that *didn't* have official trails going to them. I had assumed – without realizing that I was assuming anything at all – that if there was a dramatic or pleasant spot in the Smokies, there was a trail to take you there. This reference by Campbell was the first crack in that wall.

I next read *Out Under the Sky of the Great Smokies* by Harvey Broome and found that his hikes were frequently to places that I'd never heard of. I wondered why he kept hiking to places like Woolly Tops or Drinkwater Pool or Mount Winnesoka. Why all those obscure locations?

Then it occurred to me that perhaps these locations weren't so obscure back in the early days of the park. Broome and Campbell both lived in the Knoxville area and spent a great deal of their outdoor time in the northeast portion of the park. These obscure locations were their backyard, and they explored it frequently and got to know it intimately. If the CCC and the NPS chose not to build trails to these places, that didn't mean these places were unworthy of being visited. It simply meant that for some reason, men in offices in Gatlinburg and in Washington, DC, had decided that a trail would be built to site Y but not to site X. I began to understand that there were a lot of X's out there, and if we'd read the writings of men and women from the 1930s and 40s, we'd learn where some of these X's were.

5

One thing led to another, and before long I found myself looking for that old 1973 Sierra Club *Hiker's Guide* that used to be my Smokies Bible, but had been replaced by the more recent *Hiking Trails of the Smokies* published by the Great Smoky Mountains Association. I wondered if a thirty-five year old hiking guide might have descriptions of a few trails that had been decommissioned by the NPS. Yes, it did – Raven Fork, Porters Creek to Dry Sluice Gap, Greenbrier Pinnacle. I also discovered that the 1949 map of the Smokies that hangs on my wall had a few small, dashed lines that didn't appear on recent trail maps. Then I found the October, 1952 issue of *National Geographic* and its reference to Three Forks Pool, another place I'd never heard of.

This was starting to feel like a treasure hunt. I was uncovering clues about a parallel universe or a secret kingdom that our forbearers had known about, but the secret had been somehow misplaced. Nicholas Cage could play me when the movie is finally made. They could call it something like, I don't know, maybe *National Treasure*.

As I began to explore a few of the manifestations of this secret kingdom, I got spoiled. These places were beautiful, uncrowded, and untouched. My hiking partner and I were always alone – dirty, scratched, and bruised, but alone. I could get used to this.

As I became acquainted with these old, forgotten places, I also became acquainted with a previous generation of hikers – Harvey & Anne Broome, Carlos Campbell, Dutch Roth, Guy Frizzell – that I've come to admire as a unique breed who were tougher than us 21st century sissies. I've occasionally tried to retrace some of their paths on day hikes, and let me assure you, the going is tough. Rhododendron branches, briers, blowdowns, wet river crossings. After I've made it through these barriers and found respite at a trail or campsite, I pause to remember that I'm carrying a sleek, lightweight daypack. Harvey, Anne, and all the rest carried full-blown, heavy, canvas backpacks. They were a special breed of hikers, a vanished species. Old school.

For instance, in the summer of 1932 nine members of the Smoky Mountains Hiking Club of Knoxville became the first to hike along the ridgecrest from one end of the Smokies to the other. This was the route of the Appalachian Trail; although, it would probably be more accurate

6

to speak of the Appalachian "Trail" – the quote marks indicating that the AT through the Smokies was, in 1932, nothing more than a good idea.

The eastern end of the park was a mix of worn trail, no trail, underbrush and briers, downed trees, open fields from clear-cut logging, and burned over areas from forest fires. Carlos Campbell described it this way in *Memories of Old Smoky*.

"We soon were fighting our way laboriously through a maze of rhododendron and laurel, with a few saw briers interspersed for good measure.... It was slow travel no matter where we went, and very rough. Our packs were continually hanging on the underbrush, as was our clothing.... [Eventually we] were out of the maze of underbrush and out into an open area caused by the lumberman's ax, and the fire that had followed... only the charred remains of trees over which we were forced to climb, or go around. This was on the North Carolina side, so we tried to use the virgin forests on the Tennessee side but soon found the slope too steep for good hiking, and the undergrowth too thick" (p. 22-23).

If you've done any off-trail hiking, you know how slow and hard – even stressful – this trail-less, cluttered terrain can be. Pushing your way through a rhododendron and mountain laurel thicket is like trying to push your way through a brick wall, looking for a crack in the mortar joints to squeeze through. Climbing over downed trees is like climbing or hopping over a fence, over and over and over again, or occasionally crawling under the fence. Sometimes it's easier to just walk on the logs like a series of criss-crossed beams. *Slippery* beams because the bark has peeled away exposing the slick, inner wood. The fact that their first two or three days were like this would have been disheartening. It's a hard way to begin a week-long hike.

And then there are the backpacks.... When I backpack it's rare for me to carry more than 35 pounds, maybe 40 for a long trip. Their packs were 60 pounds. Yes, sixty. I have no idea how they carried 60 pounds. No idea whatsoever. Maybe it was because that was 1932, when men were real men. You know, The Greatest Generation: they survived the

7

Great Depression, they won World War Two, they carried Sixty Pound Backpacks.

One reason their packs were so heavy was their need to carry liquids because there was not much water on the ridgecrest. Today we have guidebooks and trail signs that point us to small springs near the trail. In 1932 the eastern end of the crest between Mount Cammerer (still called White Rock by Tennesseans in 1932) and Mount Guyot was still a mystery. Sure, lumbermen, hikers, and herders had wandered these higher elevations, but the specific details of springs and campsites had not been recorded for others to read. In fact, they ran out of water several times and had to wait while one of their group (probably the guy who drew the short straw, I would guess) would take their canteens and a canvas water bag down the side of the mountain until he found a spring. Then, of course, he'd have to hike back up carrying thirty or forty pounds of water.

Consequently, these guys broke one of the cardinal rules of today's backpackers: they carried liquids with them. To supplement their meager water supply they carried canned goods with plenty of liquids. Today that's the one thing you *don't* carry with you. All your food is dry and light. If you want vegetables, you carry dried vegetables and cook them in water that you get from the spring near your campsite, which you learned about from your trail book. You carry just enough drinking water to get you to the next spring, the location of which is thoroughly described in your trail guide. And, your campsite – rock and wood shelters so you don't need to carry a tent – is located where it is because there is a source of water nearby. Those predetermined campsites and shelters didn't exist in 1932. It was these hikers in the 1930s that were beginning to figure out where reliable water sources were and where the shelters should be.

Another problem they encountered was staying on the ridgecrest. Believe it or not, without a well-marked, well-worn trail, it's possible to get lost on the main ridgecrest of the Smokies. Occasional side ridges intersect with the main crest, and there are places where it is not entirely obvious where the main crest goes. The twists and turns of the main crest can be confusing, a confusion amplified by the intersecting side ridges. In 1932 there were portions of the AT that were vague, and these

8

nine hikers occasionally found themselves off course on a side ridge in North Carolina or Tennessee. It took them five and a half days to reach Newfound Gap, the approximate halfway point. That's roughly 30 miles in about 60 hours of hiking, which is half a mile an hour, an excruciatingly slow pace by today's standards. I'm a slow hiker, and on my slowest day with a backpack on my back, I expect to travel (including rest and scenery stops) *at least* one mile per hour. That may not seem like a big difference, but it's the difference between walking six miles by 2 pm versus 8 pm. Today, even I could hike the eastern half of the Smokies in two long days or three easy days, not five and a half. The difference is that today I have a well-marked, well-described, well-worn trail, making the hike almost easy by comparison.

While the eastern half of the Smokies was largely untamed in 1932, the western half of the Smokies was semi-civilized. They had seen no one else in their first five and a half days in the eastern half. In the western half of the park, they saw several day hikers and forest rangers. In fact, they ran out of food on their eighth day but were able to buy some food from a cattle herder named Fondes Cable who was living in a small cabin near Russell Field on the ridgecrest. Yes, in 1932 there were still people living in what would soon (1934) become Great Smoky Mountains National Park.

Obviously, that Greatest Generation of hikers was a hardy breed, willing and able to put up with a great deal of inconvenience. Many of their descriptions of their hikes involved crawling over downed trees, through shrubs and brush, over boulders, and up rock faces. It was a very different experience from our hikes today in which we have maintained trails with names and written descriptions in trail guides that we can carry with us on our hikes. To tell you the truth, reading their simple descriptions of their hikes and their simple equipment makes me feel like a sissy. There was actually a time when hikers did this on a regular basis, with more primitive equipment. It was simply the way things were.

Those of us who hike only on the maintained trails of the Smokies today have no idea of the difficulties involved in hiking in the early days of the park. I love the wilderness, so I hate what I'm about to say: compared to 1932, hiking in the Smokies today is civilized; yes, *civilized.* Even if you see no one else on your hike, you see a well-worn trail and signs to direct you. We have guidebooks to tell us where to turn, where to get water, where to sleep. It is these conveniences that enable us to meditate and relax while we hike, to "commune with nature," as we say. Those hikers in 1932 couldn't afford that sort of luxury because it's impossible to commune with Nature when she's trying to kill you. All you can do is defend yourself. Hikers in the pre-park days were busy crawling over blowdowns and through (and under and over) rhododendron thickets. They were preoccupied with finding water and a level place to sleep. They often had to blaze their own routes because back then much of their hiking was off-trail hiking. Of course, they didn't call it "off-trail hiking." They just called it "hiking." "Off trail" and "hiking" would be redundant because they were often the same thing.

I love the Appalachian Trail. I especially love those seventy miles in the Smokies. I enjoy the other trails in the park: Boulevard, Alum Cave, Bone Valley, Welch Ridge. The list could go on and on. But I've also grown to love the creeks and ridges where there are no trails, or there used to be trails, or there are still the remnants of old, decommissioned trails. I've discovered that hiking off the established trails is a very, very different experience than hiking on a trail. It's more than just "harder." It's a different world. Stepping off the trail is like stepping into the wardrobe that leads to Narnia. You really do see an entirely different world when you get off the trail. You notice things because you have to notice them. You have to pay attention to where you are going or not going or ought to be going or ought not to be going. You think more. You even worry more; worry about time and pace and injury and barriers and getting lost. Off trail hiking is just so... uncivilized. Refreshingly uncivilized.

Ironically, the Smokies are closer to pure wilderness today than in 1932, but it's a wilderness punctuated with outposts of civilization – parking lots, bathrooms, campgrounds, roads. And well-established, well-maintained trails with trailheads (aka parking lots) that are easy to get to, so we can do quick day hikes to destinations that would take several days to reach in 1932. Back then the Smokies were almost entirely corn fields, gardens, cabins, pasture land, and logged (often clear-cut, sometimes burned) forests. Only 25% of the park managed to escape the logger's saw, but even in those unlogged portions, families lived, grew corn, raised livestock, built houses and churches and even a few hotels and vacation cabins.

Two years after that 1932 hike, the young men of the Civilian Conservation Corps descended en masse upon the Smokies to construct buildings and roads, plant trees, clear campgrounds, and build trails. Yes, *build* trails; dirt has to be leveled, rocks broken and moved, culverts buried, log footbridges hewn, and limbs trimmed. (Even today there are volunteers from the local area who *maintain* the trails in the park by trimming branches.) But in 1932 that was all yet to be. The mountains were rough and only partially mapped. Gatlinburg and Pigeon Forge were still tiny mountain villages. In 1932 things were different. Life was harder. The hikes were harder, and the hikers were tougher. Yes, you can still get a sense of what they experienced, but first you have to step off the trail.

The National Park Service discourages off-trail and old-trail hiking in the Smokies. Rescuing people from the backcountry is expensive and time-consuming, and occasionally tragic, so it's understandable that their official position is that we should all stay on the roads and trails. And 99% of the time, that's exactly the right policy. Most people should stay in plain sight, for their own good. But what about that other one percent?

If you'll talk to rangers and the folks in the Backcountry Office on an informal, one-on-one basis, you'll occasionally get a story that's different from the standard roads-and-trails line, a story that's designed for that 1%. But in order to get to that 1% level, you have to prove that you are worthy of the ranger's confidence. And to do that, you have to present yourself in the proper manner, one that conveys knowledge and experience.

First of all, you have to dress for success. If you are wearing flip flops and a polo shirt or earrings and make-up, the ranger will direct you toward the roads, crowded trails, and visitor centers where you belong.

Your clothing shows that you aren't in that 1% that wants to get deep in the backcountry. You obviously fall into that dreaded 99% known as "tourists," people who belong in a car with the windows rolled up. Please don't misunderstand – I've spent plenty of my national park time as a tourist, in the car with the windows up and the air conditioner running, driving frantically to see as much as I could see – geysers, buffalo, cliff dwellings, etc. Life is short, the clock is ticking, and corners must be cut. But if you aspire to be part of the 1%, then you are going to have to make some changes in schedules, experiences, and attitude. The task will be easier if you can live with the knowledge that some folks will think you are being irresponsible for skipping those committee meetings, taking full advantage of your sick days at work, or letting your yard go wild. You'll know you've arrived when their disapproval becomes a point of pride rather than shame. After all, do you really want your tombstone to read: "Here lies a fully domesticated citizen who lived a life of quiet desperation"?

So, you must look worthy. This is typically accomplished by wearing well-worn hiking clothes, including a pair of dirty boots. And, yes, the "well-worn" part is important. New boots and freshly pressed shorts shout "rookie" to all but the most naïve tourists. If you don't have any well-worn hiking clothes, then you'll have to put in some time paying your dues because your clothes must not only *look* well-worn, they must *be* well-worn. And, of course, you must display a backpack with the appropriate number of scrapes and smudges. Cute little patches saying "Appalachian Trail" or "Yellowstone" are optional because anyone can buy them at a visitor center, so they prove nothing beyond the fact that you were willing to spend a dollar on a souvenir. Patches that say "Friends of the Smokies" or "Great Smoky Mountains Association" or "Smoky Mountains Hiking Club" will make a better impression because these are organizations that you actually have to commit to. They are a symbol that you care enough to invest time and money in a worthy cause.

Of course, there are a few cosmetic details that can help. Women should not wear make-up and earrings. Men should be unshaven and should wear no cologne. Old hats and bandanas also add a nice, weathered touch. Nothing about your appearance should even hint that

12

you care about your appearance. Rather, everything about you must say, "I'm dressed and accessorized for spending a day outdoors. Function trumps fashion. I belong in the wilderness." These seemingly insignificant details tell the ranger that you came to explore the park, not to shop in Pigeon Forge.

And your map.... At some point you'll have to pull out your map as you explain to the ranger that you've heard of such-and-such a destination and intend to go there. You must not – I repeat, NOT – use the $1 visitor map that all the tourists use. Instead, you'll need to spend $10 or $15 on a detailed, topographic map. And like all the rest of your paraphernalia, it must be worn and dirty, with various lines and stars drawn on it showing that it's a piece of working equipment, not an unblemished showpiece. Your map should be like an old truck that you still use to haul firewood and trash, not a prized antique that you keep hidden in your garage. And it should go without saying that those lines and stars on your map should point out actual trails and trips that you've done. Don't draw random markings on your map just to give the appearance of experience. After all, the purpose of all this is not to trick the ranger but to show her that you actually know what you are doing and want to learn more.

Once you've dressed appropriately and shown your map, you'll have to actually talk to the ranger. You know, open your mouth and explain yourself – what you want to do, what you already know, and what you don't know. This, of course, is where the ax meets the wood. In some ways, it's like a job interview. You have to know enough (and *prove* that you know enough) to deserve the ranger's trust, so you'll have to negotiate that wide gulf between confidence and ignorance. To land on the confidence side of the chasm you should carry your pack with you, slinging it to the ground casually but roughly. It's been through a lot and will go through much more, so you don't baby it.

The rule of thumb that I've used most of my life to hide my ignorance might be useful here: talk about what you know, not what you don't know. First, tell the ranger where you've been. This is the hiking equivalent of name dropping, something most of us prefer not to do, but will if circumstances demand it. For example, if I need to make a good impression around Jefferson County, I'll mention that I know the

Emmerts, or that the McKinneys are my in-laws, or that my daughter married into the Ballingers. That usually will start things off on the right foot. Conversely, I'll not mention that I know anyone by the name of Harrell, Landefeld, or Oakes. That would buy me nothing and in most respectable circles would do more harm than good. The same thing applies to the Smokies. You can tell the ranger that you've visited all the popular spots like Clingmans Dome or Cades Cove, but that won't buy you any credibility, and might even make you sound pathetic and needy. Ditto hiking to Laurel Falls and tubing in the Little River. Any place involving pavement or crowds just isn't worth mentioning. Even Alum Cave trail and Andrews Bald will only barely impress the rangers. Those are two great trails, and you must hike them, but they are also very civilized, being deeply worn and having a wooden sign at every trail intersection.

To gain any sort of trail credibility, you'll have to drop the names of a few out-of-the-way locations like Greenbrier Pinnacle, Indian Flats Falls, or Kalanu Prong. These will get the ranger's attention because not only do few people go there, they are not officially maintained trails. If you've been to these places then you've been "off-trail." (Sort of. They are old trails that are still used by enough one percenters to be well-worn and usually obvious, so they are good starter routes for off-trail trips.)

After dropping the right names and thereby establishing your trail cred, tell the ranger where you want to go and what you know about how to get there, then ask if she has any suggestions. Don't ask if it's okay to go there. You aren't here to get her permission. You are here to tell her where you are going and to see if she can help you in your quest. The open-ended nature of your request puts the ball squarely in her court, and since it will be her job to rescue you if you get lost, she might simply tell you not to go anywhere risky. But if you've dressed appropriately and spoken with confidence and wisdom, then she'll probably give you some useful information about where to park, how far to walk, and what to look for. After all, neither one of you wants you to end up lost in the woods, and since it has become obvious that you *will* make this trip, her only real option is to ensure that it will be successful by telling you what she knows.

And by the way, if the ranger tries to talk you out of going on your trip, listen carefully to separate the wheat from the chaff. She might be giving you the standard line: "The National Park Service recommends that you not engage in activities beyond the designated...." In this case, pretend to listen politely, smile, and thank her for her concern. On the other hand, she might be giving you some valuable advice. If she talks about dangerous river crossings or impassable cliffs, then you might want to pay attention. Some rivers can't be crossed safely (especially during the high water season of spring or soon after a good rain), and some cliffs can't be easily avoided. On the other hand again, most creeks that you'll encounter in the backcountry are small enough that they can be crossed, and most cliffs and boulders can be managed by side tracking until you find a manageable route.

Finally, there's one question that you should ask *yourself* before trying an off-trail adventure: "What will we do if we get lost?" That's "we," not "I." A hiking partner is essential on all but the simplest off-trail trips because the unexpected does sometimes happen, and it's more likely to happen off-trail because the going is rougher. Bumps and scratches are a minor annoyance, or maybe a badge of honor, proof that you've gone beyond the call of duty. Twists and breaks are more serious and can be life-threatening if they happen away from crowds and hiking partners. Your hiking partner is more than a friend; he's an essential part of Plan B if thing go badly.

Probably the best way to keep from getting lost is to spend $200 on a hand-held GPS that has a topo map loaded into it. I prefer not to use those new-fangled gadgets, but there have been several occasions in which my sense of direction told me one thing, but my GPS told me something else. In every case, the GPS was right, and I was wrong. I suppose if my tax money is being used to launch and monitor billions of dollars worth of satellites, I might as well try to get my money's worth. So I use my GPS occasionally, usually just to mark places of interest for later reference on my topo maps.

Because I rely heavily on my map, compass, altimeter, and GPS (in that order), I've never become absolutely, desperately, fearfully lost in the mountains. (Although, I have spent a few minutes here and there wondering why there was a valley in front of me when I was expecting a ridge, or why this east-west ridge was taking me south.) So I've never had to resort to "following the river" to get back to civilization. But it is true that many a lost hiker has saved himself with the knowledge that a river system is like a funnel. Just find a creek and follow it down, and it will eventually lead you to trails, roads, cars, and people. Of course, in the Smokies it's even easier than that. Just find a gully or valley and follow it down. If there's no water in it, there could or should be, and soon will be. So keep walking down and the water will find you. Of course, all that assumes that you have at least a basic understanding of the creeks around you and which river they feed into, and where that river goes. So, again, a compass and map are essential, as is knowing how to use them together, as a single piece of equipment. Really. If you think of a map and compass as two separate things, then you still need more practice in using them.

When Greg Harrell and I walked into the ranger station in July, 2007 and asked about Mill Creek Cascade, we didn't know these details about presenting ourselves to the ranger, but somehow we passed the test. We went to the desk and innocently asked about Mill Creek Cascade. The ranger flinched as if we had just exposed some sort of classified information or uttered a secret password. She looked us over – we were not physically impressive specimens, but our boots were well-worn and our day packs were old and dirty. Then she paused, looked around the room, her eyes darting left to right, looking for spies or intruders, then she leaned forward, lowered her head and voice, and whispered, "Okay, here's the thing...."

I'm not known for being perceptive and attentive to detail, but even I could tell that at that moment, we were about to be initiated into a club that we didn't even know existed. After that conversation and the hike that followed, the paradigm had shifted and a new world had been opened to us. The Smoky Mountains would never be the same again.

And neither would we.

Chapter 1

Keepers of the Secret

Our destination felt like it was unknown, but in fact it was just the opposite. It was precisely known: 35° 33' 44" N and 83° 48' 2" W. Those were, according a website we had found, its exact coordinates. So, technically, Greg Harrell and I knew exactly where we were going. Nevertheless, it felt like we didn't know anything about Molly Creek Cascade because, well, we didn't.

It seemed safe to assume that Molly Creek Cascade was on Molly Creek, so we weren't completely ignorant. The most obvious starting point would be the spot where Molly Creek crossed Parson Branch Road on the southwest corner of Cades Cove. The problem was that this waterfall was not on any recent map that we could find, and there was no clear trail along Molly Creek. We planned to bushwhack (aka "off-trail hiking") up Molly Creek until we found the cascade. Sounds simple enough, right?

If you are at least 16 years old then you've probably learned by now that nothing in life is ever as easy as it seems. Most of us guys learn that lesson the first time we are smitten by a member of the opposite sex. There ought to be a sensible, uncomplicated way to win the heart of our first love. Of course, there isn't, which we discover rather quickly.

Less heart-wrenching, but equally frustrating, examples abound: computers, tax forms, and fast food. You estimate how long it will take, then double it. The same thing applies to bushwhacking in the Smokies. Make your best estimate of the time, energy, and obstacles involved, then double it, then add some sort of injury, equipment failure, topographic oddity, or good ol' stupidity, and you'll be in the right ballpark.

Now you might think that we merely had to follow Molly Creek as we hiked, and we couldn't possibly get lost. Just stay next to the creek

17

until we found the cascade. Well, that creekside strategy works best if you are hiking downhill, not uphill. Here's why.

Let's say you are on a ridge and you need to get down to a campsite (or waterfall) down in the river valley. That river will have a watershed between two side ridges. There will be numerous small creeks and rivulets that flow downhill and converge at various points to eventually form the river that flows to your destination. As long as you start walking downhill somewhere in the right watershed, between those two ridges, then just follow any flow of water and it will eventually take you down to the river. It works like a funnel. No matter where in that river's watershed you start, if you'll keep going down, you'll be funneled toward the river.

Going uphill, from the small end of the funnel to the big end, is different. As you follow the river uphill, you'll encounter splits and channels in the river. Every split requires a decision – do you follow the right or the left fork? If you have a perfectly accurate map with every split shown and labeled, then you are probably okay. Just do what the map tells you to do. But that's rarely the case. You might encounter forks in the river that aren't on the map. Or, you'll encounter a fork that *is* on the map, but you think it's not. Or, it's *not* on the map, but you think it is. Or, it doesn't matter whether it's on the map or not because you don't know exactly where you are – "which fork in the creek am I at?"

If you know where you are on the river, then a compass might help you to decide between, say, a north versus a northwest route. But of course, estimating your speed when you bushwhack is very difficult. And when you can't accurately estimate your speed, then you'll have a hard time estimating where on the river you are. Therefore, much of the time when you are off-trail hiking, you know *generally* where you are but not *exactly* where you are.

Even so, I wouldn't think of hiking off-trail without a compass, partly because a compass can often be helpful in finding my way, but mainly because when I use a compass I'm plugging in to a long line of travelers that stretches over the centuries. We've all been told that "those who forget history are doomed to repeat it," and there's a lot of truth in that because there's a lot of history that's not worth repeating.

But some things in our past are worth hanging on to just to stay connected to our past. I'm not opposed to using GPS devices to figure out where I am, but I really like the old-school approach, doing what people have been doing for generations. That's one reason why I like canoes and kayaks, because you are paddling the way the Native Americans, pioneers, and voyageurs did for hundreds of years. That's another reason to fish for brook trout in the Smokies. When you catch one, you are tapping into a Smoky Mountain bloodline that's been there for thousands of years. This old-school bias leads me to prefer map and compass over GPS. I'm not a technophobe who thinks new gadgets are a sign of the slow decline of civilization (although I am deeply suspicious of video games and Instagram). After all, the compass was a new gadget once. I just think there's something valuable in having experiences and skills that few people have, and technological advances are making old skills increasingly rare and increasingly interesting.

One alleged problem with a compass is that magnetic north is created by flowing liquid iron in the earth's outer core, which is not the same as the North Pole. Magnetic north is moving as the liquid iron moves. However, this is not as bad as it seems because the iron is actually moving *closer* to the North Pole and will be closer than it has ever been around 2020. For the next few years compasses across the earth are becoming more accurate, not less. Another lucky detail is that the movement of magnetic north is almost directly away from the eastern US. If you'll stand pretty much anywhere in the east, hold your compass and let it point north, and then continue to stand there for twenty or thirty years, your compass needle won't move much because magnetic north is moving directly away from you, not off to one side or the other. So if you are visiting the Smokies, you might not need a GPS system to locate landmarks. A map and compass, with a little help from an altimeter, will usually work. (If you are stickler for details, in the Smokies magnetic north is only about five degrees to the west of true north. Adjust your compass accordingly.) So don't buy a GPS quite yet because they'll soon be so cheap that McDonalds will be giving them away in happy meals, and you can borrow your five year old granddaughter's.

19

The difference between magnetic north and true north is not a big problem, especially in the Smokies where the difference is only about five degrees, and any decent compass can be easily adjusted to correct for the difference. Unfortunately, there are some real problems in using a compass on a river hike. First of all, to use a compass you have to know where *something* is. If you are on a trail on a long, high ridge, you can figure out exactly where on that trail you are if you know what mountain you are seeing in the distance. You can point your compass at that mountain peak to see exactly what its bearing (number of degrees from north) is. Then you simply find that mountain peak on your map and draw an imaginary line from that mountain to the trail that you are on, using the bearing that your compass is telling you to use. Where that imaginary line crosses your trail is exactly where you are on that trail. Or, if you know exactly where you are, then you can use your map and compass to determine what all those mountain peaks, rivers, towns, etc. are.

So, to use a compass properly, you have to know where something is, and in off-trail hiking you often don't know where anything is, including yourself, which raises the other problem in using a compass in Smokies bushwhacking: you can't see very far. There are trees everywhere, obstructing your views. In the case of most river hikes, you will be down in a valley or ravine, surrounded not only by trees but also by ridges. There just aren't many clear views of distant peaks. All you can see is forest and dirt and rock. Usually, all you know is that you need to be walking in a certain direction because you know where you started and you know where you want to end. In that case, if you can keep walking in the right direction, then you'll end up at your destination.

Our hike to Molly Creek Cascade had several challenges. First, we knew exactly where we would start. The point where Molly Creek crossed the road was clearly indicated on the map. No problem. However, we didn't know exactly where our destination was. We knew the general area, but as Molly Creek twisted and wound its way down the slope from the main ridgecrest, we didn't know which twist or turn held Molly Creek Cascade. So, our compass couldn't tell us the precise direction we needed to follow.

Second, our route to Molly Creek Cascade would be uphill. There might not be countless forks in the river, but there would probably be several. The shorter the hike to the cascades, the less likely that we'd encounter many forks in the river. A longer hike would mean more forks, thus more chances for a wrong decision. And we didn't know whether our hike would be one mile or five, or somewhere in between.

We'd do the best we could in trying to figure out where we were and where we were going. We'd try to make the right decisions at each fork in the river by following what appeared to be the larger of the two. If we encountered a split in the river with two equal creeks flowing together, then we'd stop, look at the map, eat a Snickers bar, and discuss our options. If still undecided, we'd eat another Snickers bar under the assumption that chocolate is the solution to many of life's problems.

That was our initial plan. But then we found the website – the one that told us not only the exact coordinates of the cascade but also the exact location based on an old, 1931 map. According to the map, the cascade was right on the 3,000 foot contour line. Greg had several useful gadgets: specifically, a GPS and an altimeter. If we got in a bind we could use one or both of these to get oriented and find the cascade.

We got up early on a Wednesday in July and drove to Cades Cove. We locked the coordinates of the cascades into Greg Harrell's GPS, and stuffed it and his altimeter into his daypack. We didn't want to resort to using them, but they were there if we got desperate. They were our dirty, little secret.

Cades Cove is the most popular tourist site in the Smokies. This broad, comparatively flat expanse of fields and pasture is a beautiful spot, full of deer and an occasional bear, fox, wild boar, or wild turkey. There are also several pioneer cabins, churches, and graveyards. It was used by the Cherokee as a hunting and gathering ground until 1819 when they gave it up in one of their last treaties with the US government. At about this same time, white settlers moved into Cades Cove, and by 1850 its population was approaching 700. Cades Cove was not the first spot in the Smokies that was settled by whites, nor was it the largest settlement.

21

Today it is popular with visitors simply because of its beauty. The combination of meadows, mountains, and rustic cabins, churches, and mills is hard to beat.

When the park was first established in 1934, there was some discussion about what to do with Cades Cove. Some lifetime leases were signed, so a few families continued to live and raise cattle in Cades Cove until just recently. I remember as a child seeing cattle grazing in the meadows and stopping to buy homemade honey at one of the homes in the Cove. There was talk of letting it revert to its original, wooded state and perhaps of removing the historic buildings. Most visitors would agree that the decision to maintain Cades Cove as an open meadowland with historic exhibits was the right choice. It's a great spot, if you can manage to avoid the crowds, so it was perfectly fine with me that we had to drive through Cades Cove to get to Molly Creek.

Many years ago, in the midst of a career crisis, I drove a van for a small mail courier company in Atlanta for about six months. I had several friends who were also in the midst of significant life decisions, and several of us landed at the same company. One of them was my long-time backpacking buddy, Frank Hogg. We both worked the early morning shift, starting about 5 am and finishing in the early afternoon, and several times we blasted out of work early Friday afternoon and rocketed toward the Smokies for a quick, two-night camping trip. The problem was that we just couldn't seem to get to our destination early enough to hike any on Friday evening, so our trips amounted to sleeping somewhere by the car on Friday night, backpacking on Saturday, camping in the mountains on Saturday night, then hiking back out and driving home on Sunday. Of course, being back at work at 5 am Monday morning was brutal, but we were young and could sleep when we were forty.

I would guess that it was a Monday after one of these trips that Frank was in his courier van at a stop light. The light turned green, and he pushed on the gas. The next thing he knew, he was slamming his van into the back of a car in the intersection. He had managed to fall asleep between the time he accelerated and about two seconds later when he hit the car. Backpacking can be expensive.

One of these trips was to Spence Field, one of the Smokies' "balds" – mountaintops that are open, grassy fields rather than rocky crags or tree-covered forests. We drove up I-75 through Chattanooga and somewhere southwest of Knoxville we got on US 411 to Maryville and US 321 into Townsend. These are not exactly scenic wonders, but they are fine, back roads now and were even more so forty years ago.

I don't remember whose car we took. Probably my tiny Subaru because I think we quit taking Frank's car on these trips when, on one of our winter backpacking trips, we returned from our two nights on Mount Mitchell to find that two or three of his tires had frozen and disintegrated. I don't remember the details, but I'm pretty sure we were all bummed out because I'm also pretty sure Frank didn't carry three spare tires in his trunk. Actually, I admired Frank even more after that winter trip. Anyone who will take a car like that on a road trip of any sort has just the right mix of youthful irresponsibility and reckless adventurism. I mean, if you never find yourself in some sort of difficult, outdoor predicament – such as a flat tire on a gravel road miles from the nearest town or being trapped in your tent by a heavy, March snow or coming face to face with a bear or snake – then you are living too safely. From that moment on, I vowed to be more like him.

Townsend is a quiet place today and was even more so in those days, so as it got dark we skinny dipped in the Little River just outside the park to avoid committing some sort of federal crime, and then we drove into Townsend to find a place to sleep. In those days, "driving into Townsend" meant driving to the combination gas station/convenience store/campground. So that's what we did. Without asking permission, we parked in a field across the street and unrolled our sleeping bags. Those were simpler times with fewer corporate resorts and lawyers, so it was easy to convince ourselves that no one would mind our minor act of trespassing, and as far as we could tell, nobody did. A local country music band was playing next to the gas station. I've never been a country music fan, so I wouldn't know if the music was good or not. It all sounded bad to me. But, good or bad, it was the perfect backdrop to sleeping in a field at the edge of the Great Smoky Mountains.

Very early the next morning Frank and I drove to Cades Cove to get to Anthony Creek trail. Actually, the trail begins at the very start of

23

the eleven mile loop road through Cades Cove, so we didn't have to drive through Cades Cove. But we did. We were in a hurry to get on the trail to Spence Field, but Cades Cove is something you just can't miss on an early July morning. The fields were moist and slightly foggy – the kind of fog that doesn't really hinder your view but is just substantial enough to add drama to the moment. The whitetail deer were everywhere, grazing in the fields and next to the road, jumping the fences in front of our car the way grasshoppers jump out of the way as you walk along a grassy trail.

There are a couple of gravel roads that cut across Cades Cove, providing a shortcut in the eleven mile paved loop. We took one of those short cuts, but not to save time. We just wanted to get right in the middle of the cove to simply stop and absorb it all. We stopped the car and sat there, silently. There must have been other cars and visitors while we were there, but I don't remember them. All I remember is the quiet beauty of the meadows. Forty years later, I'm still searching for an adjective to describe the scene and the moment.

At that time, many years ago, I hadn't even heard of Molly Creek Cascade. In fact, I only recently found out about it while reading *Memories of Old Smoky* by Carlos Campbell. In this book he reminisces about his hiking and camping experiences in the Smokies from the pre-park 1920s through the 1960s. It's not the greatest piece of literature you'll ever encounter, but it does give a feel for the park's early years, when hiking equipment was primitive, facilities were scarce, and men (and women) were tougher. It's embarrassing to read about the level of discomfort they simply took for granted as part of a life lived outdoors.

It was my reading of Campbell's book along with Harvey Broome's *Out Under the Sky of the Great Smokies* that had re-ignited my interest in off-trail hiking. I had used a map and compass to do some off-trail hiking once or twice, but quite a few years had passed since then. Reading Campbell's and Broome's descriptions of their off-trail hikes sounded much different from a typical trail hike. Their descriptions were full of wading across creeks, crawling over fallen trees, and scrambling up rocky faces. And they never talked about how strange or adventurous these trips were. They just called it "hiking" as if it was all perfectly normal. So I decided it was time to hike like a real

24

man – on my hands and knees, through rhododendron thickets, in creeks, over boulders, without a GPS.

Let me jump quickly to the moral of this story… I'm a 21st century sissy. After our Molly Creek hike, I limped around on sore feet and legs for a couple of days, groaning every time I had to stand up or sit down or bend over or breathe or blink. I had hiked with a lightweight daypack, Gore-tex clothes, a plastic water bottle, a water purifier, etc., etc., and I still struggled and suffered. Hiking 1930s style makes you feel like you've been in an MMA fight for a couple of seconds with Brock Lesnar. How did Harvey or Anne or Carlos or any of the others manage to get out of bed and go to work on Monday mornings?

Greg and I arrived at Cades Cove at 8:30 am. And it was *crowded*, more so than I had ever seen it. The picnic area at Cades Cove was *full* at 8:30 in the morning! The reason? It was the Fourth of July, and it was a Wednesday. We had known that it was the Fourth of July, but the significance had not fully sunk deep down into the part of our consciousness that plans hiking trips. I had never actually bothered to visit the Smokies on the Fourth of July, and today's crowds reconfirmed the wisdom of that strategy. Even if the fourth is a weekday, the park (especially Cades Cove) will be full of locals who have come over to spend the day. They arrive around 7 or 8 am, grab a spot in a picnic area, and spend the entire day there. It's like one big block party. Picnickers set up tables and chairs and stereos. They eat. They meet their neighbors. They eat. They sing. They eat. They nap. Then in the evening, they drive the eleven mile loop road through Cades Cove, looking for deer and bears. They just have a good, ol' Fourth of July.

It's a quaint, home-spun event, and I tried not to get too annoyed by the crowds. After all, what better place to have a twelve hour picnic than the mountains? If I were going to have a big family picnic on my day off, I might do the same thing. But it's also very crowded, so we fled the scene as quickly as possible.

The other planning error we made was really, really stupid. It was Wednesday. Both of us knew that the Cades Cove loop road is closed until 10 am on Wednesdays to give walkers and bicyclists a few traffic-free hours in the cove. Our problem was that neither one of us had known it was Wednesday. I'm a teacher and Greg was a self-employed engineer. Neither one of us was working that week, and we weren't in the position of needing to know what day it was – so we didn't. (During the summer, I usually get re-oriented every Sunday, only to become disoriented again by Tuesday. It's a good life.)

So we arrived at Cades Cove, but we couldn't drive to Molly Creek at the other end of Cades Cove until after 10 am. We'd have to sit and wait for 1½ hours, which wouldn't have been a major disruption except that we intended to not only find Molly Creek Cascade but also continue up the creek to the Appalachian Trail. From there we would hike west to Gregory Bald. We'd then hike down the Gregory Ridge trail back to the car. The day could very easily stretch into a twelve hour hike. You can do the math and see that starting at 8:30 and hiking for twelve hours would get us back at the car before dark. Starting around 10:30 wouldn't. So we changed our plans.

We decided to begin our hike outside the loop road. We'd start on the Anthony Creek trail from the picnic area. It would take us to Bote Mountain trail, which would take us to the AT near Spence Field. From there we could hike about a mile east to one of our favorite spots in the Smokies – Thunderhead – a rocky, open peak with panoramic views of Gregory Bald, Cades Cove, the Eagle Creek watershed, and even a small sliver of Fontana Lake. It's a great, great spot, so neither of us was disappointed by our change of plans. (I'm ashamed to say that it had been over twenty years since I'd been to Thunderhead and Spence Field. I had fond memories of both of them and was eager to return.)

The most significant change was that we'd now be bushwhacking *down* Molly Creek instead of up. We'd begin the last leg of our day hike by picking up the headwaters of Molly Creek near the Russell Field shelter and following it all the way down about five miles to Cades Cove. As it turns out, this was a blessing in disguise. Trying to stay on track going upstream would have been possible but very, very difficult. It's just really hard to find your way up a creek in a steep-sided ravine. You focus so much on just trying to walk on a steep slope through or around rhododendron thickets and on rugged game trails that you can

26

easily head up a tributary without realizing that you've left the main branch, and eventually there is no main branch, just a web of tributaries. If you hike right next to the river, you can see the main branch and the tributaries, but you rarely hike right next to the river. More often, you are on the slope above the rhododendron thickets and river.

Okay. I've mentioned rhododendron thickets a couple of times. Let me just say it again. Rhododendron! That one word changes everything. When you look at the map, you think, "I'll just stay by Molly Creek all the way up (or down). I'll see the tributaries and avoid them. I'll see the cascade when I get to it." The flaw in that plan is rosebay rhododendron. This is the shrub that blooms beautiful white-pink flowers along the roadside in July and attracts thousands of sightseers. It also grows prolifically in river gorges and moist, shady ravines. It forms a heavy thicket called a rhododendron "hell" because that's how you feel, what you go through, and what you say (repeatedly) while you are in it.

Running into a thick stand of rhododendron, often with a smattering of mountain laurel to fill in the gaps, is like trying to push your way through a crowd of uncooperative people... who vastly outnumber you... and hate you... and won't listen to reason... and don't care who you are and where you are going and why you are going there. Rhododendron is the most unsympathetic plant that I know.

It was this rhododendron that forced us to hike along the side of the steep slope of the creek valley, putting us up above the rhododendron hells. Occasionally, we'd feel that we were getting too far away from the creek, so we'd work our way back down the slope a bit. Sometimes we'd pick up the faint trace of a trail along the slope. Following it would guide us well for a while, but we'd often end up being led directly into a rhododendron thicket, crawling on stomach, hands, and knees. This was a sure sign that we were on a bear trail. Deer would have a hard time squeezing through the thicket while a low-flying bear could push through the tangle.

For off-trail hiking, the significance is that the rhododendron pushes you away from the creek and up onto the slope. Not only is hiking along the side of a 45° slope physically taxing – giving you a distinctive set of blisters from what you are used to, mostly on the downhill sides of your feet – you also occasionally lose sight of the creek. If you are going *down* the creek, that may be okay. You'll sometimes get too high on the slope and have to work your way down, but there's no question about what you should do – go down. The slopes and creekbeds will funnel you down to the main river.

On the other hand, if you are going *up* the creek, you aren't in a good position to see the main branch of your creek. You might follow the route of your creek, only to find that you have accidentally followed a tributary that is leading you to the right or the left of the main branch. Of course, you might not actually discover this until you get to the top of the ridge three hours later and find that you are at Mollys Ridge, not Russell Field. Or, you may find that you don't know where you are.

So, if you are going *up* a creek, you'd like to stay near the creek to keep an eye on the main branch, but of course the rhododendron won't allow that. You can try hiking along the edge of the water which means slow progress as you climb and slip over rocks and logs. Unfortunately, the higher up you go, the smaller the creek gets, and the more the rhododendron reaches over the creek and blocks your path. One way or another, the rhododendron is going to exert its authority over you... just to remind you that you are an intruder and you are not welcome.

Fortunately, our miscalculation about the 10 am road opening had prodded us to bushwhack *down* Molly Creek. As we started down from Russell Field, I mentioned that this would be hard, but at least we wouldn't get lost: "Only an idiot could get lost going down this stream."

Greg's response was simply, "Yeah, well what about *two* idiots? Does that make us *half* as likely or *twice* as likely?" We began to worry that maybe the odds were even worse, perhaps raised to the second power. We could feed on each other's ineptness. Synergy. The whole is less than the sum of its parts. We clearly had reason to be concerned.

Miraculously, even two idiots couldn't get lost today. But that doesn't mean the hike was easy.

Because the rhododendron pushed us up the slope, we couldn't always see and hear the creek very well. We didn't know how big and loud the Molly Creek Cascade would be. Could we expect to hear it when we got there? We didn't know for sure, so we had to rely on one of Greg's gadgets, his altimeter. Hoping that the 1931 map was reasonably accurate, we decided to drop down off the slope around the

28

3,500 feet elevation point. We hoped that the cascade would be somewhere between 2,500 and 3,500 feet. Consequently, starting at about 3,500 feet, we hiked *in* the creek.

Our first hour in the creek was slow. Rhododendron hung low over the water, blocking our path. We stepped carefully on rocks and in shallow spots. We both had good, waterproof boots on, so our feet stayed dry. But the hiking was slow.

Did I mention that by this point it was the middle of the afternoon? We had already hiked up to the AT, hiked east to Thunderhead, backtracked to Spence Field and continued another couple miles to Russell Field. A total of about eleven miles, plus a couple of miles down Molly Creek. We were beginning to wonder how many more hours this trip would take. Hiking out of the forest after dark on a trail was a bit of a problem; hiking after dark *off-trail* could be very bewildering. So, we needed to speed up, but couldn't... until we got our feet wet.

At some point in the afternoon, we both managed to step into the creek in a knee-deep hole. Obviously, that was not life threatening, but it did mean that water had now poured in over the top of our boots. Those waterproof boots that had been keeping water *out* was now holding the water *in*. Our feet were soaked.

Wet feet are not really a good thing on a hike. However, getting our feet wet did give us one less thing to worry about. We no longer had to step carefully to keep our feet dry. Wet feet gave us the freedom to wade in the creek with reckless abandon. Knee deep water? Just slog on through. Don't waste time looking for rocks along the edges. Just charge ahead. A waist-deep run with huge boulders on both sides? Don't get out of the creek and climb up the slope above the boulders – just wade through the middle, making sure you don't wade so deeply that your pack gets wet. Our pace sped up dramatically from that point on, which is something I would never have imagined. But once it happened, it seemed obvious, as things in hindsight often are.

Three hours after we had begun following the creek at Russell Field, we began to encounter a series of small waterfalls, each maybe eight feet high. We wondered if each one was Molly Creek Cascade or if putting them all together was the cascade. None of them really looked like a "cascade" to us, but we did stop below each one and take a picture, just in case. I began to wonder if Carlos Campbell's favorite waterfall was a quiet, little pool in a lonely, little spot with a cute, little cascade. I couldn't remember if he had said anything about its size.

These small waterfalls also slowed us down because they were at points in the river where the creek gorge was steep-walled on the sides. It was almost impossible to get out of the creek and hike around these falls. So, we took the path of least resistance and crawled down the edges of these small waterfalls. It was wet, slippery, and tiring. And moderately dangerous, or stupid, whichever synonym you prefer. It was also fun, as stupid or dangerous things sometimes are, if you survive. At that moment we were living examples of the joke about a redneck's famous, last words: "Hey ya'll. Watch this."

After four or five of these small waterfalls, we began to wonder where we were and where the cascade was and whether we had already passed it. We both wondered aloud if perhaps the adventure of this off-trail hike would have to be its own reward. Maybe the cascade was so unimpressive that we had already seen it without realizing it. Maybe it was special only because it was a secret, not because of its grandeur. We were both okay with that. The hike had been a challenging, interesting experience so far. We were deep in the Smokies wilderness, on a creek that humans rarely laid eyes on. Yeah, that would be reward enough.

Then, without any noisy fanfare, we got to the bottom of one of these 8' falls and looked downstream once again, and we could see only the tops of trees. It was an impressive, even intimidating, sight. Peeking over the edge (I was on my hands and knees with water running under me), we saw a long, rocky, cascading descent. Looking over the edge of a cascade such as this is not very safe, but there we were, at the top. What else could we do? So, we crouched at the precipice and stared, pretty dang proud of ourselves. The challenge of this off-trail trek (which had now lasted four hours) would have been an adequate reward. Seeing a rarely-seen cascade would be a nice bonus. The fact that Molly Creek Cascade really is impressive made us feel almost unworthy of the honor of being there and seeing it.

Getting to the bottom of the cascade was hard work. It was too long and steep and wet to crawl down as we had done with the others, so we worked our way to the surrounding slopes and crawled down, around,

30

over, and through the dirt, boulders, fallen trees, and the rhododendron. It was a wild scene in a wild place. I was too focused on the hike and the cascade to grasp the significance of it all, but now I can see that this trip was everything that I want in a wilderness experience. I thought that my previous hiking trips had given me whatever it is that the wilderness is supposed to give me, but this off-trail trip gave me more. And for that reason, I'd rank it as one of my best experiences in the Smokies.

One reason this trip was special was simply that it was off-trail. Even if we had gone nowhere in particular, the fact that we were walking (and crawling, sliding, wading, and falling) away from the trails was supremely satisfying. Anything resembling a trail usually turned out to be an animal trail leading to places not fit for humans. The off-trail part of the trip was more physically challenging than a typical hiking trip.

I'm trying to not exaggerate the difficulty of this hike. The physical act was tiring, but it wasn't something that is beyond the physical capabilities of an average guy in decent shape. There were some uncomfortable moments, but nothing life-threatening. We got wet and dirty, but no broken bones. In a sense, there's no dramatic story to tell. We weren't Stanley and Livingstone. We were just two guys (more like Laurel and Hardy, actually) who had heard about a secret spot in the wilderness that might be worth a visit, so we spent a day in the wilderness to see for ourselves. There were, I suppose, a few risks, and a couple of slips and falls could have resulted in broken bones. But the main features of the entire affair were sweat, a few aches and pains, and an overwhelming sense of adventure.

In fact, the biggest risk was the potential confrontation with the Federal bureaucracy. A few weeks before this hike, I had asked one of the rangers in a visitor center about off-trail hiking in the park – were there any special regulations or restrictions? In the process of talking to me, he commented that he had been a ranger in the Smokies for over ten years, and in all that time no one had ever asked him about off-trail hiking, which means either not many people hike off-trail, or those that do don't bother to ask the rangers about it. I myself was tempted not to ask, being afraid that he might say there was paperwork involved – the National Park Service is part of the Federal government, after all. (I

31

generally live by the rule that it's easier to ask for forgiveness than permission, and if I don't get caught, I won't even have to ask for forgiveness.) As it happens, I did ask and there was no paperwork and no condescending lecture from the ranger.

The challenge of this off-trail hike was not only physical; it was also mental. We had to think about the right way to navigate off-trail. We had to consider the increased possibility of getting lost or hurt. In short, we had to do a little more homework than usual – websites, maps, etc. And during the hike we were forced to pay attention not to the scenery but to the landscape itself. Can we still hear the river? What's our elevation? Should we get in the river or continue to stay uphill from the rhododendron? What kinds of obstacles are up ahead? Is the other side of the river gorge flatter than our side, or is it just wishful thinking? (The Smoky Mountain version of "the grass is greener on the other side" is "the river gorge is flatter on the other side.") We had a deeper sense of connection with nature because we had to be more observant. But at the time it didn't feel like a deep connection; it felt like a puzzle to solve. It was more stressful than hiking on a trail.

Our off-trail trip was enhanced by that fact that Molly Creek at about 3,000 feet above sea level is a wild, beautiful place. The trees, the rhododendron, the series of small waterfalls, the boulders, the Cascade, the noise. There are no panoramic views that take your breath away by their expanse and grandeur, but there is beauty everywhere and up close.

Some people feel claustrophobic in a setting like this. On vacations out west I've spoken with several residents who said they didn't like the east because there were too many trees. At the time I just shook my head in disbelief, but now I really do understand. Preferring the landscape of your home region is a good thing. It helps us to be happy where we are, and Heaven knows there are enough things in life to make us dissatisfied with life as it is. The landscape where we live shouldn't be one of those things. As Sheryl Crow's sings, "It's not getting what you want, it's wanting what you've got."

Of course, there are many beautiful spots in the Smokies, both intimate and panoramic. You can even drive to many of them. But something is special about the inaccessible sites. Maybe it's the sense of ownership you get from being the only ones there – a sense of doing something that very, very few people have done or will do. For the few moments that we were there at the cascade alone, it belonged to us and no one else. In fact, months later I still felt like Molly Creek Cascade belonged to me, because few people know about it and even fewer will go there. For all practical purposes, it's my own personal property; although, I don't think I'll bother posting "No Trespassing" signs because no one is going there anyway.

But maybe "ownership" isn't the right word. The thing that made this Molly Creek trip a step above the others is, I suppose, that we had figured something out. We had discovered a secret – inside information that only a few people have – and we had investigated it to see if it was true. No one held our hands. No one helped us except the mapmakers in 1931. The fact that the cascade had actually been *removed* from later maps made the trip even better. Some mapmaker had consciously made the decision to take the symbol off their edition of the map. Was it a conscious effort to keep people away, to protect the secret? Likewise, the NPS no longer maintained a trail to Molly Creek Cascade. Was this purely a financial decision, or were they saving a piece of wilderness from human impact? Either way, it not only felt like we had been someplace special, but that we had done it in spite of the efforts of others to keep us away. We were now "keepers of the secret" – part of a brotherhood so secret that we don't even know who the other members are. We need a secret handshake to identify each other.

When it's all said and done, we didn't accomplish anything that will make us famous or rich. Our names won't show up on a list anywhere. But we had done something important, something worthwhile, something that just about everybody could do, but very few choose to do. And I don't understand why. Why don't more people *explore*? Why don't more people *walk*? Why don't more people *search* out secret places? Indeed, why don't *I* do this more often? Is it because it's too hard? Is it because we don't have enough time? I'd like to blame it on our soft, modern, consumeristic, materialistic culture, but I'm not sure it's to blame. After all, Thoreau wondered the same things almost 200 years ago – quiet desperation and all that. Whatever the causes, in the end, it's not that most of us *can't* get into the wilderness; it's that most of us don't want to. The thought rarely even crosses our minds.

33

Well, the end of the story is that we left the cascade with two hours of light left, and I soon slipped into the "are we there yet" mode, which meant that the trip was pretty much over for me. My head tells me to slow down and enjoy the journey, but my heart sometimes gets impatient. That's especially true when the sun is getting low in the sky. Some people like to hike in the dark, but I think that hiking off-trail in the dark bears an uncanny resemblance to being lost, which is something I try to avoid.

We stumbled upon the remnants of an old trail that sort of came and went, sometimes crossing the creek, sometimes just disappearing right before our eyes. We found the depression of a very old road and a few piles of rocks that were the signs of an old farmstead, but the road wanted to lead us away from the creek. So, we stayed near the creek and off the roadbed, stepping over and around fallen trees as the terrain flattened out. We were entering the wooded portion of Cades Cove, and we could no longer hear the creek, even though we stayed fairly close to it, because the flat topography created a slower, quieter waterway. It would have been a pleasant walk if we'd had a bit more light.

We finally stepped out onto Parson Branch Road eleven and a half hours after we had started our hike. The sun was low in the sky, behind trees and ridges. We hitched a ride with a family who were driving around the cove in their pickup truck, looking for deer and bears. As we rode in the back of their truck, we saw both.

One of the women riding in the back of the truck asked us what we had been doing. (From the looks and smell of us, we could have said "wrestling wild boar," and she probably would have believed us; although, we weren't bloody enough to be truly convincing.) We said we had been hiking in the backcountry all day. We could tell from her blank expression that she had no idea what that meant. She just smiled and nodded, and so did we, being too tired to start an explanation from scratch.

It's not that most people *can't* get into the wilderness; it's that most people don't want to. The thought never even crosses their minds, even to the point of not even knowing what "the wilderness" is. There is another reality – like a parallel universe or a secret society – out there

34

that they've never encountered. And until that day, I had never truly encountered it either.

Now that I've been doing this sort of thing for a few years, I can sometimes go into the mountains to no place special. I'll just walk out into the woods with a map and compass, but no agenda, no trail, no destination. That relieves the challenge of schedules, routes, and running out of daylight. I'll bring a couple of field guides, usually trees and birds, that sometimes I use and sometimes I don't. I do have one gadget – a digital voice recorder. I can set it on a rock and push Record and let it capture the sounds of the wilderness. Then I'll bring it back home and push Play. That kind of trip won't have the drama of a big, steep cascade, but it will have some quiet value. It will be a good reminder that being deep in the wilderness doesn't have to be exciting and dramatic, like an amusement park. It can be quiet and slow, even ordinary, yet still be good, like lying in a hammock. As James Babb has written, there's a difference between having experiences in the wilderness versus experiencing the wilderness. Both are good and both should be pursued, to keep oneself in balance.

And, who knows, maybe I'll discover some out of the way, secret spot – a grove of chestnut saplings, a field of boulders covered in ferns, a rocky alcove, a perfect lunch spot – that would be worth keeping to myself. The only thing better than being the keeper of an old secret would be discovering a new secret and passing it on to a select few. (Or, better yet, taking the secret with you to your deathbed. What a great picture: the old hiker calling his apprentice to his bedside and whispering in his ear, "North 35 degrees, 33 minutes....") Maybe that's what this book is meant to accomplish, just in case no one is at my deathbed for me to whisper to.

And by the way, everything in this story is accurate, even the latitude and longitude. However, Molly Creek isn't the real name of the creek and cascade. I've changed the name to protect the secret; after all, what good is a secret society without a secret to keep?

35

Chapter 2

The Saddest Spot in the Smokies

Because the Smoky Mountains have not only a natural history but a human history as well, there are occasional glimpses of common elements of human society: work and play, wealth and poverty, joy and sorrow, industry and subsistence, justice and injustice, life and death. This human side of these mountains can be observed in museums, old photographs, pioneer cabins, vacation cabins, rock walls, railroad tracks, mine shafts, swimmin' holes, school houses, and cemeteries.

In the broad sweep of history, there's probably nothing sadder than the injustice perpetrated upon the Cherokee people by Andrew Jackson (with a lot of help from the state of Georgia, aggressive white settlers, and President Van Buren) in the 1830s. The Congressional record calls it the Indian Removal Act of 1830 which is coldly accurate but less poignant than its more familiar name: The Trail of Tears. And while we may be tempted to declare past generations guilty and our own innocent and enlightened, let us not forget that most of us who live near the Smokies own land that was taken from the Cherokee. We are the prime beneficiaries of that past injustice and are, in a sense, guilty of dealing in stolen property.

To see this tragedy in our national park requires a solid understanding of regional history supplemented by an informed imagination because there's very little physical evidence of the Trail of Tears in the park simply because most of the Cherokee settlements and government internment camps were south and west of the park in today's Nantahala and Cherokee National Forests. There are, however, rumors of a rocky overhang on the southern slopes of Clingmans Dome where Tsali and his family hid after killing a couple of soldiers who were transporting them down the Little Tennessee River under today's Fontana Lake.

I once joined a Smoky Mountains Hiking Club hike led by Ed Fleming to Tsali's Rock. I was never quite sure if the obscure, unassuming camping spot was actually the site where Tsali hid out or if it *might have* been the spot. As far as Ed knew, there was no physical evidence (there was no "Tsali was here" scratched in the rock), but the local lore said this was the spot.

There was nothing special in the appearance of the rock – just a flat spot with a ragged boulder to crawl under and a creek nearby. It was just like a million other spots in the Smokies, which, of course, makes sense. Tsali didn't know his name would go down in Cherokee history as a martyr for his people. He didn't find a magnificent rock shelter to mark the spot of his last stand. He just found a rock and a creek and hid there. There were several hundred other Cherokee hiding in the mountains, so maybe he hid there with others. Maybe all the really good spots were already taken, and this spot was the best he could do.

It's like many other sites of historical significance. It was nothing special before the famous event happened there, and there was nothing special about it after the event… except that, for a few moments, something significant happened there. The corn fields of Gettysburg, Edmund Pettus Bridge in Selma, Holt Street Baptist Church in Montgomery, the School Book Depository in Dallas, those metal historic markers that you see along the side of the road – some of these places have simply continued their day-to-day use once their "fifteen minutes of fame" was over, others are slowly rotting away, and still others are national historic sites.

On a more personal, punch-you-in-the-gut level, there's a lingering sorrow in the cemeteries that are scattered around the park. For instance, a one mile walk up Porters Creek trail leads to a small cemetery in which one of the first grave stones you'll encounter provides a stark reminder of the harshness of life without advanced medicine. It simply says: *Mary Whaley, Born & Died, Aug 11, 1909.* Far too many grave stones in rural communities of the early 1900s have a single date etched on their surface, accompanied by that hauntingly familiar phrase: "Born & Died." The Smokies were no exception and, because of their ruggedness, they may have been worse than most. Anyone who longs for the "good old days" of rural America needs to account for such basic

37

demographic concepts as Infant Mortality Rate and Life Expectancy. As many an old timer has said, "Aw, hell, the good old days weren't that good."

I suppose there's no way of proving that one graveyard is sadder than the next. The grave stones of every cemetery are squares of a quilt that tells the story of an interwoven community in which the life and death of each member touched the hearts and lives of nearly everyone else in the cove. That closeness and connectedness which we associate with small, rural communities also created vulnerability. The death of a neighbor left a palpable void in the lives of those who remained, just as tearing a square from a quilt not only leaves a hole but also diminishes the loveliness of the pattern. Every Smokies cemetery tells a sad story. *Many* sad stories. So many, in fact, that it's easy to become numb to the sorrow.

And yet, there is one place in the Smokies, one obscure set of grave stones, which strikes me with a dull, repressed sadness. It's the same feeling I get when I hear the low tones of violin music in a minor key, the feeling of some dark memory struggling – and once again failing – to make itself known. But in the case of this graveyard, it's the sadness that accompanies the death of children; in this case, the Barnes children.

On the dirt road in the Greenbrier section of the park, there's a fork. Straight goes to the Porters Creek trail; left goes to Ramsey Cascades trail. Almost half a mile from this split, on the road that leads to Ramsey, there's an obscure, barely-visible trail that departs from the left side of the road. This is the trail to the Barnes home site; although, it is sometimes called the Cat Stairs trail because it actually passes through the Barnes home site on its way up the western end of Greenbrier Pinnacle. Like many great sites in the park, the NPS pretends that the Barnes home site doesn't exist. It's never mentioned in any of their tourist information, and the trail is not marked on any of their maps. Any "maintenance" of the trail is done informally by the folks who know about this path and occasionally move limbs and branches to the side, maybe occasionally bringing a small hand saw to cut through a large branch or small tree that can't be simply man-handled out of the way. (Interestingly, there are one or two places where someone with a chainsaw or a two-person handsaw has cut through a 3' thick log. Maybe the NPS has relented in this case and helps with occasional maintenance of this popular, but unofficial, path.)

The hike from the road to the Barnes cemetery takes about an hour. For the first minute or two the trail parallels the road but quickly turns left, away from the road. For the next five or ten minutes the trail is obvious, heading north and paralleling old rock walls, evidence of lives spent clearing fields and farming the land. Other evidence of human habitation is an occasional clump of daffodils, a holly bush, or an unnatural pile of rocks.

I often hike this path in April during the dazzling display of spring wildflowers – mostly ephemerals that bloom in the warmth of the early spring sunshine, but disappear as the leaves of the trees create the deep shade that we associate with the Smokies. Because there are some great wildflower trails in this part of the park (most notably, Porters Creek), one would hope that this secretive path to the Barnes home site would be a wildflower bonanza for those of us who know about it. It would be the perfect reward for having discovered this path and having taken the time to explore it – a wild, secret garden. Unfortunately, wildflowers are not part of this story. There are, of course, a few early violets and little brown jugs, but no profligate display of botanical beauty. Nothing to draw poets and painters, except maybe for the gravesites of the Barnes children, which is why we are on this path.

After ten or fifteen minutes from the start of this hike, the trail crosses Bird Branch, a modest creek a mere five or six feet wide and usually only ankle deep. The first time or two that I did this hike, I took special notice of this spot where the path crosses Bird Branch, and marked it with a small pile of rocks, because if we got lost or bewildered, our exit strategy would have been to walk downhill (south) back to this creek, and follow it downstream until we reached this spot, where we would reconnect with the trail that would take us back to our car.

That's one of the things about off-trailing: as you hike in, you have to be thinking about how you will exit if things go well, and how you'll exit if things don't go well. Our small, rock cairn would mark the spot where, if we got lost, we'd get out of the creek and back on the footpath. That's another thing about off-trailing: think about how things will look when you are walking the opposite direction. Turns that are obvious going one way may be not-obvious when walking the other direction. That's especially true when a small, obscure path intersects a more substantial trail. On the way out, it's easy to continue down that substantial trail and walk right past the faint intersection with that light path. The same thing applies if you are walking down a creek instead of a trail. It's easy to miss your exit path, unless you've marked it with a rock cairn.

And one more thing: piles of rocks are the marker of choice. Strips of surveyor's tape are less organic and more obnoxious, and are to be used only if a pile of rocks would be invisible in the weeds and brush.

After the path crosses the creek, it goes straight uphill for about ten yards, then bears right, paralleling the creek. (There's usually an ancient tin can hanging on a tree at this spot; if not, this is another good spot to build a small cairn to mark this obscure *left* turn on our hike out.) So for the next fifteen minutes the trail generally parallels Bird Branch, staying about ten or twenty yards above and to the left of this creek as we walk upstream which is generally northeast. In other words, the creek is ten or twenty yards to our right and below us for the next fifteen minutes.

About fifteen minutes after the Bird Branch crossing, the worn path turns left away from Bird Branch. (This left turn can be hard to see because there's actually a split in the trail. One fork goes straight and continues to parallel the creek. The left fork is the one we take. There's a small remnant of a wall or modest pile of rocks at this split.) There's an X carved about eye level into a tree (a dying hemlock) a few yards up this trail to the left; although, this marker will surely rot away in the next few years, or it may already be gone. On our very first trip up here, Greg Harrell, Keith Oakes, Charlie Roth, and I just stood at the "X Tree," wondering what it meant. Does it mean "Come this way"? Or does it mean "Don't come this way"? We eventually figured out that it means "Come this way," but it took us a few minutes of wandering and wondering to figure it out.

40

So we follow this X Tree path, which is usually very obvious, except in the fall when the ground is covered with an endless, pathless carpet of brown leaves or in the winter when a blanket of snow hides the path. About five minutes after we turn left away from Bird Branch and onto the X Tree path, we join a different, smaller, unnamed creek. My hiking partners and I call this sometimes-wet-sometimes-dry trickle Barnes Branch because of where it will lead us. This is another turn where it may be wise to mark this spot with a rock cairn because it's easy to miss this junction on the way back down. At this point we are about half way to the Barnes graves. We follow this small creek steadily up, so if the path gets hazy, we just keep following this creek's small valley uphill. This begins the part of the hike where we have to stop occasionally to catch our breath. Up to this point the hike has been surprisingly easy.

For the final ten minutes of this hike, the trail curves to the right, away from Barnes Branch – so Barnes Branch doesn't actually go all the way to the graves and home site. At this point in the hike the trail is well-worn and obvious, so when we notice the trail bear to the right away from the creekbed, we follow the trail. Finally, after walking through a thicket of rhododendron and mountain laurel for just a few, steep minutes we arrive at the saddest place in the Smokies: the Barnes graves (GPS: 35.71828, 83.35930).

Some folks call this the Barnes Cemetery, and I suppose that's technically true, but I can't bring myself to call three small graves a cemetery. The entire gravesite consists of a small plot about 6' x 6', so it's a tiny monument to human frailty in a vast ocean of ancient forests and mountains, not unlike the tiny speck called Earth floating in the midst of that vast expanse we call the Universe.

This sense of isolation is enhanced by the fact that it takes some effort to reach this spot – about an hour-long walk on an old trail, a trail "maintained" by the footsteps of the few folks who have heard about this place through word of mouth or blog. Just as a waterfall or vista is better if it requires some effort to reach, the impact of a lonely cemetery is magnified by sweat and distance. And, like most sites in the park, the more sweat and distance, the lonelier the destination will be. Death and loneliness are a powerful combination, and nowhere in the park is that more potent than at the Barnes graves.

But the real impact of the Barnes cemetery is the names and dates on those three, small graves: Delia Lenora Barnes, Oct 25, 1897 – Dec 25, 1898; Julies Barnes, Dec 25, 1899 – Feb 7, 1901; Rosey Barnes, Aug 18, 1915 – Sept 17, 1922. Two fourteen month old kids, one seven year old girl. Being a guy with two, young granddaughters, that hits me pretty hard.

This is one of those moments where an historically-informed, vivid imagination can help us to experience the sadness of the tragedy that struck John and Isabelle Barnes, perhaps the entire Greenbrier community, in the winters of 1898/9 and 1900/1. Maybe those two winters were no worse than any other, but for the Barnes they were devastating. The days and sleepless nights in December, 1898, nursing a sick child. The tears. The prayers. The loss. Then on Christmas Day one year later having the chance to start over with little Julies. It must have felt like a gift from God to give birth to a second child exactly one year after the death of their first. Merry Christmas! And then, the following winter, their family history was repeated, with a vengeance. Their second child, gone after fourteen months, just like the first. Imagine the fear and apprehension that must have accompanied their third pregnancy.

Local oral history says there were several more children and several death-free years after Julies. Perhaps John and Isabelle thought they had finally moved past their personal tragedy, or knowing the vagaries of life in the mountains, perhaps they knew better than to assume that their tragedies had come to an end. Then came 1922 and the death of seven year old Rosey. I've been told that she somehow became lost and died of exposure, perhaps in an early snow. If you read much Smoky Mountain history, that's a scenario that has happened many times in the past 100+ years – farmers, herders, hunters, hikers, and children lost outdoors and dying of hypothermia in these dangerously beautiful mountains.

And here is where we run into the flaws in oral history mixed with a vivid imagination… sometimes we get the story wrong. All that stuff about John and Isabelle's little Julies being a gift from God exactly one year after the death of their first child… it might not be true. The deaths were real. The sadness was certainly real. But there was a bit more drama than most of us would have imagined.

For many years my hiking partners and I assumed that Delia, Julies, and Rosey were three girls. I've heard people mention the graves of "the three Barnes girls." Whenever we hiked past these Barnes graves, we'd stop and pay our silent respects to those three little girls.

We were wrong: the middle child, Julies, was a boy, probably an alternate of Jules or Julius. This is according to a present-day descendant of the Barnes family.

A few years ago I was hiking the path toward the Barnes place when I met an older gentleman who was a direct descendant of John Barnes, the father of Rosey, Julies, and Delia. We talked for a few minutes, and he clarified a few details. First and foremost, Julies was spelled Jules in the old family Bible, and Jules was a boy. Second, Isabelle (Carver) was John's second wife. His marriage to his first wife, Nancy (Whaley), had recently ended in divorce, but Nancy still lived nearby. Third, Rosey had died of appendicitis, not hypothermia in the wilderness.

The most enlightening detail he shared with me was that Rosey and Delia were born to John's second wife, Isabelle. Jules was born to John's first wife, Nancy. That seemed a bit odd – two kids from one wife and a third child from another wife – all in the same, small plot. But they all had the same father, so maybe it wasn't so odd after all. I pondered these things as I continued my hike up to the gravesites.

As I stood at the three graves and reconsidered these new facts, the sadness of three dead children continued to weigh upon me. The grief felt by John and Isabelle for Delia and Rosey, must have been… wait a minute! Delia… Julies… Rosey. Delia was the first to be born and die. Julies was the second. Rosey was the third. Julies was the middle child of those three. If my new information was true, somehow John managed to father a child by Nancy (his first wife) in between his two children with Isabelle.

So all that heart-warming stuff I had imagined about little Jules being born exactly one year after the death of Delia and seeming like a gift from God, well, it's now a bit tarnished. Yes, Jules was born exactly one year after Delia's death... but to the wrong woman. I was now a member of a fairly large club – people who had a good story ruined by the facts.

I won't engage in any more speculation about John, Isabelle, and Nancy and the births and deaths of those three kids, but I must say, this is one of those times when truth is stranger than fiction... but I like my fictional version better. In fact, I deeply, truly want to believe that the gentleman I met on the trail somehow got his facts twisted, but he seemed sincere, knowledgeable, and confident. I hate it when that happens.

Wherever the truth lies, those three graves are the kind of thing that gets you to thinking about the brevity and meaning of life and our feeble efforts to be remembered by those who are yet to come – the same things that Solomon was thinking when he wrote "all is vanity, a chasing after the wind." All of us will end up in graveyards marked with stones that will erode and that people will forget. These mountain cemeteries are full of stones that are so old and worn that no words are visible, the final, fitting remnants of lives lived quietly and unremarkably in a mountain cove. Thomas Gray, writing of a common graveyard in England's countryside, could easily have been writing of the coves and creeks of the Smokies and the people that inhabited them:

> Full many a flower is born to blush unseen,
> And waste its sweetness on the desert air.

Tombstones erode and memories fade. The world will little note nor long remember the quiet lives that were lived here. They were flowers that blushed unseen.

It's ironic that one of the simmering controversies arising from the creation of the national park has been providing adequate access to these cemeteries. Some Smoky Mountain descendants still resent the government intrusion that took their land and family cemeteries from them. And yet, knowing the way children and grandchildren move away

44

to jobs in the city and lose their connection to the family home place, if the land had not been taken by the government and a national park created, these rocks and graves today might be covered by pavement, condos, and strip malls, and thus gone forever. Instead, the forced sacrifice by those mountain families has provided us all with the opportunity to put on our boots, walk to a quiet corner of the mountains, to imagine the lives and tragedies of those families… and to keep their memory alive.

Chapter 3

Don't Do It!

"No wild parties while we're gone." "Thou shalt not eat of the tree of the knowledge of good and evil." "Stay out of the cookie jar." Warnings that are wise, but hard to resist.

My old 1973 Sierra Club *Hiker's Guide* had this to say about the Porters Creek trail: "

> This trail consists of two sections which are very different in character. For four miles it is an easy walking trail through an undisturbed forest. After that it turns into an unmaintained manway and becomes very steep, rising 2,000 feet in the last mile. This section is for the experienced hiker only and even for him only one way. Nobody should attempt to descend this trail from the AT. The latter section is the most difficult and dangerous stretch of trail described in this entire handbook. Don't do it!

What I heard was slightly different from what appeared on the printed page. I heard what I wanted to hear, which was:

> Blah... blah... blah... blah... I dare you to try this one... blah... blah... blah... blah... You big sissy... blah... blah....

I took the "Don't do it" as a personal challenge, an affront to my manhood, such as it is. I may not be bold enough to try it, but I'm stupid enough. Bring it on, Sierra Club! This would be a perfect example of stupidity masquerading as bravery.

When I read the warning to Greg Harrell, his response was typical for him: "Sounds like we need to give it a try." So we did.

I had been studying the topographic map of the Greenbrier section of the park, and couldn't quite tell how the 1973 trail description fit in with the wiggles and bumps that appeared on the map. I learned that the old manway ended very close to Dry Sluice Gap, which was about a quarter of a mile east of the cliffs of Charlies Bunion on the main ridgecrest. So I knew the target that we were shooting for, but the exact route was a mystery. This trip could be pure, trial-and-error bushwhacking that might even take more than one trip to figure out. On the other hand, the 1973 trail description did talk of an "unmaintained manway" so there might be some semblance of a path. But that was 1973. If it was an unmaintained manway in 1973, what would it be thirty-five years later?

One thing that I could tell for certain was the steepness of that last mile, and especially the last quarter mile. This section of the park, the Porters Creek watershed below the main ridgecrest, was rugged and steep. Sometimes in studying a topo map, you can get a good feel for the ruggedness of an area not by a close examination of the map but by actually stepping back several feet and just looking at the overall *color* of the map. If your topo lines are brown or black, then where does the map look dark instead of the typical light green? Where does the shading look a bit deeper and darker? In looking at a topo map of the Smokies, the brown topo lines squeeze closely together and create a fuzzy, brown mass along the north side of the five miles of ridgeline from Mt. Le Conte along the Boulevard then east on the AT past Charlies Bunion to Porters Mountain. If you are familiar with land forms and topo maps, those tight topo lines speak of deep, steep, shady ravines. These are the places that get very little sunlight, and even less during the winter months when the sun is low in the sky, so they are moist. The springs and rivulets high on a north-facing slope will probably freeze over in December, providing beautiful walls and columns of ice until deep into March, maybe April. If these sites are off trail, then you can be sure that very few people have seen them.

Lest I exaggerate the trail's danger and our bravery, let's get something straight. I strongly suspect that if a trail or manway was truly dangerous, the *Hiker's Guide* wouldn't even have mentioned it. So, we'd take their warning to heart and be careful, but we knew this trip would probably rate about a 5 or 6 on the danger meter, maybe less – where 0 is walking across the parking lot at Sugarlands Visitor Center and 10 is pulling a wild boar's tail.

It's also important to understand that there's sometimes a fine, nearly-invisible line between bravery and stupidity, between fearlessness and cluelessness. Some people are brave. Some lack good judgment. A guy might pull on a wild boar's tail because he's incredibly brave, or incredibly stupid, and it's sometimes difficult to tell the difference. We had to investigate the trail guide's "Don't do it!" because we both are well ensconced on the clueless side of that fine line. I'm not being humble. I'm simply recognizing the overwhelming weight of the evidence.

As usual, when exploring the Smokies, timing is important. We were able to make our schedules mesh in the third week of December, but that meant that we'd be trying this in cold weather on one of the shortest days of the year. Although the total trip would only be about twelve miles, about four of these miles would be off trail – ruggedly, steeply, slowly off-trail. This probably would not be a simple six hour trip.

Early on a Friday morning a few days before Christmas, we met at Greg's house and hopped on I-40. We exited onto US 321 near Newport and drove through the hamlet of Cosby and toward Gatlinburg. Before reaching Gatlinburg we crossed the Middle Prong of the Little Pigeon River and turned into the park at the Greenbrier entrance. The narrow road was deserted, with the Middle Prong and then Porters Creek on our left. We arrived at the Porters Creek parking area at the end of the road after a brief, bumpy drive.

This Greenbrier area, like virtually every other river valley in the park, was once fairly well populated. There were Ramseys and Partons, but Whaley is the most common name in the small cemetery less than a mile up the Porters Creek trail. The headstones show that 1909 was a hard year for the families that lived along Porters Creek.

The Greenbrier community once boasted several hundred residents and even a hotel near the confluence of Porters Creek and the Middle

Prong of the Little Pigeon which served mainly hikers and fishermen in the pre-park 1920s. Harvey Broome described this hotel in his book *Earthman*. The hotel was about fifty feet square, made of wood with a tin roof and was owned by the Whaley family.

> The hotel was situated in the peninsula between two big mountain streams which ran within fifty yards of it on one side and a hundred on the other and joined perhaps one hundred fifty yards below. The ceaseless, restless, hollow roar of this stream made a welcome music for our outdoor-living souls.... Water, drawn from faucets on the porches which surrounded the building on three sides on both floors, came from a captured stream some half mile or so up the mountain, and we could use it with lavish, wasteful frequency (p. 13).

After an overly-thorough briefing of the terrain above them by J.W. and Kimsey Whaley, Broome and his hiking partner shouldered their twenty-five pound packs and hiked up the Middle Prong past Buck Fork Cascade and Drinkwater Pool to Mt. Guyot. That was 1926.

At about the time the park was established in the early 1930s, the hotel was abandoned, but Broome and his companions in the Smoky Mountains Hiking Club built a small hiking cabin in Greenbrier that they used until 1976.

Greg Harrell and I would be heading not up the Middle Prong but up Porters Creek, past the old hotel site and past the SMHC cabin. (We didn't know it at the time, but Broome's route up the Middle Prong to Drinkwater Pool would soon become an obsession for us. But not yet.)

As we stepped out of my truck, the sky was cloudy, threatening rain or snow, with the temperature hovering around freezing. Dressing for such cold weather hikes is always a bit frustrating. You are cold and it feels good to wear a light fleece jacket, but you also know that in about ten minutes you'll be too warm for a light fleece. It's not a problem to stop and stuff your jacket into your pack, but stopping so early in a hike

49

always gives the sense of incompetence. You are trying to get off to a good, quick start, but here you are, half a mile up the trail, stopping to adjust your equipment. Even though the stop takes about one minute – hardly a major setback in your schedule – it feels unnecessary, like something done by people who don't know any better.

The Porters Creek trail follows the course of the river – occasionally rising a hundred feet above it then dropping down next to it – so it ascends gradually, moderately for its four miles to the Porters Creek campsite. Along the way Greg and I were both impressed by the size of the river – it's not what most people would call large, but by Smokies backcountry standards it's sizable. Both of us being trout fishermen, we pay a little extra attention whenever we walk along a Smokies stream. Neither of us had fished Porters Creek, but we decided that it should be placed high on our "to do" list. Actually, it looked like much of the river would be hard to get to because the trail is often high above the river. And, the river was fast and noisy, making it difficult to fish. So there were at least a couple of factors that might make this river less-fished than most. Those factors, plus the fact that it was new water for us, gave Porters Creek a special allure, even though we were confident the rainbows and occasional brown trout in Porters would be just as small as in any typical Smokies stream because, really, that's what Porters Creek is – another beautiful, noisy, typical Smokies stream.

The 3.7 miles to the end of the trail was a fine, typical Smokies hike. The sound of the river stayed with us almost the entire time. The forest was mixed hardwood and hemlock. There were a few old rock walls and foundations along the way. During April and May, this section of trail is one of the most popular wildflower hikes in the park.

About a mile up the trail, near its intersection with Brushy Mountain trail, is the old cabin, built in the mid-1930s, that once belonged to the Smoky Mountains Hiking Club. This hiking club was responsible for scouting some of the trails in this portion of the park. In fact, it was reading excerpts of Harvey Broome's hiking journals that kindled my interest in this Porters Creek – Dry Sluice trip. Today, if things went well, we would not be blazing a new trail; we would be following in the footsteps of the members of this hiking club who hiked this route a generation ago. And, on these trips they usually spent the

50

night in this old cabin that still stands as a testament to their lives and their passion for these mountains, especially this Greenbrier area. Yes, the CCC built many of the Smokies' trails, but the Smoky Mountains Hiking Club scouted and blazed many of the routes that those trails would follow.

It took us about an hour and a half to reach the backcountry campsite at the end of the trail. It looked fairly well used – more so than I had expected. Since this is a dead end trail, I would have expected it to receive light attention, but I doubt that is the case. In fact, at the end of the day as we returned from our hike, there were several tents set up and four backpacks hanging from the bear-proof cables.

This Porters Creek campsite lay in the midst of some large, old hemlocks. I love these trees because I see them so often along the rivers where I hike and fish. I can't see a hemlock without thinking about the Smokies. So I hate to see them go.

Yes, they are following the pattern of the chestnuts and firs in the park – near extinction. Just as the chestnuts had their blight and the firs have their balsam adelgids, so the hemlocks have their hemlock adelgids. Whenever I encounter a stand of hemlocks I look up to see how they look. These at Porters Creek campsite don't look healthy. I'm not a botanist, so I'm sure there are symptoms that escape my notice. However, here at Porters Creek it was fairly clear to see that the hemlocks were not doing well. They weren't barren. They didn't look brown and sickly. They were, simply…sparse. We could see too much sky through the branches.

Unless something wonderful happens, we'll tell our grandchildren about hemlocks the way a few, remaining old-timers still speak of chestnuts. And then, after a few more decades, the last of us who actually saw and touched and sat under hemlocks will join the hemlocks. Just as the last WW2 or Vietnam War veterans will one day die, so will those of us who knew and loved the hemlocks. Living witnesses, those with real memories and first-hand experiences, will pass away. And unlike the war veterans, there will be no plaques, no monuments, no memories – just a few paragraphs in old books and newspaper articles.

So we paused for a couple of moments, the way most folks around here will pull over to the side of the road as a funeral procession passes.

A sign of respect for the recently departed. I've never actually prayed for a tree or a forest, but in retrospect that probably would have been appropriate.

Okay, time to go. Time to shift gears and think about what we should do next. We thought about going down to the river a few yards down slope. We could begin there. However, the old trail guide hadn't said much about the river, so maybe we should go back to the trail and look carefully to see if it continued up the river valley.

We walked back to the small, wooden campsite #31 sign. The trail had appeared to end at this sign, but a closer inspection showed that was not the case. It continued south (left) as we had hoped. So we followed it, and it soon began to pull away from the river and proceed east up the side of Porters Mountain. After a mere five minutes, we realized that this wasn't right. The lay of the land and the old trail description indicated that we should follow Porters Creek at least a mile. So, we decided that this trail wasn't for us. If it were named, it should probably be called Porters Mountain trail, not Porters Creek. So we pushed our way through the rhododendron, down the slope toward the river. It was looking like our day would be a long, tough march through a trail-less mess of rhody thickets. Then, suddenly, we encountered another lightly-used trail running south, parallel to the river. This just might be the old Porters Creek manway we were hoping for.

We took this route simply because it was going in the general direction that we wanted to go. This trail was barely discernable as a slight indention in the thick layer of leaves – but it was discernable. It became even more distinct whenever it would lead us through a rhododendron thicket because it would form a narrow, but obvious, passageway through the tangle of branches and leaves. It soon became obvious that the unmaintained manway described in my Sierra Club *Hiker's Guide* was still here. Unmaintained, but here. So, in spite of our mistake in getting on the wrong path, we quickly realized our mistake and stumbled upon the right trail. Things were starting well, but I was concerned that we had already used up a portion of our day's allotment of good luck, and the day was still young.

It soon became clear what "unmaintained" means. It means that no one trims the branches and shrubs that grow up along the sides of the trail. On a maintained trail, you don't notice while you are on it, but someone has been diligent about trimming the branches and bushes on both sides of the trail. On a maintained trail, you are rarely slapped on the shoulders and face by rhododendron branches. On this unmaintained trail, we were being constantly slapped by wet leaves. No big deal, but it did give us a deeper appreciation of the fact that trails do have to be maintained by people with shovels, clippers, and saws.

"Unmaintained" also means that blowdowns – trees that have fallen across the trail – are not cut and removed. Blowdowns happen on maintained trails, too, but they are usually removed within a few days or weeks by trail maintenance crews. So every Smokies hiker has encountered a few of them, and they are only a mild annoyance. You either climb over them, crawl under them, or walk around them. The only difference with unmaintained trials is that you encounter more of them. But even on this old trail their number was not excessive. Not a big problem.

"Unmaintained" also means that you'd better have waterproof boots because there are no log footbridges over the river. You cross the river by rock hopping and quick stepping. It's kind of fun and adds an unusual element to your hike because this is something, again, that you just don't think about on a trail hike. Maintained trails usually have quaint, pretty, narrow, single-log foot bridges. These little bridges are great for posed pictures. They even look like they'd be fun to make. But an unmaintained trail doesn't have them. So you hop, step, slip, and slosh your way across the river.

As we were crossing Porters Creek for the fifth time, it occurred to me that Harvey Broome's descriptions of his hikes in the 1920s and 30s included frequent river crossings. That fact hadn't really stuck with me until this hike.

Why cross the river several times? Because the lay of the land and the turns in the river (plus the random thickets of rhododendron) sometimes make one side of the river excessively steep and the other side a bit more open and flat. As the river weaves its way down the river gorge, these steep and flat sides switch back and forth, so you find yourself being pushed by the terrain from one side of the river to the other. Thus, the river crossings. That's another detail you don't notice when hiking on a maintained trail.

Days later, after reflecting on this hike, it occurred to me that trail hiking vs. off-trail hiking is similar to the difference between driving a car and being the passenger. The driver pays attention to the route and knows where she is, while the passenger often just goes along for the ride and has no idea about the potholes and detours and street names. Trial hiking can be like just going along for the ride – you walk and chat and enjoy the day without giving a second thought to the fact that you are walking on a trail that was *mapped, planned, constructed,* and is *maintained,* just like roads.

There was one other, very interesting feature of this manway – one way in which it is maintained. There were occasional rock cairns to show you where the trail was because it wasn't always obvious. These rock cairns are small, simple piles of rocks placed at strategic intervals along the path. And the word "strategic" really is appropriate here. They aren't every thirty feet. They aren't even at every turn in the trial. They are only and exactly where they need to be – no more and no less. In other words, in places where the trail is obvious and well-defined, there are no cairns. But whenever you'd suddenly realize that you weren't sure where the trail went next, just look around, there will be a small cairn sitting somewhere ahead of you to show the way.

I love these little piles of rock. Yes, partly because of the security that they provide to the bewildered hiker, but mainly because they are a spontaneous act by people you've never met; yet they were willing to expend a little energy to help other, future kindred spirits. It's like someone in the past thought about me and decided that if I was interested enough in this hike to get out here and try it, then they were willing to share their secret with me. Without getting too mystical here, I'll just say that those little piles of rock are like a connection with the past, like a passing of the torch. Most of these cairns were standing intact, but occasionally one would have tipped over, and we'd stop and repair it. It was our small contribution to future hikers. Someday someone will be writing or thinking the same thoughts that I'm expressing right now – and they'll be thinking about Harvey Broome and the Smoky Mountains Hiking Club; and the many anonymous hikers who aided in "maintaining" this old trail, four of whom would be Greg Harrell and me… and you and your hiking partner, when you do this trip.

I wouldn't exactly call these cairns altars, but I would call them monuments. They are messages from the past to the future, saying "Thanks for coming. Follow us. You can trust us." As a matter of fact, after an hour of hiking and wandering, Greg and I developed a slogan that we'd repeat to each other whenever we'd have a decision to make: "Trust the cairns." That's it. Simple. Direct. True. For the entire day, if we drifted away from the cairns because we thought we saw a better route, we'd quickly learn that we had made a mistake. If we followed the cairns, things would be fine. We were putting our trust in past generations of hikers, and they were worthy of our trust. Their words, as shown in the placement of these little piles of rock, were true.

And I'm especially pleased that no punks and thugs have come along and knocked them down. This just isn't the kind of place where you'll encounter folks like that. These little rock messages from the past remained intact, threatened only by natural elements such as wind and ice. As we walked, I wondered how many years these small signposts had been in place, with the same rocks being reused whenever a pile fell over; maybe a century or more.

There's another potential threat to these cairns that hasn't materialized – the Federal government. Again and again over the years I have been reminded – usually in the form of a helpful NPS employee – that the National Park Service is an outpost of sanity and compassion in a governmental world of insanity, retribution, and hubris. If the NPS were a different government agency, it might sweep through this area knocking down and scattering these rock cairns in a vulgar display of authority: "We said unmaintained, and we mean unmaintained, damn it!" That hasn't happened yet. Actually, I give the Federal government more credit than most people do. I believe that many government employees are kind, reasonable people who mean well. Nevertheless, when committees are formed, agencies are created, and rules are established, enforcing those rules can take on a life of its own, and those reasonable people must enforce the rules, regardless of the consequences. Like any bureaucracy, rules exist for a reason, and even if we've forgotten what that reason is, rules will be enforced.

So we spent the rest of the day trusting the cairns. There was one particularly memorable moment when it seemed that we were going east when we should be going south. We had pulled away from what seemed to be the main channel of the river and were following the cairns as they led us along a small tributary. We thought that perhaps we should backtrack and return to the main river. After stopping to discuss our options, we decided to continue on the small tributary because backtracking isn't something you want to do unless absolutely essential. In other words, "The best thing about here is that we're here." So we spent the next hour following the cairns as they led us up a sometimes wet, sometime dry, always slippery streambed. It was fun and tiring and getting steeper by the minute. We didn't know where this route would deposit us – somewhere on the AT, but where exactly? But things were going well. This off-trail hiking stuff isn't too hard when you have a marked path to hike on! It was somewhere on that streambed that we learned to fully, deeply trust the cairns.

We spent most of the last hour of our ascent in the creekbed. The higher elevation meant that the creek narrowed, so of course the rhododendron took advantage of the situation and squeezed in even tighter. Greg, who stayed a few yards ahead of me, would alert me with his standard rhody warning: "I see some rhododendron in our future." The water was flowing, so we'd stay to the right or the left of the water, trying to keep our feet dry but giving the rhododendron branches their opportunity to reach out and grab us. If rhododendron is anything, it is *relentless*. It fights its battle through attrition – slapping, taunting, and grabbing; bending but not breaking, dodging and weaving – the Muhammad Ali of the botanical world. It's like being pecked to death by a duck.

Then, without warning, the water simply disappeared underneath us, and we were walking in a dry creekbed. A dry sluice.

Did I say dry? Well, in common parlance that's true. It was a waterless creekbed. However, this cold, shady piece of land was very moist. The rocks were consistently slippery. It was slow, careful hiking. We were often using our hands as well as our feet as we would scramble

56

slowly up the rocks, boulders, and tree trunks that littered the creekbed. Let me say it again: the rocks were slippery. I was reminded of the warning that the NPS gives about climbing on waterfalls. We were on a steep slope; although there was rarely a chance for any tumble farther than five or six feet. However, we also knew that it's very, very possible to get bruised and broken by just a short, quick off-balance fall. Greg had one potentially disastrous spill in which he ended up hanging upside down from a log, but he managed to survive. I spent the rest of the day asking him to not get too far ahead of me. I wanted to actually witness his next dance of clumsiness. But other than an occasional slip or slide, there were no dramatic, bloody pirouettes, but to tell you the truth, there easily could have been. We had to be very careful in choosing our footing, and our years of experience in fishing and wading Smokies rivers really did seem to help. In fact, once the hike was over, I considered this part of the hike to be the riskiest – more than the final, steep quarter mile when we were on a 45° slope and pulling ourselves up to the top with the help of roots and small trees.

As we got above 4,000' elevation, we began to see a few, small spruce trees in this mostly deciduous forest. Then, around 4,500' on a sizable ledge in the creekbed, we came upon an unusual cairn – it was a well-designed pyramid about four feet tall. What did that mean? Was it a sign that this was the last cairn and from here we were on our own? Did it mark the spot of a death or battle? It seemed like it should mean something, but what?

Above 4,500' we saw some fine walls of ice where a modest trickle of water in a shady gully or north facing slope had frozen over. The final thirty minutes were risky but manageable – assuming you didn't do something stupid. There were a few places where we could stand up, vertical, on two feet and walk up the slope – but very few. We spent much of our time on all fours, dragging ourselves up the muddy, rocky slope. We were still in a forested area, so there were small trees, rocks, and roots that we used to keep from sliding backward. In such places, standing up and trying to walk really could have resulted in significnt injury. It wasn't a straight, vertical drop, but a lengthy, head-over-heels, rolling tumble over rough ground could do just as much damage. The secret was to not do something stupid, and somehow we managed not to.

Yes, this last quarter mile deserved about a six on the danger meter – far below climbing on a waterfall or grabbing a wild boar's tail, maybe about the same as poking a copperhead with a long stick.

About 4½ hours after walking away from the car, we arrived at the AT with a surprise. For the past hour we thought we had been headed far east of Charlies Bunion and Dry Sluice Gap, farther east than we had hoped. Instead, we came out onto the AT where we had originally intended – just a few yards away from Dry Sluice Gap and just a quarter mile east of Charlies Bunion. Trusting the cairns all day had taken us up the tough, "don't do it" route, exactly what we had wanted to do. While we had been ascending I had been thinking: "If this is an easier, safer route then I really won't be able to come down the old 'don't do it' route. I'm not even sure I can descend this easy route." But as it turned out, we had ascended the hard route, the "don't do it" route, the route we had wanted to ascend. Trust the cairns.

Once we were on the AT we spent a few minutes walking to Charlies Bunion – just a ten minute walk to the west. But we soon had to make a decision. It was getting close to 2 pm, so we didn't have a lot of daylight left on this mid-December day. Should we walk about twenty minutes to the east and try to find an easier route down Porters Mountain? What if such a route doesn't exist? What if it does exist, but its intersection with the AT isn't obvious? What if there is more than one? If we walk twenty minutes and haven't found an easier route, how much longer do we walk looking for it? What if we do find it, but it's *not* easier?

We could potentially waste an hour looking for another unmaintained manway that we weren't certain even existed. So, we decided to go down the way we had come up. This would be exactly what the old Sierra Club trail guide had warned against: "Nobody should attempt to descend this trail from the AT. The latter section is the most difficult and dangerous stretch of trail described in this entire handbook. Don't do it!"

Until that moment I had assumed that we might not do it. We might ascend that segment, but we wouldn't try to descend it. But lack of daylight pushed us down the way we had ascended. So we stepped off the AT and back onto the old Porters Creek manway. We were able to

58

stay on two feet most of the time, but occasionally I'd switch to a crab walk using all fives – two hands, two feet, and my butt – to slide down the slope. The result? Dirty hands and feet and butt, but otherwise fine. There was some slipping and sliding and holding on to those same trees, rocks, and roots that had helped us on the ascent. But it was scenic and enjoyable – as long as I kept my butt on or near the ground and descended crab style in the steepest spots. In fact, descending in this manner enabled me to see more of the surrounding forest, slopes, and valleys than on the ascent. Like before, being cautious and deliberate made it a bit stressful, but interesting – just the right level of adventure for a couple of middle-aged hikers in decent, but not great, shape.

We got past this steep, topmost section in about fifteen minutes, re-entered the creekbed, and soon encountered the four foot cairn again. It had been our warning: "Boys, it's time to fasten your chin straps and head UP." This giant cairn had probably been built by the SMHC in the 1920s, or maybe pioneers in the 1800s, or maybe a Cherokee warrior in the 1700s. We were following the lead of hundreds of years of adventurers and warriors. We were carrying the torch that they had started.

At least, that was our fanciful interpretation at the time. A few years later we learned that long-time Smokies off-trailer, Brian Reed, and his hiking partner, Seneca, had stopped there to rest in the mid-1990s and had built an over-sized cairn just to keep themselves entertained while they ate lunch. Since then, off-trail hikers had added some stones and made it a little bigger. End of story. No Cherokee warriors. No impending dangers. No torch being passed. Just a couple of young guys messing around. They built it on a whim, nothing more.

Once, just once, I'd like to be right about some grand scheme, about some noble venture that I can carry forward into the future. I want so badly to be part of a legend, but reality keeps intruding. I just can't seem to find someone who will pass me a torch.

The hike back was beautiful, long, and uneventful – as most hikes in the Smokies are. We arrived back at the truck just as dusk was settling in. Sometimes when you are warned not to do something, it's best not to do it. But this wasn't one of those times. Instead, we had been careful, managed not to get lost, survived without injury, and loved every minute of it.

   And next time we'll be better prepared. I've always thought of walking (on two feet) as being the best way to prepare for a hike. Now I can add crab walking to that list. On flat land. Up stairs. Down stairs. Just keep your butt near the ground and scamper around on your hands and feet. When someone asks what in the world you are doing, you can casually say, "Getting in shape for a hike" as if the answer should have been obvious.

Chapter 4

The Hunt for Drinkwater Pool

Choosing the best waterfall in the Smokies is like trying to choose the best movie of the year, or the best song. Ask a hundred people and you probably won't get a hundred different answers, but you might get several dozen. It's all in the eye of the beholder. If you ask a hundred Smoky Mountains enthusiasts to name the best waterfall, a fist-fight might break out. I don't know why, but some folks get really passionate about their waterfalls.

My favorite waterfall is one that doesn't even show up on today's maps. It's sort of a secret, so I can't reveal much information. I'll just say that it's a beautiful waterfall that's really hard to get to. There's no discernable trail, so it involves some interesting off-trail hiking. And that's what makes it my favorite. I'm not one who thinks that Nature can teach us the answers to life's most pressing questions, but it does occasionally provide us with a nice, sensible lesson, such as: the harder you work to achieve something, the more you'll appreciate it.

Maybe that's one reason why Ramsey Cascades is a favorite for a lot of people. Not only is it high (about 90') and noisy, it's four miles from the nearest road. The trail's length, incline, and elevation change are remarkably close to that of Alum Cave trail to the top of Le Conte. So there's some work involved. It only takes a little exertion to keep most people away, which is too bad, because it's the exertion that makes it worthwhile. Nevertheless, Ramsey can be a bit crowded on summer day. Even if only one tenth of one percent of the park's visitors hike to the cascades, that's about 10,000 people a year. So, it's best to visit it during the off-season, unless you intend to get wet in the river or under the falls... or above and beyond the falls.

I suppose I could add that the hike to it is beautiful, but you already know that. They all are. But there are some unique features. The first mile of this trail is littered with car-sized, truck-sized, and house-sized boulders – more than the typical Smokies trail. At 1.5 miles the Ramsey Prong converges with the Middle Prong of the Little Pigeon River. The first time I ever fished this part of the Middle Prong, I caught only two small fish, but they were both brook trout, which changed two small fish into a significant event. The second half of this trail was only lightly logged, so it has some big trees, with several particularly impressive tulip poplars called the Roman Columns at 2.6 miles.

I don't remember when I first made the hike to Ramsey Cascades, but it was probably in just the past few years because the Greenbrier area didn't even exist until the last ten or twelve years. Or rather, it didn't exist *to me*.

There are very few hiking trails in this section of the park and even fewer campsites, so in my pre-bushwhacking days there seemed to be no reason to visit this part of the park. Now the lack of trails and campsites are the very reasons why I am drawn to this area. Most of this Greenbrier area is hard-core wilderness. That's the nature of paradigm shifts, I guess. What didn't make sense before, now does, and vice versa.

Up until 2008 Ramsey Cascades was, for me, just a nice waterfall at the end of a nice trail. For many years I had simply assumed that every interesting feature in the Smokies had a trail going to it. If a trail stretched four miles to Ramsey Cascades, then stopped, it must be because there's nothing more to see. It was as if the water cascading down that rock face didn't actually come from anywhere. It just magically appeared at the top of the cascade and came tumbling down.

It was my paradigm shift to off-trail hiking combined with the writings of Harvey Broome that got me to thinking: "I wonder what's above Ramsey Cascades?" As it turns out, there's a lot, and the story of my obsession with answering that question is a long and winding road encompassing seven trips above Ramsey Cascades, about 60+ miles of hiking, plus several emails and websites, all spread out over five years. To make sense of it, I'll start at the middle and work backwards, and then forward. Like I said, it's complicated.

In June, 2012, Greg Harrell and I led a Smoky Mountains Hiking Club hike beyond Ramsey Cascades. The description (which we had written) in the SMHC 2012 Handbook went something like this:

> **Upper Ramsey Prong**. After hiking four trail miles to Ramsey Cascades, we'll follow a safe route to the top of this 90' cascade and continue upstream (perhaps in the river) about a half-mile to another wide, unnamed falls mentioned by Harvey Broome in his book *Out Under the Sky*.... (See his entries for 7/7/55 and 7/7/57.) We'll explore a bit beyond this falls as time and interest allow (and perhaps debate the location of Drinkwater Pool), then return via the same route. Total trip: 8 trail miles and 2 off-trail (river) miles, 8 hours. Strenuous.

A few months later in the Club's June newsletter, we wrote the following:

> **Upper Ramsey Prong**. After hiking four trail miles to Ramsey Cascades, we'll follow a path to the top of this cascade and continue upstream (in the river, ankle to knee-deep) about a half-mile to another large, unnamed cascade. We'll explore a bit beyond this upper cascade (to Drinkwater Pool?), then return via the same route. Wear waterproof boots and gaiters to keep feet dry, or wear mesh boots and settle for wet feet.

You might wonder why I dropped the word "safe" from the second description, but the real question is why I included it in the first. Aside from that, both descriptions mention an upper cascade and Drinkwater Pool, the objects of my five year obsession. At the time we made this 2012 hike, Greg and I were 90% sure that we knew where Drinkwater Pool was. We also knew that we probably should be calling the upper cascade Buck Fork Cascade. But we weren't 100% sure, so I put a question mark after Drinkwater Pool. A few months after the SMHC hike we were 100% sure.

We had planned this hike for June because it's a wet hike, meaning you spend a lot of your off-trail time in, actually *in*, the river. Greg and I had discovered over the years that it's nice to keep your feet dry, but on some river hikes it becomes a slow and tedious task to pick your way around or across every pool and cascade. Sometimes it's quicker and easier to get wet and stay wet. Once you commit to being wet, it's fun. This Upper Ramsey trip is one of those.

On the morning of the hike, eight of us gathered at the Ramsey Cascades trailhead. The introductions were brief because we all knew each other, which is common on these off-trail trips. Those SMHC members who are passionate about off-trailing are a rather small group, like a deviant subculture or rogue agents embedded in an otherwise reputable organization. There are no passwords or secret handshakes (that I am aware of), but we do know who we are.

This trail is very typical in one important way: its gradient is almost exactly a 500' rise per mile. That seems to be the magic formula that the CCC used in constructing the trails in the Smokies. In fact, that's my personal method of determining how hard a hike will be. This 500' rise is very manageable. Anything steeper is, well... steep.

Today's bible of Smokies hikers, *Hiking Trails of the Smokies*, gives a helpful diagram – a trail profile – of the gradient of every trail in the Smokies. Once you know that 500' per mile is about right, then you can look at a trail's profile, and you'll immediately know how difficult it will be. For example, look at the trail profile of the Chimney Tops or Alum Cave trail. Their first mile is a little easier than 500' per mile. The second mile of Alum is a little harder than 500' per mile. The hard part of the Chimney Tops trail (in its second mile) is over 1,000' per mile. Or, learn your favorite trail's elevation gain from the diagram. Once you've done that you can compare every trail profile to it – "It's steady uphill like Alum Cave trail's upper half, not the Chimneys' second mile."

So, the elevation gain of the last mile of Ramsey Cascades trail is about 750', which doesn't sound significant, but as you walk, it is definitely noticeable. It's steeper than upper Alum but not as bad as

64

upper Chimney Tops. And, the steep part is short-lived, so you hardly have time to lose your breathe before you arrive at the Cascades.

Greg is a fast hiker who thrives on those internal, personal challenges that some folks create for themselves. While he appreciates the majesty of the outdoors, he does like to get from point A to point B as quickly as possible, just to see how fast he can do it. I, on the other hand, don't. So, on more than one occasion he's bragged to me about how quickly he did a solo trip, and I'll respond, with as much sarcasm as I can muster, "Well, good for you. That's the point." He'll nod in agreement, as if he hadn't noticed the sarcasm, which is aggravating to me and heartening to him. So we each follow our own muse: he, to prove some obscure point about vigor and manhood, and me, to not prove anything, except maybe that I'm getting old and slow, which is so obvious that it needn't be proven at all.

So, I was the leader on paper, but he was the leader on the trail. If I weren't so gracious and humble, we'd probably have had a fight by now over this leadership thing. So, as usual, I brought up the rear. On these club hikes one leader is supposed to be in front and the other leader is supposed to bring up the rear, so in that respect (and only in that respect), Greg and I are the perfect team.

My notes from that trip are sparse, but they do mention that we saw a few remaining bluets and wood sorrel, the last vestiges of the spring wildflower extravaganza that the Smokies should be famous for. Most visitors are here to see the mountain views and vistas and the bears, which are impressive. However, there's not as much wildlife in the park as one might expect. Going to the Smokies is not like going to Yellowstone with all its high status mammals: bison, antelope, elk, grizzlies. Instead, the Smokies really stand out in a couple of understated ways: plants and salamanders. I don't see a lot of salamanders on our hikes, but I've been told by people who should know that there's more sheer tonnage of salamander than bear in the park. As on most of our trips, we saw no bears, no deer, no elk, and no salamanders, but we did see a few chickadees and juncos, heard a veery, saw some flies and grasshoppers, and were constantly surrounded by millions of plants, everything from tiny bluets to towering spruce and poplars. Just another day in a botanical paradise.

We averaged a little less than two miles an hour, so we arrived at Ramsey Cascades in about 2½ hours. We followed the obligatory routine of sitting and resting/snacking on the big rock near the base of these beautiful falls. It's the big rock just past the sign that warns that four people have died here, the implication being: don't play around on the top of the falls. This rock is the most obvious spot to sit and enjoy the moment, so it is gradually being worn smooth by the boots and butts of a few thousand visitors each year. It's kind of like that statue of St. Peter in the Vatican that has its toe worn off every few centuries by the millions of pilgrims who kiss it every year. Or maybe it's nothing like that, except that both are holy places visited by pilgrims.

A moist spring had made the river and its cascades full and loud. We let the noise of the rushing water – one of life's few loud noises that I actually enjoy – work its cleansing magic. I understand that "cleansing magic" sounds overly poetic, and I'm not normally a poetic guy, but honestly, I do feel somehow cleansed by the roar of a river. It is like music for the soul, and when you walk away from that thunderous water-music, the silence is beautiful and overwhelming.

C. S. Lewis, in his classic book *Screwtape Letters*, speaks of music and silence as characteristics of heaven. Screwtape, a senior-level demon in the hierarchy of hell, complains:

> "Music and silence – how I detest them both! How thankful we should be that ever since our Father [Satan] entered Hell... no square inch of infernal space and no moment of infernal time has been surrendered to either of those abominable forces, but all has been occupied by Noise.... We will make the whole universe noise in the end.... Melodies and silences of Heaven will be shouted down in the end."

I think Screwtape would love the infernal noise of a Harley "shouting down" the music and silence of the mountains as it rumbles through the park, but he'd hate Ramsey Cascades, which is also loud, but musically loud, like the final notes of the *Hallelujah Chorus*. It's probably just a coincidence, but Handel also wrote a symphony called *Water Music*. (The actual story behind that name isn't very impressive

66

or poetic, but I love the phrase *water music* almost as much as I love Aldo Leopold's phrase *goose music*.)

After our moment of appreciating the moment, we crossed the slippery base of the falls with no mishaps, then pulled and crawled our way up the rock-and-dirt side of the cascade. This part of the route is messy but safe, but the problem (if you are concerned about the safety of a group of people of which you are allegedly a leader) is that this route emerges at the top edge of the cascade – the most likely spot where the four deaths were initiated. The open rock provides about a four foot wide corridor between the rhododendron on your right and a 90' nearly-vertical drop on your left.

There is a safer route on the other side of the river and cascade, but it involves a losing battle with a horrendous rhododendron thicket, so this dangerous route is the one we usually take. Greg takes it because it is dangerous; I take it because it is easier than pushing through all the rhody on the other side of the cascade. Once at the top, I will sometimes walk the rocky corridor upright with semi-confidence; other times I'll crawl on all fours like a soft, little kitten.

It is possible to angle away from the edge by tightrope walking a blown-down tree that leads in the general direction of the river, away from the edge, but before I had a chance to say anything about it, the entire group had walked or crawled along the edge and into the river a few feet back from the edge. Of course, today was one of those times I walked upright on two feet like a hominid instead of on all fours like a feline. I didn't like it one bit, but such is the nature of peer pressure and male ego. It's a combination that can push you out of your comfort zone to do things you normally wouldn't do, which can have its advantages. On the other hand, those were probably the last thoughts of those four people, right before they fell to their deaths. Once again, the fine line between bravery and stupidity. Happily, no one died today. The number on the sign is still four.

Once we were across the ledge and in the river, we began to slog upstream. This type of river hiking is not usually intimidating, but it can be slow and tiring. The cold water feels good on a hot, humid summer day, but that same cold water sucks the internal heat right out of your core. We stepped from one spot to the next with no dramatic slips and slides, and for the most part, the cold water felt good because we rarely got in over our knees.

Within fifteen minutes we encountered a 20' waterfall consisting not of boulders but a wide wall of rock. It was the kind of obstacle that can't be climbed, only avoided. So, we waded to the shore and found a path leading around and up, with one small piece of pink surveyor's tape marking the way. Apparently, a few people know about this trip and do it occasionally – enough to maintain a lightly-worn path at the spots where you are forced out of the river and onto the riverbank. The tape seemed unnecessary, so we had a brief discussion of whether the person who did this wanted to be helpful to others who would make this hike later versus they wanted to show that they had been here first, like a dog peeing to mark his territory. As I recall, the dog peeing hypothesis was accepted unanimously, simply because anyone who came upon this 20' high barrier could see that he'd need to get out of the water and walk around, and the route was obvious. There are a few overly, unnecessarily helpful people in society, but the general consensus was that most of them were little, old grandmothers who give you a blanket when they are cold but you aren't. Not many of them would make it past Ramsey Cascades.

Less than an hour later we came upon the second cascade, about a half mile above Ramsey Cascades. It was magnificent. It is well over 100' high, maybe 150', consisting of a magnificent series of cascades, falls, and pools, one immediately after the other, for a horizontal distance of about 200'. It is big, wet, and slippery, so the only reasonable route is to get out of the river and go around. There was never even any discussion about that point. It was obvious to all. And, of course, as we got out of the water there was a little piece of pink surveyor's tape hanging from a branch. I think it was at this point that one of us (who I shall not name) began tearing down these unnecessary little hints. By this time they had become insulting and had to go.

In my opinion, this Second Cascade is better than Ramsey Cascades, but I don't really know what I mean by "better." The Second is higher, but not as vertical. Still, the Second simply seems so massive – it curves a little, so there is no place where you can stand and see the entire cascade. Its sheer mass seems overwhelming. Maybe that's what I mean by "better." Or, maybe it's "better" because it is harder to get to and very few people have seen it. Or, maybe it's not better. Maybe it's just one more great spot in the Smokies, and on the "Best Of The Smokies" list it is tied for first place with about a thousand other places in the park.

Somehow the very unimaginative name of Second Cascade was stuck in my head and still is, so that's what I usually call this cascade. I realize now, but wasn't quite certain at the time of this SMHC hike, that I should have been calling this cascade Buck Fork Cascade because that's what Harvey Broome called it. It took me a long time to figure that out.

At the top of the Second Cascade, we stopped and enjoyed the view back down the valley. Whenever you get to the top of a mountain you have to stop for the "mountain top experience." The same process is at work at the top of waterfalls, but the phrase "cascade top experience" isn't poetic enough to ever catch on. Nevertheless, the experience at the top of a long, massive cascade accompanied by its water music is every bit as powerful as the experience on a mountain top.

At the top of the Second Cascade the streambed leveled off for a few hundred yards, after which there was a Third Cascade, sort of. Rather than being a single, continuous cascade it was a bit more spread our horizontally, so that it was more of a series of small falls and pools, separated by 20', 40', maybe 50' of level creekbed. So it's not exactly a single, continuous cascade but rather a series of adjacent plunges and terraces, but it's reasonable to talk about these as a single, Third Cascade because there is a very clear beginning and a very clear end where the streambed smooths out and heads up toward Mt. Guyot.

At the top of this Third Cascade we, of course, stopped for another cascade top experience, but this time there was a little more at stake. This final pool of the Third Cascade is the spot that Greg and I had concluded – with about 90% certainty – was Broome's beloved Drinkwater Pool. We got some decent pictures of our group scattered around the pool, including one of Charlie Roth (Dutch Roth's grandson) lying on a flat rock at the lower edge of the pool. It was a good moment; although, that missing 10% of our confidence level was nagging at me.

In the decades since Broome lived and wrote, the knowledge of the exact location of Drinkwater had become increasingly fuzzy until there seemed to be few alive who had been there and/or could remember where Drinkwater was. I suppose it wasn't technically the SMHC's responsibility to keep track of Drinkwater's location, but if not them, then who? It had been maintained as part of the oral history of the club, but was about to disappear. It is a blemish on the Club's otherwise strong resumé that they had lost Drinkwater Pool. Their last trip to Drinkwater had been in late 1970s or early 80s. After that, knowledge of Drinkwater had quietly, slowly disappeared, which was unforgivable.

Greg and I had developed an obsession with Harvey Broome's life and writings and particularly the location of Drinkwater Pool, and that obsession had led us to this moment at the top of the Third Cascade at the spot we were confident was Drinkwater Pool – ninety percent confident, not a hundred, which was unacceptable.

The obsession had begun for me about a year after my conversion to bushwhacking. In March, 2008, Greg Harrell and I explored some of the ridges and rhododendron thickets near Ramsey Cascades with rather miserable and uninspiring results. As an afterthought we wormed our way through rocks and rhody to the top of the Cascades and stood in the river and looked upstream. It looked like a nice stream but nothing out of the ordinary, but now we both could say we'd been to the top of Ramsey Cascades, which is something very few folks do. (I suppose the sign about four people dying there might have something to do with that.) We stood in the river, several feet back from the edge so that a slip wouldn't end in tragedy, and enjoyed the wild music of the river and the open view of the sky and Mt. Le Conte in the distance. I made a mental note that one might, with a good pair of binoculars, be able to see Ramsey Cascades from Myrtle Point on Le Conte.

After soaking in the scenery for a few minutes we turned upstream, scanning the riverbanks for some sign of a gap in the rhododendron, perhaps indicating an old trail. What we actually found were a few, small pieces of pink surveyor's tape tied to some of the rhody branches

70

hanging over the riverside. At first we thought this might be where we would leave the river and enter the thickets and forest, but we soon saw more pink tape leading upstream. The *river* was the trail. We'd have to rock hop (a slippery undertaking) or wade (not only slippery, but also wet) upstream. The going would be interesting, but very, very slow. We desperately wanted to see how far and where this route would lead us, but we would run out of time and daylight rather soon.

We ended our excursion sooner than we would have liked, after sloshing about a hundred yards upstream, but we were able to console ourselves with the knowledge that we'd seen one of the best waterfalls in the Smokies from the bottom and the top on a fine spring day. We also now knew that someone had blazed (can you use the word "blaze" if you're talking about little, pink pieces of plastic?) a route upstream – a route that probably went somewhere. So we had another potential adventure to add to our Smokies "to do" list.

All in all, I'd call it a successful trip. We also had the satisfaction of knowing that very, very few people explore up here because it's hard, dirty, uncharted, and maybe a little bit dangerous. Those things that keep most people away were the things that had brought us here. We weren't disappointed.

After this first, aborted trip, exploring well beyond Ramsey Cascades was pretty high on our list, and we had merely scratched the surface. After that visit, I began reading Carlos Campbell and Harvey Broome's writings, and it quickly became clear that there was more above Ramsey Cascades than Greg and I had suspected. Broome talked about Drinkwater Pool and Buck Fork Cascade, neither of which shows up on any maps, unless the old Buck Fork Cascade were today's Ramsey Cascades. Since they assumed their readers were familiar with these places, they didn't give any detailed information about access and location. It also became apparent that some of the names had changed since Broome wrote his stories. For instance, Ramsey Prong used to be Buck Fork, and Buck Fork Cascade was on today's Ramsey Prong (yesterday's Buck Fork). So, was Ramsey Cascades once known as

Buck Fork Cascade? (Simply changing the name of the cascade when the stream's name was changed made abundant sense.) And where was Drinkwater Pool?

I asked around and no one seemed to know for sure. Even the Smoky Mountains Hiking Club off-trailers were a bit uncertain about the locations of these places. It had been decades since the club had made any hikes to them, and the number of people who had ever knowingly visited these places was shrinking fast and memories were getting fuzzy. In other words, Drinkwater Pool and Buck Fork Cascade were about to become lost, permanently, like the language of a dying culture. So, for a couple of years I became obsessed with the river above Ramsey Cascades and the lost location of Drinkwater Pool and Buck Fork Cascade.

In 2009 I hiked to Ramsey Cascades by myself with the intention of fishing above the Cascades and getting a better glimpse of the territory above Ramsey Cascades. I hiked in carrying all my fishing gear. Once I got above Ramsey Cascade, I unpacked my fly rod, assembled it, and tied on a Light Cahill, a yellowish, tanish mayfly imitation about the size of a dime. I spent the next hour gradually working my way upstream, casting to likely looking chutes and pools. Whenever I fish I fight the urge to get my hopes up, but if there was ever a piece of water that had potential, this was it. The number of people who fish this stretch of water in a year must be incredibly small. In that respect, this water is every fly fisher's dream, about as close to virgin water as can be found east of the Mississippi. If any fish were there, they had to be native survivors from fifty or a hundred years ago, or they had to have been stocked in the days when the NPS still stocked these Smokies rivers, decades ago. Migrating from below was not an option.

I desperately wanted to catch a fish, partly as a reward for all my effort, but mainly so I could put this stretch of water on my list of secret fishing spots, which I must say is a very short list, but it was not to be. I didn't get a single strike – no splashes, no tugs, nothing. This, of course, was the worst possible outcome, not only because catching fish is better than not catching them, but also because of the nature of proof. Catching a fish would prove that there are fish in this water, but *not* catching a fish proves nothing. The river could be fishless, or it could full of fish, but I just couldn't entice any of them to show themselves on this particular day.

Which means I still don't know about the fish. Which means I'll have to keep coming back until I either catch a fish or am skunked enough times to convince myself that there are no trout up there. Of course, if I come back and manage to catch some fish, then I'll have to keep coming back because I will have found a lonely stretch of good water – an angler's dream. Such is the gloriously twisted logic of fishing new water. Whether you catch fish or you don't, both lead to the same conclusion: keep fishing, even if – no, *especially* if – you have to walk three hours and past a waterfall to get there.

In the process, I did manage to reach the base of a second cascade about a half mile above Ramsey Cascades. So now I had seen the second cascade but knew very little about it, and for some reason that I can't remember, I didn't explore any further. I suppose I thought that merely seeing the second cascade from the base had somehow answered my question: Is there a second cascade? Now that I knew the answer was "yes," I turned around and left because I was tired and it was getting late.

It was a long hike back, but within fifteen minutes I was already disgusted with myself. I should have explored the Second Cascade (as I was now calling it in my head). I had stopped at the base, but hadn't crawled around to the top of it to see what was further upstream. Were there more cascades? Did the landscape level out? Were there fish upstream? The answer to all those questions was, "I don't know because I didn't bother to find out."

I had to live with that on my conscience for quite a while, but eventually, a couple of years later, I decided that previous trip would be my mulligan, so I went back, hoping to get it right this time.

And I did… almost. I hiked the four miles to Ramsey Cascades, scrambled to the top, hiked the half mile in the river to the Second Cascade, then hiked along the side of it to the top. My altimeter told me that it was about 130' high, which was significantly higher than Ramsey Cascades, but it was not near-vertical like Ramsey Cascades is. Still, it was really impressive, and I was pleased with myself for finally seeing all of this remote cascade. I had undoubtedly waded through or at least seen Drinkwater Pool, but there was no way to know exactly which pool was Broome's Drinkwater. Mission Accomplished!

In the days following this successful trip, I decided to read Broome's descriptions one more time to give myself a sense of closure. But as I read Broome and Campbell carefully, I realized there was still more work to be done. Drinkwater pool was an "achingly beautiful" pool at the top of a series of plunges and pools that covered a few hundred yards, and there was a gap in the adjacent ridge call Drinkwater Gap that provided a quick route to the river immediately south of Ramsey Prong. Where was this gap and how close was it to Drinkwater Pool? To further muddy the water, Carlos Campbell mentioned in his book and Ann Broome mentioned in a footnote in Harvey Broome's book that the SMHC (including Broome) didn't even know Ramsey Cascades existed for many years. I also noticed that Broome's description of Buck Fork Cascade as being a few hundred feet long (horizontally) didn't fit today's Ramsey Cascades.

All this seemed to indicate that today's Ramsey Cascades was not the old Buck Fork Cascade. Also, my Second Cascade wasn't several hundred yards long; it was maybe fifty or seventy-five yards long from bottom to top. So Drinkwater couldn't be in the Second Cascade. Nothing was making sense. Where was Buck Fork Cascade and where was the long (several hundred yards, according to Broome) series of plunges and pools that held Drinkwater Pool? Did they really not know about Ramsey Cascades in those early years? Was I even on the right river?

At about this time Greg Harrell joined me in my obsession over Buck Fork Cascade and Drinkwater Pool. In 2011 Greg and I and a friend who was in desperate need of some mountain time, Megan Lynch, chased our obsession once again. We hiked beyond Ramsey Cascades to the Second Cascade, then to the top of the Second Cascade. We continued upstream and soon encountered a long stretch of small cascades and pools. These plunges and pools continued for a few hundred yards and finally flattened out and opened up as Ramsey Prong headed up the slopes of Mt. Guyot.

We now knew that there were three cascades: Ramsey Cascades, the Second Cascade, and now the Third Cascade (the long series of plunges and pools). At the top of the Third, the stream finally settled down to become a tame, gradual flow. Now that we finally knew the real topography of the stream (i.e., three cascades, each one becoming less vertical and more horizontal than the one before), but we still couldn't determine the location of Drinkwater Pool. And, which one of these three cascades was the old Buck Fork Cascade?

I read Broome's writings yet again, and the pieces finally began to fall into place. Broome's Buck Fork Cascade was not today's Ramsey Cascades because Broome's description of Buck didn't match the size and shape of Ramsey, but it did match the size and shape of our Second Cascade, plus for many years while they visited Buck Fork Cascade they didn't know today's Ramsey Cascades existed, plus when they did discover Ramsey Cascades they began speaking of Buck Fork Cascade and Ramsey Falls (today's Ramsey Cascades) as two separate entities. Our Second Cascade is Buck Fork Cascade.

Another piece of the puzzle... Drinkwater Pool was at the top of the series of small pools and cascades far beyond Buck Fork Cascade (the Second Cascade). This series of pools and cascades that culminated in Drinkwater Pool was a few hundred yards long, much longer than the Second Cascade. Drinkwater Pool is at the top of the Third Cascade, not the Second. We knew it was at the top because it matched Broome's description perfectly – after Drinkwater Pool, the stream opened up and leveled out.

Now Greg and I were confident enough in what we had discovered to lead a SMHC hike to Drinkwater Pool – at the top of the Third Cascade. We had found Broome's beloved Buck Fork Cascade and Drinkwater Pool again. They had been lost but now were found.

In the spring of 2012, a few months before our SMHC hike, Greg and I made a final scouting trip to our three cascades, to make sure we were clear on what we were seeing and thinking. We wanted to be able to tell the group with some conviction that "this is Broome's Drinkwater Pool" and "that ridge above us is Drinkwater Gap." As we hiked along the Second and Third Cascades we noted the pools and cascades. We had Broome's descriptions with us and we compared them carefully with what we were seeing. We hiked up the adjacent, southern ridge, looking for a gap that fit Broome's description. And we found them all.

Broome's descriptions could fit only one scenario. Our Second Cascade was Broome's Buck Fork Cascade, and Broome's pools and plunges beyond Buck Fork Cascade were our Third Cascade. Drinkwater Pool was the last plunge pool of our Third Cascade. Drinkwater Gap was on the ridge almost directly above (south of) Drinkwater Pool, at the top of the Third Cascade. This was the story we told the SMHC club group on our June, 2012 trip. As we lounged around Drinkwater Pool, there wasn't much debate. There simply was no other place Drinkwater Pool could be, based on Broome's writing.

After lying on the rocks and basking in our accomplishment – having rediscovered Drinkwater Pool and Buck Fork Cascades – we made the quick and leisurely hike back; it was all downriver and downhill. Greg and Charlie Roth sped away from the group while the other six of us strung along, with me in the rear. Somewhere below the Second Cascade but before Ramsey Cascades, Amanda Beal managed to slip on a wet river rock and dislocate her shoulder. I came upon Amanda and her husband Adam as she was sitting in the river, head down, trying to shake off the pain and dizziness. It was the kind of injury that could happen in any river, anywhere, and had a random feel to it. It's like winning the lottery – it's going to happen to someone, sometime, somewhere, usually someone else.

After a few minutes, Amanda stood up and starting wading, rock-hopping, and hiking. It was that simple. I'm sure she wasn't having fun – she was holding her bad arm up by the elbow with her good arm – but she did what had to be done. She cowboyed up and hiked herself out. Much pain but no whining.

I've since heard of one or two people who have been hiking on Smokies trails who have fallen and dislocated their shoulders – and have called Search & Rescue teams to come and carry them out. These were people who were on trails like the Gatlinburg tail or Laurel Falls trail, each probably a ten minute walk from the main, paved road and their car. Without making any accusations about those S & R incidents, I'll simply say that Amanda continued down the river to Ramsey Cascades, scrambled down the side to the base of Ramsey, and then the four miles down the trail to the car. She was a stallion that day.

76

Greg and Charlie had finished so far ahead of the rest of us that they drove to McDonalds on the outskirts of Gatlinburg, bought cheeseburgers, and had them waiting for us when we arrived at the trailhead. So we ate cheeseburgers, told a few stories, and got in our cars and drove away, pretty proud of ourselves. Just another day in a wet, secret paradise.

Except... Greg and I were 90% confident in our conclusions, maybe 99%. But there were a couple of nagging details. First, Broome had mentioned a casket-shaped rock on the "shelving rim" at Drinkwater Pool. We had seen several rocks that day that looked "casket-shaped" to us, but none of them were at Drinkwater Pool. There were several flat rocks around Drinkwater Pool that an active imagination might call "casket-shaped," but my imagination is not that active. So there was that tiny bit of doubt: where is the casket shaped rock?

One hypothesis was that it had been washed away by the heavy flow of the creek after a rainstorm. That's a very plausible idea. Rocks do move, especially in these kinds of rivers on the steep slopes of the mountains. However, an old Dutch Roth picture from the 1930s or 40s of our Drinkwater Pool (I wish Dutch had labelled it "Drinkwater Pool," but he didn't, but it was clearly the one we claimed was Drinkwater) showed the pool to be nearly identical to today. Harvey Broome had mentioned the casket-shaped rock as late as the 1950s. The pool looked the same then as it does now, as far as we could tell from the picture. No rocks had moved.

Here's a more likely explanation. Looking for a casket-shaped rock makes us think about this backwards. It pushes us to walk up the river, looking for the best, casket-shaped rock we can find, or maybe second-best, or third; we go upstream looking for casket-shaped rocks. The problem with that approach is that's not how hikers name things. We talk about house-sized boulders that don't look like houses. We talk about table-rocks to describe flat or level rocks that you can lay your equipment on, that don't really look like tables. In other words, we use a few common, familiar items, like cars, tables, microwaves, footballs, columns, etc. to describe the general size or shape of a rock, even though the rock doesn't really look like that object. We use those common objects to provide a quick, general description. That's probably what Broome was doing. For some reason, he chose a casket as his object whereas someone else might have chosen a table or a bed or something else. In other words, a "casket-shaped rock" needs to bear some, vague resemblance to a long, flat thing. The rock might look exactly like a casket, but it doesn't have to because of the way hikers name things.

I was pleasantly surprised when fellow SMHC member and off-trail guru, Ken Wise, told me that he had seen the casket-shaped rock at our Drinkwater, but it was only casket-shaped if you approached from a certain angle, not from directly downstream. I am embarrassed to say, that thought had never occurred to me. We had always approached it from the downstream or slightly across stream angle. I believe that it is important, when discussing important political or social issues, to try to see it from the other guy's point of view. I believe that all cultures have something to offer in customs, laws, and world-views, but it never occurred to me to look at a rock in a river from more than one point of view.

That helped a lot. I was now 99.5% certain that we had found Drinkwater, with Ken's input pretty much sealing the deal. But it sure would be nice if we could find someone who had hiked with Broome or had hiked to Drinkwater and actually remembered where it was or how it looked. Or, better yet, had taken pictures...

In 2013 Brian Reed, who is presently living in exile in Florida, informed me that he had found some online pictures by Herbert Webster of Drinkwater Pool. Apparently, Webster knew Harvey Broome and had hiked with him to Drinkwater and had taken pictures of it. These pictures had recently been posted on the UT-Knoxville library website by Ken Wise. Here's an excerpt from the UTK library page:

> Within a few years, he was visiting the mountains regularly, venturing into the backcountry with many of those whose names are synonymous with early twentieth century exploration of the Smokies — Dutch Roth, Jim Thompson, Carlos Campbell, Guy Frizzell, Wiley Oakley, and Harvey Broome — and capturing on film the vanishing way of life of the mountaineer, the Smoky Mountain

backcountry, and his own adventures in the wilderness. The images in the Herbert M. Webster Photograph Collection rank with those of Dutch Roth and the Thompson brothers as an enduring historical record of the Great Smoky Mountains.

The Herbert M. Webster Photograph Collection is maintained as part of the U.T. Libraries' Great Smoky Mountains Regional Project.

I visited this website (http://kiva.lib.utk.edu/webster/) and searched for Drinkwater: The pictures match perfectly our pictures of the pool at the top of the third cascade. This was the eyewitness evidence from the past that had been eluding us from the start. We were finally at that elusive, 100% confidence level.

In retrospect, I'm glad these pictures were the last piece of the puzzle, not the first. If we had stumbled across these pictures at the beginning, we might have given up immediately because there's nothing more useless in finding a specific location in the mountains than a picture, just a picture. I might have looked at the picture and thought, "That could be anywhere," and given up. Studying Broome and Campbell's writings and making several hikes above Ramsey Cascades allowed us to recognize the picture when we saw it. The sequence of events was long and circuitous, but perfect.

Drinkwater Pool is now a regular destination for SMHC hikes. About every other year, someone (sometimes Harrell and I, sometimes Ken Wise, sometimes others) leads a trip to Drinkwater Pool. To tell the truth, it's not the most dramatic trip of the year. There's a lot of sloshing and wading, which can be slow and tiring, not to mention cold. Nevertheless, it's a good trip if for no other reason than we get to see what's above Ramsey Cascades, which only a very few folks have done.

In addition to the beauty and drama of the hike, the historical significance to the SMHC of Buck Fork Cascade and Drinkwater Pool is unavoidable. This trip should be a rite of passage or a required pilgrimage for every club member.

On a SMHC hike in 2015, Ken Wise and I sat on Broome's casket rock watching Kinsey and Montana and Clayton jumping repeatedly into Drinkwater Pool, Ken suggested not only the annual pilgrimage to Drinkwater but also the need for baptism in Drinkwater as a requirement for membership in the hiking club – a self-baptism performed by jumping into the pool from the rocky ledge above.

While some folks may be offended at the frequent comparison of off-trail hiking and religion, I think the comparison is apt and interesting. I wouldn't go so far as to say off-trailing *is* a religion, but there are similarities having to do with commitment, perseverance, special knowledge, a sense of awe, pilgrimage, holy ground, rites of initiation, peace & serenity, music & silence, and of course, following the straight and narrow path, or better yet, no path at all, that only a few will find and even fewer will follow.

Chapter 5

Place of the Balsams

On one of our very first off-trail hikes, Greg Harrell and I looked down the creek valley which we were to follow and commented, "Just follow the creek. Easy. Only an idiot could get lost." Of course, we both knew what that meant for our impending hike: we could get lost.

One of us asked, "What if there are *two* idiots? Does that make it *half* as likely or *twice* as likely?"

A couple of years later on Anakeesta Ridge we discovered the answer: *twice* as likely....

It's amazing to me that people will pay $20 or $30 to stand in line for an hour for the opportunity to be jostled and scared by a roller coaster, but they'll run indoors if it starts to rain for free. They don't want to get wet; although, I'm sure the threat of lightning also has something to do with it.

Of course, you've heard that your car is a safe space during a thunderstorm, and as far as I can tell, that's not just an urban legend. So, if you are ever caught in a heavy rainstorm in the Smokies, just pull off the road, stay in your car, and enjoy the show. If you'll do that, it will be like the roller coaster – all thrill, little actual danger (except to the electrical system of your car). But there's one important stipulation here: don't park on Newfound Gap Road between the Chimneys Tops trail and Newfound Gap. The water and lightning probably won't get you, but the mud, trees, and boulders might.

There's an area of the park that has been especially susceptible to flash floods and landslides. They don't happen often – maybe one major event every decade – but when they do, they are impressively dangerous. This danger zone runs roughly from the Chimney Tops trailhead along the main ridge of Mt. Le Conte and the Boulevard to

Charlies Bunion, then west along the main crest to Sugarland Mountain, and down the spine of Sugarland Mountain to the Chimney Tops. Or, another way of saying it: the upper watershed of the West Prong of the Little Pigeon River, consisting of Walker Camp Prong and Road Prong, plus their numerous tributaries.

The heart of this triangle of danger is Anakeesta Ridge, which is easily recognizable from the road. It's the one that's missing big chunks of soil and vegetation on its high slopes. These rocky scars are seen clearly from the top mile or two of the road leading from Gatlinburg to Newfound Gap. Stop at one of the parking pullouts near Morton Overlook (milepost #14) and look north across the valley. That beaten and bruised ridge with exposed, rocky scars is Anakeesta Ridge. (Behind it lies Mt. Le Conte, also bruised and scarred.) It's weathered but still standing, yet it seems to be evolving in the opposite direction from most mountains. We've all heard that the Rocky Mountains are young, but the Smokies are older, having that smoothed, rounded, ancient look. As time passes, mountains are supposed to become softer and gentler. Apparently, Anakeesta Ridge didn't get that memo. It has shed huge slices of soil and trees, exposing steep, rocky scars that would look at home west of the Mississippi.

The geologists call this landslide-prone section of the park the Anakeesta Formation, which is very different from most rock in the Smokies. My *Hiking Trails* describes the geological underpinnings of this region, but I'm not going to repeat it all because I'd just be repeating words that I don't fully understand. Instead, here's a short, and possibly even accurate, summary. This section is composed of a particular type of metamorphic rock closely related to slate that is easily broken and eroded. So, the landslides that plague this section are the result of storms racing up the West Prong valley and raining on land that has thin soil on steep rocks that aren't particularly sturdy. The soil and rock give way, then when it begins to slide, it not only pushes the landscape below it, but it also pulls down the landscape above it. Those who have witnessed these slides report that the trees seem to be surfing, leaning back, roots forward, on top of the landslide. The trees fall not from being blown down the slope by wind but by having the rug pulled out from under them – thus the "roots forward" surfing analogy.

I assume this underlying slate is the reason why most of the steepest cliffs and mountain slopes are in this section of the park: Eagle Rocks, Charlies Bunion, Jumpoff, Anakeesta Ridge, Alum Cave Bluff, Duck Hawk Ridge, Myrtle Point, Cliff Top, Chimney Tops, and dozens of unnamed rocky scars and ridges. If you like rugged terrain, including frighteningly steep cliffs, this Anakeesta section of the park is the place to be.

By the way, "anakeesta" is a Cherokee word meaning "place of the balsams." This ridge just south of Mt. Le Conte has long been called Anakeesta Ridge. The unique, erodible rock formation in this section of the park was named after that ridge. That was a good call by the geologists because the most dramatically visible scars are on the slopes of Anakeesta Ridge.

So it seemed to me that a guy looking for a good time might want to wander around the steep slopes and exposed rock of this Anakeesta Triangle, to get a sense of the power and drama that Mother Nature exhibits every now and then in the form of heavy rain, landslides, and mud-surfing trees.

Greg Harrell and I stepped out of my truck at Newfound Gap on a Saturday morning in the middle of February. We were on the tail end of an unseasonably warm stretch, so the weather was bearable, although a bit on the moist side. Our plan was simple: hike about three miles northeast on the Appalachian Trail to the Boulevard trail and then about two miles on the Boulevard to its intersection with Anakeesta Ridge. That would be the point where the real fun began because we'd step off a popular, maintained trail and onto a ridge that had no official trail, so it would probably be littered with blown-down trees, mountain laurel, and briers. It would also be rocky and narrow, with a smattering of sand myrtle and rhododendron. Perfect.

This stretch of the AT and the Boulevard is often fairly crowded, being a good route to Mt. Le Conte. The fact that there is a backpacking shelter near their junction means that many a hiker has made this route into a two night trip, the first night being spent at Icewater Spring shelter and the second on top of Le Conte. The fact that the Jumpoff and Charlies Bunion are nearby adds to the appeal of this route. It's one of the premier weekend backpacking trips in the Smokies.

So at about 1:30 pm, Greg and I stepped off the Boulevard and into the tangle of Anakeesta Ridge. Because we'd be gone maybe two or three hours at most, I decided to fill my pockets with granola bars and my GPS and stash my daypack by the side of the trail. I'd be waterless for a few hours, but I had been drinking heavily and was pretty sure I wouldn't die of dehydration. It would be nice to squeeze my way through laurel thickets without being encumbered by my pack.

Sometimes off-trail hiking is a pleasant walk in the woods; sometimes it's a slow, exhausting slog through a steel curtain of mountain laurel and rhododendron in which you are on your hands and knees, looking for a path of least resistance, only to find that there are only paths of *most* resistance. You're fighting a losing battle because you are tired and outnumbered.

Our first order of business was to crawl and push our way over logs and through mountain laurel and briers to the top of Anakeesta Knob. We then began a steady descent down the narrow, rocky ridgecrest toward a deep swag in the ridge about a half mile away. As with many of our off-trail jaunts, there was a barely-existing remnant of an old path along the crest, occasionally visible and clear, more often overgrown and tangled. It was dirty, wet work as the wind and lingering clouds kept us and the underbrush dripping wet. Forty degrees and wet is not one of my favorite combinations, but calories from granola bars and the exertion of pushing and weaving our way down this steep ridge kept hypothermia at bay.

The route was difficult to manage but easy to see. It was a nice change of pace from those off-trail excursions where you aren't really sure which ridge to climb or which creek to follow. This route was obvious – stay on this narrow ridge. We didn't have any particular destination in mind. We would simply follow the ridge as far as daylight would allow, looking for interesting sights, and then backtrack to the Boulevard and the AT before it got dark. So simple even a caveman could do it.

So for the next hour and a half we enjoyed the challenge of a steep, rocky, tangled, ridge hike. On a clear day, the views toward Le Conte to the north and the main crest to the south would have been fabulous, but today the clouds and mist meant that visibility was just a few yards. I would have preferred warm sunshine, singing birds, blooming flowers, panoramic views, and a tailwind, but clouds and mist are useful for reinforcing our delusion that we are a couple of manly guys who aren't afraid of some scratches, bruises, blood, and mud.

After a particularly difficult section which kept us descending faster and farther than we had expected, we stopped to rest and wonder. I looked at my watch and commented, "It's three o'clock. We're gonna run out of daylight."

Greg muttered, "Yeah, I know."

"Really? How long have you known?"

"Since we stepped out of the truck," Greg responded. I giggled under my breath and braced myself for yet another comment about my age or pace or propensity for frequent rest stops – all of which are favorite topics of Greg's commentary during our hikes. Instead, Greg added, "And that's not our only problem."

"What is it?"

"We've been heading south for the last ten minutes."

I understood the significance immediately: "No way! Are you sure?"

"Yep. At least ten minutes."

Greg and I both like compasses, and we use them on these untested hikes. I don't recall where Greg carries his. Probably in one of his pockets. I hang mine around my neck, tucked under my shirt so it won't get caught on branches. I hadn't even thought of pulling it out and looking at it because our route along this narrow ridge was so obvious. Greg held out his compass to show me. I looked back north up the ridge we'd been descending and looked south down the ridgecrest in front of us. Yes, south.

Anakeesta is an east-west ridge with an occasional north-south wiggle, but not a tenth of a mile, and not where we were standing. South simply wasn't supposed to happen. So I did something that I hate to do on these hikes because it feels like I'm cheating – I pulled out my GPS and poked around on it until the electronic bread crumb trail popped up on its topo map. And there it was, a blue line about a tenth of a mile long showing us traveling straight down toward the bottom of the screen – south, straight south.

The next five minutes involved a lot of staring down the foggy ridge, staring back up the foggy ridge, staring at each other, shaking the compass, poking more GPS buttons, and general bafflement. It's like those moments when my truck dies, and I open the hood and stand there staring at the tangle of wires and metal, wondering what it all means. Because I know nothing about the mysteries of internal combustion engines, I have no business looking under the hood, but I do it anyway in hopes that there will be a flashing, neon sign with an arrow pointing to the problem saying, "Replace this." There's never a flashing arrow under the hood, and there was no flashing sign for us on that side ridge.

Without going into the details of our conversation, I'll just say that we had no idea how we wandered off Anakeesta's main ridge and onto an obscure, south-going, side ridge. No idea whatsoever. We had stayed on what seemed to be not merely the *main* ridge, but the *only* ridge. There was just no other route to take. I've sometimes seen the trail under our feet just disappear into the dirt, rocks, and leaves, but this was the first time an entire ridge simply dissolved into clouds and thin air. I wondered if we had wandered into the Anakeesta Triangle where planes, ships, hikers, and ridges disappear.

But there we were, on that small, unnamed ridge. As we stood there dazed and confused, the only reasonable option was to backtrack up to the main ridge. We'd try to find the split in the ridge where we had made our mistake, but because it was getting late – we still had about five miles of hiking to get back to the truck – we'd have to hustle back to the Boulevard and the AT. The point where we were standing would have to suffice as our "destination" for the day. But then we heard cars below us…

In the distance below us an occasional car would pass along the base of Anakeesta, to the south, at the end of this side ridge. Greg pulled out his map, and we discovered that we were only about a half mile away from Newfound Gap Road. Greg later told me that at that moment he saw the gears start turning in my head as I began considering our

86

options and doing the math: we could push our way for an hour or more, back to the Boulevard then hike two miles up the Boulevard and another three miles on the AT... or... we could hike about a half mile down hill and catch a ride back up to the truck. In my mind, the choice was obvious – hike down, then hitchhike.

I explained my thinking and my preference to Greg, who just stood there, listening patiently, which made me a bit suspicious. He listened as I went on and on about daylight, gravity, old age, and the value of exploring new territory. I probably even covered some politics, history, and theology to drive home my point. PhD dissertations have been shorter and simpler than my exhaustive monologue. MLK's "I Have a Dream" speech was mere chatter compared to my impassioned "I Have an Idea!" speech.

When I finally paused to take a breath, thinking that I had an airtight case and that we would be going down, not up, Greg looked down in the direction of the road and said, "Sounds good to me."

I was a bit surprised at how easily he agreed with my analysis of the situation, but I assumed that even he, when faced with the overwhelming weight of unadulterated logic, had no alternative but to yield to the inevitable. Then he paused for effect and said, "Hey, pal..." – another pause, for even greater dramatic impact – "... where's your pack?"

What followed can only be described as a conniption for the ages. I jumped and screamed and spun and kicked. Greg giggled. I wailed and moaned and ranted and spit. Greg laughed. Like Job, I recounted the unfairness in life, the capriciousness of fate. Greg chortled. Coyotes howled in the distance. Mothers in Gatlinburg covered their children's ears. Rabbits and bears fled in terror. My disappointment was deep, reaching to the marrow of my bones and the core of my being. Greg bellowed. He showed no pity, no sympathy. He seemed happy with our fate. Backtracking up through the tangle and rocks of Anakeesta Ridge was a small price to pay to witness my tantrum.

Then I paused and began a mental inventory of the contents of my daypack. Could I just leave my pack where it was? It was old and ratty. It held a water bottle and a fleece jacket, so I'd be losing a few dollars, but it might be worth it. It was hidden well, so I could even come back

87

in a few weeks and retrieve it if the mood struck. Yes, there was a ray of hope, a chance for redemption – which Greg saw written on my face.

At that moment Greg Harrell, Mind Read & Sadist appeared. He seemed to know what I was thinking because he looked at me as I pondered, paused for effect, and said rhetorically, "Hey... (another pause to heighten the drama)... where are your keys?" Insert a picture of my face with a momentary blank stare, followed by a flicker of recognition, and finally sadness and gloom. If this were a passage from the Bible, I believe it would say, "...and his countenance fell...."

In my pack. My keys were in my stinkin' pack.

I swooned as the sun was blotted out and the moon turned to blood. I cursed the day I was born. I cursed the mountain. I cursed life and fate. I just plain cursed.

I'm not very fond of golf, but I am very fond of the concept of a mulligan. That trip would be our Anakeesta Mulligan. We'd try again, and I'd keep my pack in plain sight.

So on a crisp, clear March day, we parked Greg's car at the parking spot where Walker Camp Prong flows off the slopes of Mount Kephart and under Newfound Gap Road and began walking up Conniption Ridge, our side spur of Anakeesta Ridge that we had stumbled upon a month earlier. Our hike to the ridgecrest would be steep, which became immediately apparent. Greg's calculations (he's the statistician on all our hikes) showed that we would ascend from 4,600 feet to 5,600 feet in 3/10 of a mile. Yes, 1,000 feet vertical in .3 mile horizontal. Compare that to the typical Smokies trail which rises 500 feet in 1 mile.

I never know what to call this type of hike. I tend not to use the word "climb" because the rock climbers with ropes and carabiners are the ones who "climb." On the other hand, the word "hike" implies walking upright on two feet. The first hour of this hike was somewhere in between. We'd walk steeply but upright for a while, then we'd switch to hands and feet, using rocks, roots, and limbs to pull ourselves up. I've heard people use the word "scramble" to describe this, but somehow that sounds quick and energetic, which definitely doesn't apply here.

Whatever it was we were doing, it wasn't dangerous, but it was dirty and slow. Greg the Statistician told me the next day that this was the slowest hike we had ever done. We covered one mile in five hours; although, in our defense, there were more than the average number of stops for pictures which is a sure sign of a memorable trip.

There was a lightly worn path running right up this narrow crest, meaning that this route was occasionally used by others. Who these others are and how they discovered this route are mysteries to me; although, I have a hunch that few, if any, of them are human. Sometimes a path is clear from head to foot, but others are only about knee high. Those knee high tunnels through the brush are almost certainly bear paths, which adds another layer of drama to the trip. Walking on a trail is fine. Walking on a manway has a greater sense of discovery to it. Walking on a *bearway* is wildly enticing, as long as the bear is black, not grizzly.

Whatever mammals they are, *homo* or *ursus*, they keep their secrets well, and I found myself thanking them for their covert trailblazing. Pushing one's way through a pathless tangle of rhododendron and mountain laurel is the hardest, most frustrating part of off-trail hiking. Yes, off-trail hiking is a lot easier when there's a path… and I've been surprised at how often there is one, however faint and narrow.

On the other hand, the presence of rhododendron, mountain laurel, and sand myrtle means that you are in a beautiful, wild place that becomes outrageously beautiful in May, June, and July. In fact, when it's all said and done, I think these lonely, rocky, narrow ridges covered in heath thickets are my favorite genre in the Smokies. There's always a good view of the surrounding terrain, there's always work and sweat involved which makes the destination all the more special, and there's a gradual progression of spring blooms which is so outrageously outrageous, so extravagantly extravagant, that redundancy is necessary but not quite sufficient.

After about two hours of hiking, scrambling, and picture-taking, Greg and I reached Anakeesta's main crest, and we found the unbelievably obscure spot where a month earlier we had taken a wrong turn and stumbled upon this side ridge. We followed the faint trail leading west along Anakeesta's crest, giving magnificent views across the Alum Cave and Styx river valleys. The broad crest of Mt. Le Conte was visible: Myrtle Point, High Top, Cliff Top, West Point, Balsam Point. Looking down we could clearly pick out Alum Cave trail leading to Inspiration Point and Peregrine Peak. There are many reasons why people hike, but views like this are high on everyone's list. It's good to know early in the day that your hike has paid off handsomely in the form of vast panoramas, and this one had. If we had quit right then, the hike would still have been a success, but the really unique part of this hike was yet to come: the landslides and their scars.

There have been several large landslides since the park was established in 1934, and numerous smaller ones. A storm on September 1, 1951 and another on June 28, 1993 struck the south slopes of Mt. Le Conte around Peregrine Peak. From our vantage point on Anakeesta Ridge, rocky scars from these downpours and subsequent landslides were clearly visible high on the south slopes of Mt. Le Conte.

Another large landslide was actually a pair of landslides that occurred on August 10, 1984. After a heavy, evening thunderstorm two sections of mountainside slid off the southern slope of Anakeesta Ridge and onto Newfound Gap Road, between Alum Cave trail and Newfound Gap. About thirty cars were trapped on the road between these two slides for several hours. Amazingly, while there were several near-misses, no one was seriously injured. These are the prominent rocky scars that are visible from the Morton Overlook parking pullouts. It was these scars that we would walk above today.

My wife is skeptical when I tell her this, but it's true: those rocky scars are not quite as dangerous as they appear. Looking at them from a mile away, they look slick and vertical, but as we walked on the ridge above them we could see that some spots were dangerously vertical, but plenty of others were not. Many of these scars had small shrubs beginning to repopulate their cracks and gullies. In fact, small spruce forests were developing along the edges of these scars where there was enough soil to support trees.

As the day wore on, Greg and I began to ask each other what our plans were. We had originally thought that we'd hike along the ridgecrest, enjoy the views, and be flexible. We might follow the entire crest all the way to the Alum Cave trail parking area. Or, we might hike

90

down some other side ridge or creekbed. But as we looked down the rocky scars below us we began to consider another possibility: would it be really, really stupid to scramble down these rocky scars? And if so, should that stop us? We've done stupid things before; why stop now?

After letting that thought simmer for a while, the answer became obvious to both of us. One of our reasons for coming to Anakeesta had been to see the landslide scars up close. Finding a route down them would probably be interesting, maybe educational, and definitely up close. So, stupid or not.... This wouldn't be the first time that a burst of adrenaline had trumped sound judgement.

This may have been the moment when I realized that there are many things in life that I like the *idea* of doing, but not *actually* doing. I love the idea of organic gardening, but actually doing it is too much work, as are beekeeping, reading the novels of Tolstoy and Dostoyevsky, and joining the 900 mile club. As we prepared to step down off the ridgecrest, I wondered if exploring Anakeesta's landslide scars belonged on this list. It may have been somewhere in here that one of us recalled that famous battle cry of Crazy Horse: It is a good day to die!

At the low swag in the ridge where we were having our lunch, the landslide scar looked less treacherous. I'd guess it was at least a 45° but not quite a 60° angle; not easy, but 30° or 40° shy of vertical. In fact, along the western edge of this scar, a small forest of young trees and bushes was growing up. About twenty-five years worth of leaves had begun to create a layer of soft dirt that actually made crab-walking and two-footed-walking possible.

So we left the ridgecrest at the swag and angled our way through this young forest, down the slope, and to the bare rock scar. Once we reached the bare rock below the crest, we gingerly worked our way down the scar. In situations like this, I tend to be a bit more cautious than Greg. He says I'm a sissy. I say he's too stupid to be scared. We're probably both right. So I crab-walked down the scar on all fours with my butt dragging the ground as an emergency brake. It's a slow process, but that's sort of the point. Thus, we both managed to travel down and across several rocky scars with a few, small bumps and bruises but no near-death experiences.

In most places these scars are barren and still crumbly. In other places there are long cracks in the rock that have filled with dirt and have sprouted various species of shrubs. I would guess that a hundred years from now, this will be another Smoky Mountain heath bald – one of those smooth-looking evergreen swaths that punctuate high, rocky ridges. It was a perfect laboratory for what we've all learned in school – that given enough time, a rocky surface can turn into a forest or field (or, in this case, maybe a heath thicket). If I were a young botanist, I'd study these scars on Anakeesta Ridge to track their progress. I suppose it would be a rather long, drawn-out project that would outlive several generations of researchers, but it would beat sitting in a laboratory watching petri dishes.

So we zigged and zagged our way down the barren slope to lonely outposts of vegetation that would provide a chance to stand up and relax. There were also a few small ridges that had their sides scoured by the landslide, but their crests were still covered with small trees and shrubs. All in all, the terrain was scrubbed and sterile, with occasional islands of life scattered about. I guess it's really just a large version of a driveway or sidewalk – mostly clean and well-swept, with the occasional dandelion or tuft of grass poking up through the cracks or along the edges.

After an hour or two of scrambling and exploring these rocky acres, we entered phase two of the landslide – the debris field, consisting of all those acres of soil, shrubs, rock, and trees, all thrown together into a tangled mess. Those high elevation scars are frighteningly beautiful and make for dramatic pictures. If you want to impress your friends, point to one of these scars on a mountain slope across the valley and tell them you've scrambled or slithered down it.

The debris field at the bottom of the scar is a different matter. It's wild and chaotic and not at all photogenic, definitely not postcard material. If you watch the welcome video at Sugarlands Visitor Center, you'll see images of creeks, deer, mountain tops, and foggy mornings, but one thing you won't see is a debris field. If the Smokies were a city, a debris field would be a ghetto or maybe the municipal landfill. It's just not the sort of thing you advertise to the tourists because it isn't pretty.

Debris fields are also difficult to maneuver because they consist mostly of tangled, criss-crossed trees and piles of rocky dirt. It's bumpy going with plenty of opportunities to step into a hole or a soft spot or to slip off the tree trunk that you are walking on or climbing over. Then, of course, there are the snakes.

To be honest, I've walked through dozens of debris fields, and I've never seen a snake in any of them, but there's no question in my mind that these places must be full of them. When I'm hiking in the Smokies, I rarely think about snakes and other creepy, crawly things because dwelling on those possibilities would probably get me too spooked to go. So I put them out of my mind. Except, that is, for when I'm picking my way through a debris field. The rattlesnakes I've seen in the Smokies are usually lying in the middle of a tangle of rocks and tree branches -- and that's exactly what a debris field is, multiplied by about 10 gazillion. For that reason, I try to avoid this tangled habitat in warm weather, preferring those cold days that push those cold-blooded critters into dormancy.

The particular debris field that Greg Harrell and I picked our way through near the bottom of Anakeesta Ridge was impressive in a big, nasty, tangled sort of way. It's impressive not because of its beauty but because of the sheer power that was required to create it. You can't look at this sort of scene the way you look at Cades Cove or a sunset. Those sights are breathtakingly beautiful. No, you have to look at the debris field at the bottom of a landslide the way you look at the wreckage after a tornado or a tsunami. There's a mixed sense of sadness and awe at the raw power that was momentarily unleashed to do its destructive work.

It's funny, then, that the spot where this mass of wreckage meets Newfound Gap Road at the south base of Anakeesta Ridge appears as a modest, little creek full of broken rock and young, birch trees. You'd never know, as you drive past, that the remnants of a massive, natural catastrophe lie just a few yards uphill from the road, hidden from view. When this landslide happened back in 1984, tons of mountainside were funneled down into a narrow valley and sped down the chute and out onto Newfound Gap Road. Bulldozers and dump trucks did such a good job of cleaning up the mess on the road that the typical car tourist hasn't a clue that several hundred yards of debris begin just a few yards above the road.

The best indicator that something out of the ordinary happened here is the pure stand of yellow birch trees, all about four inches in diameter, filling up that narrow creekbed. There's a similar stand of yellow birches along the bottom 1.5 miles of Alum Cave trail where landslides of 1951 and 1993 both came roaring down the river valley. Yellow birch trees are a pioneer species which specializes in the disturbed soil of a landslide. You can recognize these distinctive birches by their golden, papery bark that peels off in horizontal strips. I would have been tempted to call them paper birch, but my tree books tell me that paper birches don't live in the Smokies. So these papery birches are actually yellow birches.

As far as I know, there's no law against exploring Anakeesta Ridge – *as far as I know* – because being firm believers that it's better to seek forgiveness than permission, we didn't ask. Luckily, our national parks really are, in most ways, parks for "the people," and I've been pleasantly surprised at the lack of restrictions on our right to wander in the Smokies. If we had asked permission, we probably would have received a brief lecture about safety and discretion, and then when it became obvious that we would not be dissuaded, we'd have been told to have fun and be careful – which is exactly what we did, without having to be told.

Chapter 6

A Gorge, A Ranger, and Raven Fork

This trip started in October, 1952. That's when *National Geographic* published an article entitled "Pack Trip Through the Smokies." I didn't run across this article until about 55 years later as I was searching for old articles about the Smokies. I had been on my off-trail jag for a few months, and I was looking for old trails from the past that were no longer maintained. (I was still under the mis-impression that off-trail hiking was really old-trail hiking, not yet having realized that every stream, every ridge, and every landslide scar is a potential off-trail option.) This article described several trails that do still exist and one that doesn't. The one that no longer exists led to Three Forks Pool on Raven Fork in the southeast quarter of the park, which the article described as "the most beautiful spot in the Smokies." Of course, just about any article you read about any national park will describe its location of interest as the most beautiful spot, so you have to take all these claims with a grain of salt. Nevertheless, it all sounded interesting.

I was able once again to find a little bit of information in my old 1973 edition of the Sierra Club's *Hiker's Guide to the Smokies*. This guide had been my Smokies bible back in the 1970s and 80s when I was a young, rabid backpacker. I have since replaced it with updated hiking guides, but in recent years it has resurfaced as a treasure chest containing a few hidden jewels. The particular gem I found this time was the Raven Fork trail, the route of the wilderness backpacking trip described in the 1952 article.

This trail no longer exists on recent maps and guide books. (It barely existed in 1952.) In fact, my most recent hiking guide specifically says that there is NOT a trail along Raven Fork. That sounded a bit suspicious to me. It's one thing to simply not mention the presence or lack of a trail. It's entirely different to specifically point out that there is no trail along Raven Fork. If Phyllis came home and asked me what I'd done all day, I'd be foolish to say, "Well, one thing I didn't do was eat all the Oreos and take a three hour nap on the couch." She'd know immediately that I'd been up to no good instead of cutting the grass. So, I strongly suspected that the guide book wasn't telling the whole truth. Maybe it was helping the NPS to return the old trail to pure wilderness by promoting the idea that there's not a trail. Yes, this had all the markings of government sanctioned disinformation. It was time to blow the lid off this cover-up!

My 1973 *Guide* actually described Raven Fork trail as a manway, not a trail. In other words, it still existed as a faint trail, being maintained not by the NPS but by the feet of outdoorsmen who fished and hiked along the banks of this fine stream. So it was certainly possible that thirty-five years later the manway could be completely overgrown. On the other hand, thirty-five years worth of fishermen could keep it trampled and visible, so on a warm July afternoon Greg Harrell and I took off for Big Cove Road on the Cherokee Indian Reservation. This road would lead us to the Round Bottom parking area where our excursion would begin on Beech Gap trail (called Hyatt Bald trail in some books because it goes to Hyatt Bald, not Beech Gap; makes sense.).

Some of life's mundane details kept us from leaving Jefferson City until 5 pm, so we didn't get on the trail until 8 pm, and the last hour of our two-hour hike to McGee Spring campsite was in the dark using flashlights. The moon was full so, although it was bright, it was too low in the sky to provide much light during the first hour or two of night. After setting up our tents in the dark, we had a quick bite to eat and crawled in for the night.

The equipment that we carried on this trip was pretty sparse, but not sparse enough to weigh less than thirty-five pounds. As the years have gone by, I've shifted my backpacking philosophy from "How much can I stuff in my backpack?" to "How few things can I get by with?" (I think that would make a good philosophy of life, but for now let's just stick to backpacking.) This has resulted in a change in priorities from cooking and clothing to sleeping. I'm willing to commit a few extra pounds in my pack to a comfortable tent, a good sleeping pad, and a small pillow but am less inclined to carry the poundage of clothes that I used to carry. On this trip my wardrobe consisted of the clothes I was wearing, plus one extra T shirt, one extra pair of socks, and a light rain jacket. No warm clothes because it was the middle of July, and if the evening got chilly (we were camped above 5,000 feet), I'd dance a jig while I ate and then crawl in my sleeping bag.

According to one expert (my wife), by the end of these trips I smell like a wet goat and have occasionally just thrown some of my clothes in the garbage. Not a glorious end for hiking clothes, but sometimes the only realistic option. So on these trips it's important to wear clothes that have no sentimental value; so don't wear the NASCAR T shirt you were wearing when you proposed to your wife or the Vol T shirt with the mustard stains from the 1999 Fiesta Bowl. On the other hand, after you complete a trip like this with lots of sweat and dirt and fond memories, your clothes may *gain* some sentimental value.

The closest I've ever come to having a special backpacking T shirt was when I ran out of toilet paper near Mt. Le Conte and had to tear strips off the bottom of my T shirt for two days. I wore the surviving 50% of that T shirt whenever I'd backpack as a memorial to that trip. Of course, any guy who saves a memento like that had better have several keepsakes and cards from his wife or girlfriend (one or the other, not both) publicly displayed in prominent spots around home. Otherwise, trying to explain your choice of memorabilia is a lost cause: "Yes, Dear, I did throw away your anniversary card – which, by the way, really warmed the cockles of my heart – but I kept that Springsteen backpacking T shirt, and here's why...." That sentence is exactly like our war in Iraq – there are no good options for ending it.

On this trip I carried a roomy one-person tent that weighs more than it should, but it's a pleasure to sleep in at the end of the day. I have an inflatable sleeping pad that is entirely too bulky, but makes a world of difference in blotting out those inevitable rocks and roots that are nonexistent when you set up the tent but magically appear when you lie down for the night. I also brought a small pillow. A few years ago a pillow would have been an extravagance worthy of ridicule and shame, such as: "Don't forget your night light" or "Where's the remote?" Yes, what were once luxuries are now essentials.

Of course, if you're going to carry a pillow, pad, and tent then something significant has to go because what were once essentials are now expendable. My ultimate solution has been to stop cooking, thus eliminating pots and pans, stove, and fuel. That's a couple of pounds of stuff, which may not sound like much, but keep in mind that this is a sport in which guys have been known to cut the tags off clothes and tea bags to save weight. Instead of rice, macaroni, and stew, I now rely on granola bars, crackers, and beef jerky, which can get a bit monotonous after a day or two, so I include an occasional can of tuna or bag of chips to spice up the menu. If eating were important to me, I don't know what I'd do on these trips. Fortunately, eating on a backpacking trip is just something I do to stay alive and keep moving, so I don't need cooked veggies, smores, hot chocolate, and a hot breakfast. And of course, with no cooking, there's no clean-up, which is important to a guy who scores above average on the laziness scale.

When tromping around outdoors I know it's best to always be prepared, as the Boy Scouts say, but over-preparation can make a backpack pretty heavy, which becomes an issue for a guy who's flirting with senior citizen status. That's one of the ironies of backpacking. You are more likely to get into trouble (broken bones, hypothermia, exhaustion) when you are old – the very stage at which it's impossible to carry equipment to cover those emergencies. Of course, one way to resolve this dilemma is to hike with young guys – preferably former Boy Scouts – who are still willing and able to carry all the extra stuff. It's sort of like life insurance. Traveling in groups spreads the risk – or, in backpacking, the weight – to manageable proportions, and if you can free ride on someone else's equipment without their realizing it, so much the better.

For example, I have been known to suggest to some of my younger friends that one should never backpack without a first aid kit. If they see the wisdom in that and stuff one in their backpack, then I won't have to carry one. The same ploy works for water filters, tarps, rope, knives, can openers, magazines, maps, even extra food. Of course, this strategy isn't always successful because many of my "younger" friends are in their 40s and 50s, so they aren't exactly wet behind the ears. But some of them are still conscientious enough to carry stuff that we might need but probably won't, thus lightening my load.

So that evening at McGee Springs campsite we hung our food bags on the bear-proof, steel cables and retired to our tents. It was a quiet, uneventful night, as most nights in camp are – no bears, no deer, no skunks, no noise; at least none that we noticed. We slept pretty well under the spruce, buckeye, and birch trees. I enjoy sleeping outdoors, but the real purpose of this trip would come tomorrow: Raven Fork – the long, beautiful river that flows from the slopes of Hyatt Ridge, Hughes Ridge, and the main ridgecrest between Pecks Corner and Tricorner Knob – the large, wild watershed that forms the heart of the southeastern quarter of the Smokies.

The old Raven Fork trail begins high on Hyatt Ridge near McGee Springs. Its first mile weaves along the crest of Breakneck Ridge, which Greg insisted on calling Brokeback Mountain a few times, just to annoy me. Breakneck sounds intimidating, and I suppose there might be an interesting and perhaps tragic story about its origin, but the hike itself wasn't too formidable. Greg and I lost the faint trail a few times in tangles of briers, rhododendron, and dog hobble resulting in a few scratches and blood, but for the most part the old trail was still recognizable.

There was even an occasional piece of old, brittle, blue tape tied to a branch to help us stay on course. Greg and I are both typical guys who like to be self-sufficient and to figure things out for ourselves, but these small, plastic clues are perfectly fine. They are fragile reminders that others have been here before and were kind enough to share their knowledge with those who would come later – namely, us. Those little, blue messages from the past let us know that we are the latest incarnation of "wilderness enthusiasts," as some of the books say. Sometimes you can derive a lot of satisfaction not by being the first to do something, or the best. Occasionally just being a link in a chain is enough. People have done this before us, and people will do this after we are gone. The fact that we don't even know these people adds a bit of intrigue to the story. As we continue these off-trail and old-trail treks, I may start bringing a roll of surveyor's tape with me, so I can add a few pieces along the way so that a few years from now another hiker – the next link in the chain – can find her way. She won't know who put the tape along the path, which is not a problem because it's the where and why, not the who, that's important.

It took about two hours for Greg and me to work our way along Breakneck Ridge and down its north slope to Three Forks Pool on Raven Fork. Three Forks is a pleasant spot in the river where three small creeks converge to form the main branch. Here the terrain flattens just enough to slow the river's flow and to provide a flat, riverside area to rest or camp. Actually, camping here is now illegal, but that doesn't seem to have completely deterred everyone. There were several campfire rings and small piles of firewood nearby – remnants of small acts of civil disobedience. Or, just spots where some guys decided to flaunt federal law and play hide-and-seek with the rangers. It's a nice spot, but I wouldn't call it the most beautiful spot in the Smokies as the old *National Geographic* article had done.

In fact, it was here that Greg and I decided that we would start our Top 1,000 list – our list of the 1,000 "best places in the Smokies." The point is that there is no single spot that is the best or prettiest or whatever, and anyone who claims there is needs to get out more and look around. There are hundreds or thousands of river valleys, pools, waterfalls, heath balds, grassy balds, beech gaps, meadows, cliffs, boulder dens, rhododendron thickets, hardwood forests, log cabins, rock walls, old churches, mountain top panoramas, wildflowers, and spruce forests that could all qualify as the most beautiful sights, but none are better than the others. Don't even try to come up with a single best location. Just put them all in the top 1,000 and move on. So, is Three Forks Pool the most dramatic, impressive, beautiful spot in the Smokies? Absolutely not, because there's no such thing, but Three Forks, like many other bends in the river, is in the top 1,000. It's tied for 1st with 999 others.

But Three Forks is special because it's so hard to get to. In fact, that is probably the secret ingredient that qualifies some sites for special recognition within the Top 1,000. Knowing that you are enjoying a spot that only a handful of people see each year is not only good for the ego ("We walked four hours to get here. How many people would do *that*?"), it's also good for the soul. The stillness is somehow stiller, the wildness is wilder, and the isolation is that healthy kind of loneliness that you get when you separate yourself from the pack because you are following a different drummer, taking a path less traveled. In this case, *literally* a path less traveled, or no path at all. There are reasons why people use phrases like "off the beaten path" or "the road less traveled" to describe their great, solitary, life-changing experiences.

The route we took from our car at Round Bottom up and over Breakneck Ridge to Three Forks takes a total of three to four hours. However, because we started our day at McGee Springs campsite, we were less than two hours into our hike when we arrived at the river. After lounging and fishing (Greg caught three brook trout and one brown on a Thunderhead dry fly) for about an hour, we were ready for part two: Raven Fork. We hoped to find remnants of the old Raven Fork trail leading us downstream for about 4 miles down to the Enloe Creek trail and campsite. The fact that there had still been a light trail across Breakneck Ridge was encouraging because the river would probably be more heavily traveled.

To make a long story short, if more people travel along the banks of the river, we weren't able to prove it. We followed a faint trail out of the old (illegal) campsite at Three Forks for ten minutes. It then disappeared into the river, never to emerge again. No pieces of blue tape. No rock cairns. No unnatural openings in the riverside bushes. No worn trail. No government cover-up.

Of course, there could be a trail. On those hikes where we do find an old trail, there is usually no clue to its presence until we step on to it. It makes such a small dent in the underbrush that you can be standing three feet away without seeing it. I suppose that's good news because you can push your way through a thicket of briers or rhody with the feeling that you are nowhere close to the old trail, only to suddenly find that you are standing on it. Although, I suspect that it's just as common to step on and across the old trail without realizing it. Or, to bushwhack your way almost to the trail only to give up just a couple of feet shy of your destination. That may have happened to us on Raven Fork, but of course we don't really know how close we got to the old trail that may or may not still exist.

So for about four hours, we walked along and in Raven Fork. The water level was low, and there were many exposed, streamside boulders and gravel beds for us to walk on, but at some point I chose to walk *in* the water... as usual. While Greg hops and skips and sloshes along the rocks at the edge, happy to stay dry, I find joy in being sloppy and wet and not caring. I don't know why. It's easier, but it's also uncomfortable to have wet feet in wet boots, so ease and discomfort tend to cancel each other out. Instead, I seem to be drawn to the water by some primordial, mystical urge that I can feel, just beneath the surface, but can't explain. To quote Norman Maclean, "I am haunted by waters," but only if those waters are moving waters, in the mountains.

I was exposed to my first mountain river when I was young and as impressionable as a baby duck, so it's one of my most vivid childhood memories. I still remember the time: a summer night in 1961; the place: a pullout by the Oconaluftee River; the moment: sleeping in our family car; the feeling: thrill and awe. To steal a line from C. S. Lewis, I was "surprised by joy." A mountain river isn't the only thing that can still elicit these glimpses of joy, but a mountain river was my first.

Hiking in the river is a bit slippery, but on a hot, summer day it's delightfully comfortable and clean. Sweaty and dirty? Just take off your pack and dunk yourself. The water can be breathtakingly cold or refreshingly brisk. Your choice. And the soggy boots and socks are but a small price to pay.

This river hike was such a pleasant, easy, off-trail experience that I felt our purpose shift as we worked our way downstream. At some point we were no longer simply on an off-trail adventure; we were now looking for good fishing spots for our next trip here. And there were plenty of them – dozens of runs, riffles, channels, chutes, and plunges. And, best of all, lightly fished. Surely not <u>un</u>fished, but several miles from the nearest road.

Sure, lots of other fishermen have had the same thoughts: drive deep into the mountains, hike away from the road, fish virgin water. And some of them have pursued those thoughts all the way to the river with a fishing rod in their hand. But how many do it, how far do they walk, and how often? The answer is probably "not" – not many, not far, not often. In other words, Raven Fork is not such a secret that fishermen will get

102

mad at me for divulging its name in print. It's not an untouched secret. But it is remote, so we will come back... eventually, but maybe not often. It's a three hour drive to get here, after all, and then the walking begins, mostly uphill.

The day ended with a 3.6 mile walk on Enloe Creek and Hyatt Ridge trails back to our tents. After a day of rough, wet, off-trail hiking, an officially-maintained trail feels like a four lane highway. You can shift into overdrive and set the cruise control. However, the fact that almost every step of the first three miles of this final stretch was uphill caused my transmission to grind to a halt several times. At least we were carrying ten pound day packs, not thirty-five pound backpacks. We had covered ten miles today.

That evening we ate our uncooked meals consisting of granola bars, peanut M & M's, and a few other items that I can't remember. One thing about going cookless is that the meals are not memorable – unless you have no fear of fat grams and sugar. Then you can eat wonderfully and recklessly – chips, cookies, nuts, candy. It's like being let off your leash with the gate open. But if you have any dietary scruples at all, then you look forward with anticipation to bedtime, but not to supper. Supper is just something you have to do. I don't know how the younger guys feel, but at my stage in life, that's fine with me. Bedtime is usually the highlight of my day anyway.

As darkness settled in we heard a couple of calls from a Barred Owl asking, "Who cooks for you? Who cooks for ya'll?" He seemed to know we were eating a cold, uncooked supper and took this opportunity to taunt us a few times before he began his nightly hunt and feast. Mice would die tonight. He would eat like a king while we slept, but I wasn't jealous. I had my tent, sleeping pad, pillow, and memories of another good day in a wild part of Creation. I fell asleep while he was still taunting us.

Since that first trip, I've been to Raven Fork only twice: once by myself and once with fifteen other people. Both trips were great, for different reasons.

103

The solo trip was a year or two after the first trip. The best part of it was the fact that I was actually making good on my promise to return, a promise I've made and broken many times in other places. It's nice to actually keep a promise every now and then, you know, just to remind yourself of how it feels.

As I recall, I finally reached the Enloe Creek campsite around 1 pm, maybe 2 pm, with a day pack and my fishing gear. Just a few minutes after I had spread all my stuff on the ground and had begun assembling my rod and reel, a park ranger appeared from downstream. He was soaking wet because he had just waded up The Gorge section of Raven Fork, looking for illegal, bait fishermen.

We talked for a few minutes about hiking, fishing, trout, picking blueberries, and an assortment of mountain-related topics. We seemed to be getting along swimmingly, so I (jokingly) suggested that we throw rocks at a nearby hornet's nest. It was obvious that I was kidding. Only a blithering idiot would provoke hornets; plus, you don't do damage to the park or its inhabitants, especially in front of a ranger. Everyone knows that, right? I was obviously kidding because he could tell that I wasn't a fool. It should be obvious.

It wasn't obvious. About ten seconds into his "National parks are federal property with a clear set of regulations established for the protection and..." monologue, when he momentarily paused to take a breath, I interrupted him and said, "Really, I was just kidding. I don't aggravate the wildlife. I like the rules that protect this place." He seemed skeptical.

Lesson for the future: a person with a badge and gun doesn't have a sense of humor. Or, maybe I'm not as funny as I think I am. Or both.

Since he was now doubtful of my scruples, he asked to see my fishing license, which I showed him. That seemed to pacify him, so we finished our now-awkward conversation, and I picked up my fishing pack... and a salamander was clinging to it.

I saw a cute little resident of the park who had crawled under it, thinking it seemed like a nice cozy rest stop. The ranger, on the other hand, saw *bait*. As in: "The possession and use of live bait is prohibited on the streams of Great Smoky Mountains National Park. Violators will be prosecuted."

Remember the part about people with badges and guns not having a sense of humor? Well, they are also a very, very suspicious breed. I suppose their encounters with tourists and the occasional criminal has taught them to trust nobody about anything. I hope, for their spouses' sakes, they are able to flip that switch to "off" when they go home at night, because when standing by a river with a salamander dangling from your fishing gear, suspicious rangers can be really, really annoying. Convincing him that I was fly fishing, not bait fishing, took a lot more time and energy than I thought it deserved. I think the convincing piece of evidence was the tiny Elk Hair Caddis that I had tied to my leader. Thankfully, this humorless ranger knew enough about fly fishing to see that I'd have trouble impaling the salamander on the tiny hook and even more trouble casting such as conglomeration of elk hair, peacock herl, rooster feather, and salamander. Maybe he believed me, or maybe it was close to quitting time and he'd had a long day. Whatever the reason, he didn't arrest me for bait fishing nor for molesting the wildlife. He bought my story about the salamander being an inadvertent hitchhiker, which just happened to be true.

As far as I know, I've never committed a federal crime worthy of imprisonment, but if I ever do, I hope it will be little more exciting than kidnapping a salamander. I'm not sure how I could explain that to the other inmates in the federal penitentiary. For the sake of gaining some respect, I'd claim to have killed it... in cold blood (literally)... with my bare hands. "So don't mess with me, bro. I'm bloodthirsty."

After all the driving and hiking and the brief encounter with the ranger, I only had a couple of hours to fish. So I picked my way upstream and fished one of a thousand beautiful Smokies rivers. Although, one thing that really does set this portion of Raven Fork apart from the rest is that it is big and wide and open, as mountain streams go. There was plenty of backcasting room, which is an important part of fly fishing. I didn't lose a single fly in branches and weeds behind me.

And, by the way, I caught a few brook trout. Except for the five hours of driving, three or four hours of hiking, and almost being arrested for molesting salamanders and threatening hornets, it was easy.

My third trip to Raven Fork was with fifteen other people, which at first blush sounds horrible, but it wasn't. It was a Smoky Mountains Hiking Club off-trail hike consisting of sixteen hearty, fit, adventurous souls. Those three adjectives – hearty, fit, adventurous – are not just a random set of adjectives. Our off-trail hikes occasionally attract some folks that aren't quite ready for what's about to happen to them. Either, they aren't physically prepared for the rigors of the trip or they aren't mentally prepared, or both.

In short, it's best if you are in reasonably decent, physical condition, and have a sense of adventure, and have the toughness you'll need to cope with the crawling, sliding, wading, sweat, dirt, bruises, and blood of hiking off-trail. Of those three traits – hearty, fit, and adventurous – you need at least two of them to have a good time. A sense of adventure can compensate for being somewhat out of shape. But occasionally someone with none of those three attributes will give it a try, and while I appreciate their desire, it usually becomes obvious pretty quickly that they just aren't up to the task.

Or, I should say, it becomes quickly obvious to *everyone else*. It's not always obvious to the victim. That's when things don't go well. In those cases, there may need to be an intervention in which the hike leader tells the straggler that we care very much about him, and that's why we are kicking you off the island. It's time for you to turn around and go back to the car.

On our SMHC trip, all 16 of us were up to the task, both mentally and physically, even though the section of Raven Fork that we explored was the tough, even dangerous, lower section – The Gorge.

To get a real, full-blown taste of this part of the river, go to YouTube and search: *raven fork gorge kayak*. That's right, *kayak*. This section of Raven Fork has become one of the top high-energy, adrenaline-pumping kayak trips in the eastern US. In the spring, or after a decent spell of wet weather, young kayakers with no fear of death or disability will carry their kayaks several miles up to the Enloe Creek area, and run the chutes and rapids down to the Cherokee Indian Reservation. If they survive the Headless Horseman, the Mangler, and Mortal Combat, then they'll have some great GoPro videos to tell the

106

story. It's only a matter of time until the NPS adds to The Gorge's legend by erecting a warning sign listing the number of deaths, which will be like a "Welcome" sign to these swashbuckling kayakers.

Hikers, on the other hand, wait for a time when the weather has been dry and the river's flow is low and slow; that would be *relatively* slow, not *absolutely* slow. Only then can you set foot in the stream without being swept away.

The Gorge is about a mile of massive boulders, deep pools, fast chutes, steep cascades, sliding rocks, and frothy falls. It is as wild a scene as the Smokies have to offer. On our trip David spent much of his time diving and swimming, James tried to keep the group intact but wisely gave up and watched us wander and explore (he settled for taking an occasional head count to see if we'd lost anyone), Mike the Elder had a momentary attack of adulthood in which he worried that we were doing too much playing and not enough actual hiking (he got over it), the three Page sisters were their enthusiastic, delightful selves as they zigged and zagged their way upstream looking for the fun routes, Ken took a few tumbles as he always does, and the rest of us just gawked and wondered at the Gorge's untamed beauty. And, best of all, there were no interventions.

And whatever injuries we sustained were perfect – not so serious as to be life threatening, but serious enough to draw some blood and create bruises, all of which would be displayed proudly to our friends and family upon our return to civilization.

We spent the day wading, swimming, hopping, and occasionally even walking up the river, and in the process I discovered that there are two types of people: those who enjoy being wet and those who don't, like the difference between dogs and cats. Some of our sixteen tended to stay on dry land – either the boulders in the river or the rhododendron-infested soil along the slopes just above the river. They would get in the water only when all their dry options were exhausted. Others of us were like Labrador Retrievers – wet and happy, and maybe a bit careless at times. There were several occasions where we looked like those explorers of Africa in the old Tarzan movies, wading in single file, holding our packs over our heads to keep their contents dry, but without the piranhas and quicksand.

To get to The Gorge, we had bartered our way into permission to park on private property on the Cherokee reservation. After that there was a bit of uphill road walking, which transitioned into following an old, elusive railroad grade, which deteriorated into wading through waist high stinging nettle, which eventually led us (with the help of a handheld GPS and some "points of interest" pins) to a spot just a bit above the borderline between the national park and the Cherokee Reservation. I believe it was the spot the kayakers call Mike Tyson's Punch Out. It was every bit as impressive as being hit in the face by Iron Mike. (Of course, I've never been hit by Tyson, but I've smashed my face into rocks a few times, so I think I know the feeling.)

The most straightforward way to make this trip would be to start and end the off-trail portion of the hike at the Enloe Creek campsite, which would have been fine, but would have added about an hour of additional uphill hiking to the trip. Instead, we got permission to park on a family's land on the reservation. While you certainly couldn't blame any Native American family for being suspicious of a bunch of white folks wanting to make some sort of deal, in this case everyone seemed happy with the exchange of gifts, and no one was hurt or victimized. In fact, I wish most of the world worked this way. There was no paperwork, no consent forms, no lawyers; just some folks asking for the favor of parking in your yard, some money or other items changed hands, and the deal was done. Thank you... You're welcome... Ya'll have fun.

And we did.

Chapter 7

Friends in High Places

I'm secretly glad that it's illegal to hike on the upper end of Little Duck Hawk Ridge near Peregrine Peak on the southern slope of Mt. Le Conte. The $20,000 fine (yes, a twenty followed by a comma and three zeros) is a bit stout for my budget. I'm glad for two reasons. One is that it protects the nesting peregrine falcons from disturbance by curious humans. That's the noble, environmentally sensitive reason.

The other reason is that Little Duck Hawk Ridge is extraordinarily rocky and narrow, and it scares me. It looks dangerous, which of course means that some of my friends would feel compelled to give it a try, which also means that the peer pressure from them would force me to give it a try, which, to be honest, is something that I'd rather not do. It's just too rocky and steep, and yes, it intimidates me. I know from past experience that I may see a narrow, rocky ridge and think that a hike along the crest would be awesome. Then we work our way up to the ridgecrest and reality sets in. It's too much for my psyche to handle. My partners tightrope their way along the narrow spine while I crawl on all fours, or I simply give up and find a safer route. And, let the record show, there isn't always a safer route. Sometimes the only option is to give up and go back where we came from, but no one, including me, wants to be the guy who ruined everyone's trip by getting scared and quitting. I've never quite done that, but Little Duck Hawk could easily have been my first. Among my hiking friends, I'll continue to pretend that I resent the government's $20,000 threat, but deep in the secret places of my soul, I'm rejoicing that Uncle Sam has let me off the hook.

The name "Little Duck Hawk" isn't the kind of title that strikes fear in the hearts of those who hear it. A name like Devil's Razor or Deadman's Wall would be appropriately intimidating names, but, as it happens, Duck Hawk is also fitting because "duck hawk" is another name for a peregrine falcon.

109

These birds nested on this narrow ridge for many years (probably centuries or millennia) but disappeared sometime during the 1940s or 50s. According to Margaret Brown in *The Wild East*, a falcon nest on Little Duck Hawk Ridge was one of the last falcon nests in the eastern US as widespread human encroachment and the use of DDT as an insecticide nearly eliminated them from North America. During the 1970s several programs were working to save the falcons from extinction, and in 1984 several females were released on Greenbrier Pinnacle, and several more were released in the park over the next few years. None of these birds nested and bred in the park until 1997, when a nest with three falcon chicks was sighted in June on Little Duck Hawk Ridge. The falcons had returned from the brink of extinction, and today they continue to live and breed there.

Events like this – near-extinction followed by a recovery – are a reminder to me that, first, our actions matter to the other occupants of the planet, and second, we are a part of something that is much, much bigger – a regional ecosystem connected to other regional ecosystems, which are parts of larger climatic zones and weather patterns and migration routes, and... well... those things are bounded and crossed by roads, cities, state lines, national borders, and various cultures with varying attitudes toward nature and our relation to it. In short, we matter to the falcons, even if they don't realize it, and the falcons should matter to us, even if for several centuries we wouldn't admit it.

Getting an occasional glimpse of these larger places and processes and interconnections is one of those things that's most likely to happen when we slow down and look around, and think, and care. Seeing the ring-billed gulls gather on Cherokee Lake every November is a reminder that for every gull I see, there are probably thousands of them on other southern lakes, doing the same things for the same reasons. Then one day in March or April, they're gone, in the blink of an eye. It's a pleasant coincidence that I know where many of them go because I see them in the fields and ponds in northern Michigan when I fish the Au Sable River every year in mid-June. Keith Oakes, Tim Landefeld, and I, along with hundreds of other trout fishermen from across the nation, migrate to northern Michigan every summer to take advantage of the

110

cycles of mayflies and trout. So, both gulls and humans are tiny cogs in the large wheels of seasons, temperatures, bugs, and fish.

The warblers that I see in my back yard or in the Smokies every spring (they pass through in the fall, too, but they are so drab I hardly notice them) are another, colorful example of a big thing that happens right under our noses, yet we see just a tiny part of it, if we see it at all. It's not that different from, say, seeing my first movie at a theatre in downtown Orlando in 1960, but almost all the rest of my subsequent movie watching taking place at a mall in the suburbs. The cultural and demographic shift from downtowns to suburbs was happening across America in the 1960s, and I was a tiny part of that larger process, even though I didn't realize it until a few decades later as I began to read about such things. That's one of the benefits of growing older: you can look back and remember specific events that were small pieces of a larger puzzle. For some of us, it was the theatre at a mall, for others it was the loss of the family farm or the loss of a factory job. Whatever it was, we weren't alone, even though it may have felt like it at the time.

The easiest way to see these falcons is to walk two miles up Alum Cave trail to a rocky observation spot called Inspiration Point. There's no sign at this spot, but it's not hard to recognize. The first 1.5 miles of Alum Cave trail leads to Arch Rock where the trail tunnels through a large rock on a set of rock stairs. About five minutes after Arch Rock, the trail crosses a modest creek called Styx Branch on a small, log footbridge. From this footbridge, the trail begins ascending away from the river for about fifteen minutes at which point the trail makes a sharp right turn at Inspiration Point where there's a small, open, rocky area surrounded by rhododendron and mountain laurel and providing nearly 360° views of Anakeesta Ridge, Sugarland Mountain, the Chimneys, and the entire upper Sugarlands valley. This spot gives you a lot of bang for your buck because the views are worth a lot more than the seventy minutes you've invested to walk here. It's a great view of the Tennessee heart of the park.

As you stand at Inspiration Point looking out across the valley, directly to your right (west) the closest thing you'll see is the rocky face of Little Duck Hawk Ridge. (Look closely and you'll see a couple of holes, or windows, through the spine of the ridge.) Unless you go to a zoo and look at peregrine falcons in a cage, you are now in one of the two best spots for watching these survivors who, with a little help from some caring humans, have managed to survive the holocaust that nearly destroyed their species.

The other great viewing spot – the place where I saw my first peregrine falcons – is Big Duck Hawk Ridge, the ridge just beyond Little Duck Hawk.

Sometime in 2009, after a trip to the top of Mt. Le Conte, my friends had been talking incessantly about exploring Big Duck Hawk Ridge on Le Conte's south slope. The views from Alum Cave trail to Big Duck Hawk Ridge had been enticing. It looked rugged and rocky and, therefore, worthy of inclusion on our To Do Soon list. The fact that peregrine falcons were nesting on nearby Little Duck Hawk Ridge made this section of the park doubly appealing. I had never seen one of these rare falcons before, so my hopes were high that they'd make an appearance.

I had been distracted by some of life's obligations, so most of the thought and planning for our July (2009) trip to Big Duck Hawk had been done by my hiking partners, not me. I've been the planner and navigator on many family vacations ever since I was young, so I'm not used to just showing up and having a map and itinerary handed to me, but that's what happened on this trip. As we stepped out of Greg's car, he gave me a topo map with a blue line showing our intended route. We would start at the Alum Cave trail parking lot but would immediately cross Alum Cave Creek, hop off the trail, and work our way up the south side of Big Duck Hawk to its ridgecrest. We would then follow the crest north and east to its junction with Alum Cave trail near Alum Cave Bluff. It was pretty much the same route that I would have chosen, so there were no great surprises or debates about the route, but I felt a bit bewildered as we started, simply because I hadn't spent a few days ruminating about the pros and cons of the various routes that we could choose from. Considering how dirty and nasty some of these trips can be, the planning is actually the fun part. After that, the real work begins.

After crossing the creek, we immediately dove into a rhododendron thicket that was actually more help than hindrance. It was thick and low enough to force us to weave and crawl, but the branches provided convenient handles for us to grab as we slithered our way up the steep slope. It's not at all unusual after a hike like this for our arms and backs to be just as tired as our legs.

Without going into all the gory details, I'll make a long story short by saying that we spent a lot of time thrashing against walls of briers, bushes, and vines on this small side ridge. At one point I actually found myself looking for a rhododendron thicket because that would be *easier* terrain. Yes, you know you are having a rough day when a rhododendron hell is the *easy* route.

After about thirty minutes of thrashing of bushes and gnashing of teeth, Greg Harrell suggested, "You guys know I love hiking up ridges, but it's time to try something new...." There were absolutely no arguments, so we bailed out of our intended path and found a tiny creek to follow. Hiking up these slippery ravines is not easy, but they often provide a much needed reprieve from the brush and thickets that can form impenetrable green walls. It was a good choice. This small creekbed led us to the crest of Big Duck Hawk Ridge, maybe a tenth of a mile east of our original route.

The crest was exactly what we've come to expect of these open side ridges in this part of the Smokies: narrow, rocky spines adorned with mountain laurel, sand myrtle, and gnarled spruce and pines. And the views were fabulous, even though we were only about 4,800' high. There were plenty of ridges and peaks that were higher than we were, but there's something about being totally alone on a rarely-visited ridge that makes us feel like we are on the top of the world. These rocky ridges are, in our opinion, one of the great, undisclosed secrets of the Smokies. There are few, if any, official trails that lead to settings such as this. The reason for the secrecy is obvious: these rocky ridges are too fragile and risky to advertise to the general public. There would be too much damage done to both the landscape and the tourists.

It's a sign of a good trip when most of your stops are for the scenic views, not for resting and recuperating. So this was a good trip. As we sat on a rocky spot surrounded by the ridges and valleys of Mt. Le

Conte, Anakeesta Ridge, and Sugarland Mountain, we looked up and ahead toward our junction with Alum Cave trail. It was appropriate that the name of the peak where we were headed was Peregrine Peak because that was where we caught a glimpse of them – a pair of falcons circling their domain between Big and Little Duck Hawk Ridges.

When I first heard the name "duck hawk," I visualized some sort of hybrid bird – a mix of a hawk and a duck. It's not a very majestic image – maybe a hawk with a big, Daffy Duck beak or a big butt better suited for floating than soaring – but all that changed when I learned that "Duck Hawk" is just a quaint, old name for a peregrine falcon, based on the fact that they are particularly fond of killing and eating ducks. I didn't know much about falcons, but my image of them was sleek, fast hunters who live by catching and killing other animals. That put them in the same category as eagles and hawks which is pretty elite company if we'll ignore the fact that eagles frequently feast on dead, rotting fish, the aquatic equivalent of roadkill.

There are three main species of falcons in the eastern US: American kestrel, merlin, and peregrine falcon. These three are sleek, modest-sized birds with black-and-white face markings like the rock band Kiss. The kestrel and merlin are about the size of a blue jay while the peregrine is about six inches longer, about the size of a healthy crow. I'll occasionally see an American kestrel sitting on a power line overlooking a field. They have rusty-orange colored backs and those distinctive Kiss face markings. Merlins are rare in our area, passing through occasionally during spring and fall migrations.

Peregrine falcons are permanent residents in the eastern US. In fact, they are permanent residents across almost the entire planet, being one of the most widely distributed animals in the world. But that doesn't mean they're common. At the time of our BDH trip, there were only three well-documented, breeding pairs in Tennessee: one on Little Duck Hawk Ridge, one near Charlies Bunion, and another pair at the Chickamauga Dam in Chattanooga. The owners of Rock City were participating in a falcon "hacking" (the release of captive falcons) program at Lovers' Leap, so if that project succeeds or if the falcons simply find those cliffs on their own, it will give us another reason to See Rock City.

114

There's no reason to expect them to restrict themselves to East Tennessee; they'll soon spread to central and west Tennessee but not north or south Tennessee... because there's no such thing. There's just East (with a capital E, like a sovereign nation), central, and west. Ironically, as they move west the places where they are most likely to settle down are Nashville and Memphis.

Aside from the banning of DDT, the other factor that has strongly contributed to their comeback has been big cities with tall buildings. For example, the first nesting pair of peregrines in the state of Ohio was found in Toledo in 1988; afterwards, they spread to Cincinnati and Cleveland. Chicago and Indianapolis both have peregrine families living in their downtown areas. Not very inspiring stuff. In my mind, that diminishes the glamour of these birds a bit because they appear to occupy the same environmental niche as pigeons, their favorite food.

I'd prefer that they live only in wild, lonely places that are hard to find, but that isn't how Mother Nature and urban architects wrote the script. They nest on rocky cliffs and ledges, but apparently the concrete walls of bridges, dams, and skyscrapers fit that description well enough to satisfy the falcons. The fact that cities lack the primary predator of falcon chicks – the Great Horned Owl – also makes high-rise, urban areas favorable falcon habitat.

Beside their near extinction, peregrines' other claim to fame is their speed. On a good, downward dive toward their prey, they can reach speeds over 150mph, making them the fastest animal in the world. In the wild, these falcons will swoop down like a dive bomber and crash talons-first, mid-air into their prey. They seem to prefer birds that fly in flocks rather than alone, so it's like shooting fish in a barrel, which isn't very sporting but is ruthlessly efficient. I guess most wild animals are ruthlessly efficient, but falcons do it with more panache.

They have been captured and trained for at least three thousand years, and in the days before guns, they were a useful way of hunting birds. During the Middle Ages in Europe, falconry became "the sport of kings," a form of entertainment for the elite, perhaps arising from the fact that falcons would sometimes nest on the walls of Medieval castles and cathedrals; although, the fact that only the wealthy nobility would have the leisure time to pursue sport of any kind would also have been part of the equation. So, in spite of their penchant for eating urban pigeons, they do have a trace of nobility in their blood.

So, as we stood at a wide spot on Big Duck Hawk Ridge, looking upon the southern slopes of Mt. Le Conte, near Peregrine Peak, the duck hawks made their appearance. The entire show lasted only five minutes, but it was the grand finale to an already fine day. We had grandstand seats for a brief, simple encore by a couple of birds, but it was a show that had been repeated for hundreds or thousands of years, at this very spot with few human witnesses, and then had come to a sudden, almost-permanent halt.

I've seen falcons many times since then – above Alum Cave Bluff, near Charlies Bunion, near the White Rock on Mt. Cammerer, the Cat Stairs of Greenbrier Pinnacle. I've seen them chase ravens, vultures, hawks, and even a bald eagle at amazing speeds. They circle and soar, then tuck their wings back and dive... fast, just like the books say. No one puts up a fight against them. The victims just evacuate the area as quickly as possible.

We didn't see them fly with mind-boggling speed that first time on BDH Ridge. They didn't capture any prey. They simply circled and soared and squealed, claiming their territory and just plain showing off, enjoying the fact that they were home again, alive and well in a beautiful place – exactly as God intended.

After that trip, the value of Big Duck Hawk's stock appreciated rapidly. It became one of my favorite places in the park, mainly because I really like those open, airy, narrow, rocky ridges. I have a warm, fuzzy attachment to sand myrtle because it grows in such beautiful places, and it is abundant on Big Duck Hawk.

But the problem was our entrance and exit ramps. We made five BDH trips over the next three years, but each time we found ourselves floundering in rosebay rhododendron hells and greenbrier thickets, plus an occasional wall of mountain laurel thrown in, just to keep us humble. We found some nice side ridges that were tough but fun, but we couldn't seem to find THE route. You know, the route that has the perfect balance of effort and reward. Not too hard, and not too easy, but absolutely fabulous.

By the end of 2011 our most likely candidate for THE route was to start near the mouth of Trout Branch (a modest creek that runs along the northwestern slope of BDH ridge) at about 3,800' and rock hop up Trout Branch, bear right at 4,000' onto a modest tributary, then bear right again at an even more modest tributary at 4,400'. This route led to a small, manageably steep, rocky scar that provided an open route to the ridgecrest of BDH. The creek part of this route was a bit overgrown and a bit slippery, but it was much, much better than fighting briers and dog hobble up a wooded slope. We'd exit by the same route.

It was fine. Really. It was fine. Trout Branch was fine. Its small, slippery tributaries were fine. The scar on the upper slope of BDH was more than fine, and the ridge was great. That route was much, much better than the alternatives we had tried and abandoned, so it was fine, really. Of course, we'd prefer some sort of loop route rather than an in-and-out, but that was fine, too. Really. I mean it.

But we all knew in our hearts that it *wasn't* fine – it was not THE route. It wasn't quite worthy of being the standard route that we'd take on a typical Trout-BDH trip. You know you have a standard route to a destination when you and your partners can say, "Let's go to X" and everyone knows the route you'll take to X... because it's the best route. It's your standard route. THE route. We still didn't have that for Trout Branch and Big Duck Hawk Ridge. After six trips scattered over three years, we still didn't have it... until Greg Harrell made a remarkable discovery.

In August, 2012, he hiked to the Chimneys and looked across the valley to the southern slopes of Mt. Le Conte. A heavy rainstorm had pounded Mt. Le Conte a couple of days earlier, and he wondered if perhaps something interesting had resulted.

It had. The storm had produced a new landslide scar on Trout Branch – a wonderfully long, beautifully bare, scraped-down-to-the-bone scar. Our route to BDH had been scoured and rearranged, probably for the better (because we are big fans of landslide scars), but maybe for the worse.

Greg's gentlemanly side took over, a side I didn't even know he had. Rather than rush up into the new Trout Branch scar to claim rights as the first one to explore it, he came home and told me about it. I still consider this to be one of Greg Harrell's finest moments, a genuine, selfless gift to his hiking partners. I doubt that I'll ever be able to repay him... so I've decided not to try.

The next weekend, Greg Harrell, Keith Oakes, and I made the trip to Trout Branch's new scar, and we quickly discovered that the landslide had vastly improved the route. From that moment on, this Trout-BDH trip became one of my favorite trips in the Smokies, maybe at the very top of my list; although, that's a tough call. There's no hike in the park that gives more bang for the buck. Almost every step of it is fun and dramatic, and the whole trip can be done in six hours, with very few rhododendron-and-brier dues to pay.

At the base of every landslide, there's a big, nasty tangle of logs, rock, and dirt. The debris field. Or, as we sometimes metaphorically call it: the train wreck. Now and for the next few decades, there is a magnificent train wreck in Trout Branch at 4,000' consisting of an impressive tangle of trees, rocks, and dirt. I haven't measured it carefully, and probably never will, but I'd estimate it to be fifty to sixty feet across and maybe twenty or thirty feet high. Just below it, in the stream, there's a faint sulfurish or metallic smell that, as best I can remember, is iron oxide or sulfuric acid or something like that. The water and rocks at that spot have an orange tint to them. It's a mess, a glorious, stinking mess.

Getting past the train wreck requires some bobbing and weaving as you tightrope walk the length of logs that get slicker and more slippery with each passing year. Then you squeeze through openings at root balls or intersections of logs and boulders, hoping that this isn't the moment when the tangle above you decides to settle a bit more.

When you finally pop out on the top, there's a barren moonscape awaiting you; although, the acre or two of bare, dirt & rock plateau is gradually becoming green again as various grasses and shrubs take hold. This plateau doesn't last long, however, as the bare, rock creekbed climbs out from under the dirt plateau and heads up the valley.

118

Here the real fun begins. This is the beginning of a scar that begins at 4,000' and ends with its junction with Alum Cave trail at 5,000'. It's the Thousand Foot Scar, but using a little math tells me that, since it's roughly a 45° angle, the actual, on-the-ground length is closer to 1,400 feet. And every step of it is dramatic and powerful. There's some scrambling up white, sandstone ledges. There's maneuvering carefully up a long stretch of wet, slippery Anakeesta slate. There are several great vistas back toward the Chimneys. And although it's all less than a mile from the road, there's are no tourists, no trails.

On our August hike we followed the scar all the way to its end at Alum Cave trail. It ends literally at the trail between Alum Cave Bluff and Gracie's Pulpit. That's where you'll finally encounter tourists and trail hikers, which you'd think would make for some interesting encounters, but it usually doesn't.

We've discovered over the years that even serious hikers don't usually grasp what off-trail hiking is. Whether you've just popped out of the mountain laurel on top of Mt. Cammerer or scrambled to the top of the Thousand Foot Scar, when they ask where you came from, you point down the slope into the wilderness and say, "There." Sometimes they'll ask, "What trail is down there?" Sometimes they'll ask, "What *road* is down there?" Sometimes they'll just say, "Cool" and walk away. Only on rare occasions do you see even a small glimmer of understanding in their eyes. So rather than basking in the envy and adoration of these tourists and hikers, we just have to content ourselves with the knowledge that we are privy to the whereabouts of streams and cascades, ridges and cliffs, scars and train wrecks that they will never see, never understand.

I try not to get puffed up under such circumstances, but it's hard not to feel superior to such creatures. They are mere mortals, and we must live among them, but they will never fully understand us. This must be how Zeus, Hercules, and those other Greek gods felt, bless their hearts. They weren't capricious, petty, and jealous… just misunderstood.

So we made our way to the top of the scar at 5,000', then walked about one minute on the trail to the top of another, older, overgrown scar. We slid and crab walked down toward its junction with our new scar, at about 4,600'. While we were pushing our way through some of the brush and sliding down this older scar, a voice from above us, on the trail, shouted down to us, "Are you okay?" We shouted back that we were fine, exactly where we wanted to be. After a short pause, the voice shouted again, "Are you sure that's where you want to be?" Again, we shouted that we were headed to Big Duck Hawk Ridge, which successfully ended the conversation, probably because they had never heard of Big Duck Hawk because no trail goes to it. As an afterthought, I shouted up, "Thanks for checking on us" but they were gone. I guess they had better things to do than converse with crazy people, which was fine because we had better things to do than converse with sane people.

Near the junction of the old and new scars, we cut south, up the north slope of BDH Ridge. After about ten minutes of pushing through rhododendron – the only real dues that we paid all day – we reached the crest of BDH. We found ourselves in a stand of red spruce, but as we walked along the crest, that quickly changed into bare, jagged rock, moss, and sand myrtle. We had found THE route up.

After loitering for about an hour, we dropped down into the small scar that we had been using as our exit ramp for a couple of years; it's now THE exit route. It is steep, and there are some spots that should be avoided, so we avoided them.

The day was a blazing hot afternoon in the middle of a blazing hot August. There had been no shade on the crest, of course, and even this north facing scar was sunny and hot. One of us commented that "a small dose of hypothermia would hit the spot," which made sense in a twisted sort of way. Fortunately, like most scars, big or small, this soon turned into a creek – a small one to match the small scar – that led us quickly into the shade of the trees.

The trees higher up the slope were a variety of old, established hardwoods with a few spruce and dead hemlocks mixed in. The trees in the ravine – the ones we'd actually grab onto to keep our balance on the wet rocks – were mainly young yellow birch, maybe ten or twenty years old. Since yellow birch are a pioneer species – among the first to re-populate a landslide scar – this told us that the scar that we had just descended had happened ten, twenty or maybe thirty years ago. I love the fact that some of these landslides are ancient, but it's also satisfying that some have happened, and continue to happen, during our lifetimes.

120

About an hour after we had left the ridgecrest, we arrived at the Thousand Foot Scar at about 4,400', about 400' below the crest. We hadn't noticed the small opening of this tiny creek into the scar on our way up, but we were happy to see that it deposited us just above the white, open rocks that we had scrambled up about three or four hours earlier.

It's nice to have some fun stuff to do near the end of the trip because many of our trips "end" with us standing on top of a mountain, with a three or four or ten mile hike back to the car. On those trips, we just put our heads down and go down whatever trail will take us to our car the fastest. This Trout-BDH hike is different. There's a fun thirty minutes scrambling back down the rocks to the train wreck. From there it's about thirty minutes of rock hopping down the stream back to the car on Newfound Gap Road. Wet. Cool. Easy.

A recent visit to Trout's Thousand Foot Scar and BDH was a quick trip with Ken Wise and the Page sisters – Kindel, Kamrin, and Kinsey. It was a Saturday in mid-September, the middle of the off-season between summer and leaf season. We were meeting at Sugarlands Visitor Center at 8:30 am, so instead of *Car Talk* or *This American Life*, I was listening to the *Weekend Edition* news – ISIS plots, Syrian refugees, bombings in Afghanistan, Donald vs. Hillary. I miss the simpler times of the Cold War, Mutually Assured Destruction, and the Nicaraguan Contras.

As I got off I-40 at exit 407 and entered Sevierville, I began to feel a bit uneasy. Some of the motels had full parking lots, which isn't supposed to happen this time of year. Clearly the local Chamber of Commerce had been at work. Something was amiss, but as long as it wasn't a Rod Run, things would be fine.

It was a Rod Run. As I entered Pigeon Forge I immediately began seeing block after block after block after block after block of shiny, classic cars parked with their hoods up in the parking lots along the sides of the road, accompanied by just as many blocks of lawn chairs facing the road. Apparently, later in the day, half the visitors in Pigeon Forge will sit in their chairs on the side of the road watching the other half of the visitors drive their classic cars up and down the road. I don't know if at some point they all switch and repeat.

To each his own, I suppose. It's not my cup of tea, but if you like old cars, I suppose it's great. If you like old cars and crowds and traffic and exhaust fumes, it's better than great, I suppose. Of course, I have to keep saying "I suppose" because I don't really understand the whole thing, and I'll never actually witness it, unless I'm bound and gagged and taken by force.

So, trying to be the tolerant, non-judgmental person I claim to be, I thought "to each his or her own" as I snuck through Pigeon Forge, just trying to make it to that last traffic light. I made it through alive, so I didn't spend the rest of the day cursing the Chamber of Commerce under my breath, but in the future I do hope they'll consult with me and my schedule before they plan these things. Their Rod Run nearly thwarted my plans this morning and would certainly complicate my life later that day. To get home I'd have to drive through Gatlinburg (keeping my fingers crossed that the Gatlinburg hadn't planned a competing event) and take US 321 through Cosby. But in the spirit of "When life gives you lemons, buy apples" I would stop at Carver's apple orchard on the way home and buy some Honeycrisps, so all's well that ends with fresh apples.

The rest of our day went so smoothly, there's almost nothing to tell. This was the Page sisters' first trip up our standard Trout-BDH route, so they were even more enthusiastic than usual. When we were in the actual scar and standing on top of some nice, sandstone cliffs, the views behind us provided perfect pictures of the Chimneys, nicely framed by the trees on both sides of our Thousand Foot Scar. There were lots of stops for views, pictures, and general appreciation of where we were and what we were doing. No one was in a hurry because on this trip, you don't have to be.

Ken took a good tumble early in the trip, before we even got to the train wreck and the scar. Kamrin, being the only witness, described it in vivid detail, so we could all vicariously cherish the moment. Kindel, trying to be kind, mentioned that it was good to get the accident out of the way early in the trip, so Ken could enjoy the rest of the day. Having hiked with Ken several times, I felt compelled to remind her that in order to meet his quota, he'd have to fall two or three more times, so this first one was just a start, not an end. She immediately saw that logic in that and promptly withdrew her kind, but misguided, assessment. (He fell once or twice more, so his average is still intact.)

We reminisced about an earlier trip we had made to the Raven Fork Gorge. It was a wet, wild, wonderful trip, but Ken was concerned that some folks were giving too much off-trail information in their blogs and on GoSmokies. It may have been Kinsey who innocently asked, "Ken, didn't you write a book about off-trail hiking a few years ago?" (Maybe her question wasn't so innocent. She knew he had written not only *a* book, he had written *the* book on off-trail hiking in the Smokies, even though it claims to be about trails. Ken's definition of "trails" is broad to the point of being delusional.) Ken, of course, claimed that a book was different; although, he never quite got around to explaining how.

Once we got to the crest of BDH, we spent at least an hour roaming its length. It had been a while since I've spent that long on the ridge and even longer since I've actually walked up and down much of its length. We ate cookies, yelled at hikers on Inspiration Point, and got a little sunburned. I climbed a red spruce until the branches got so thick that I couldn't get higher than about twenty feet. Ken got stuck in a brier patch. We learned that Kindel gets woozy when she sees blood on hands; anywhere else is okay, but not on hands.

Some off-trail hikes are a pleasant stroll in the woods, while others are fifteen hour slogs though the botanical equivalent of quicksand. This Thousand Foot Scar & Big Duck Hawk trip is near the easy end of that spectrum – it's not exactly easy, but it is fun, and it can be leisurely if you want it to be. You could even shorten it by hiking past the train wreck to the first or second set of white cliffs, sit and eat lunch with a grandstand view of the Chimneys to keep you company, then go back to the car. Three hours. More if you decide to take a nap.

So it's the kind of trip that can involve hot chocolate or tea heated on a backpacking stove. Or a nap. Or a good book. Or continuous, lively banter among friends because you actually have a little time and oxygen to spare. It's a good place to go solo or to be with friends in high places, whether those friends are humans or falcons.

123

Chapter 8

The Land of Sharp Edges

One of the most intimidating spots in the Smokies is near the top of Mt. Kephart, where the Appalachian Trail and the Boulevard intersect. Near this junction there's a side trail that leads about half a mile, past the actual summit of Mt. Kephart, to the eastern edge of this mountain. Yes, the eastern *edge*.

When speaking of the Smoky Mountains, the word "edge" probably seems out of place. There aren't a lot of edges in the Smokies because the southern Appalachians tend to have an old, rounded look to them. It seems that all the sharp edges have been worn off, and that's mostly true for most of the park, but there are sections of the park where that is definitely, dramatically, unequivocally *not* true. One region of sharp edges is the bowl formed by Mt. Le Conte, The Boulevard, and the AT to Charlies Bunion and the Sawteeth. These sharp edges were all formed by some sort of erosion, sometimes gradual but often sudden landslides caused by a heavy rain. Occasionally, human abuse (such as 1920s logging followed by forest fires) contributed to the landslides, but ultimately the underlying culprit is the fragile slate that provides a weak base for the accumulation of soil on these slopes.

Right in the middle of this bowl stands Mt. Kephart with its steep eastern edge, the top of which is called The Jumpoff. I suppose I could spend a paragraph expounding on the meaning of that name, but it's probably pretty obvious: it's high and steep.

Of course, many places in this Le Conte-Boulevard-Bunion bowl could be called the Jumpoff, but the name was apparently attached to this particular location by the Smoky Mountains Hiking Club. One of the most obscure, but interesting, Smokies-related documents I've ever encountered is the script of a skit that was put on by several members of the SMHC in 1944 celebrating and reminiscing about their first twenty years of existence. These old, yellowed papers were passed down from Dutch Roth (one of the SMHC's first members) to his daughter,

124

Margaret Ann, and to her brother's son, Charlie Roth, who has been one of my occasional hiking buddies. In one scene of the skit, one of the actors (probably Guy Frizzell) commented:

> Did you know the Hiking Club had a part in naming a lot of places on the state line and the Tennessee side of the Smokies? Yeah, four of our members and Hodge Mathis of Johnson City were designated as an advisory committee to the U.S. Geographic Board of Names. Jim Thompson was chairman and Brockway Crouch, Robert L. Mason, and Paul Fink were the other members. They collected folk lore, old maps, talked with the old-timers of the mountains – I remember Andy Gregory was a big help – and then they recommended the adoption of names most generally accepted; but in many instances there were duplications to be avoided. There were Big Creeks, Mill Creeks and Fork Ridges everywhere. Well, this gave the Committee an opportunity to slip in some real old Hiking Club lingo, such as "Wooly Tops," "Boulevard," "Charlie's Bunion," and "The Jump-Off."

Yes, Jumpoff was the name that the SMHC used among themselves to describe this high, eastern edge of Mt. Kephart.

My hiking partners and I have had the experience of hiking in some out-of-the-way places – ridges, creeks, and cascades that have no names. For a while we have to stumble around whenever we talk about them, saying things like, "the path that starts at Tremont and goes to Thunderhead" or "the big cascade a half mile above Ramsey Cascades," but we eventually settle in to using names that emerge naturally out of the conversations, without forming a committee and taking a vote. So, the old path from Tremont becomes Thunderhead Prong trail, the rocky overlook a quarter mile east of Charlies Bunion becomes the Rocky Crag, and the three tributaries feeding Lester Prong above Porters Creek become First Trib, Second Trib, and Third Trib, starting low and moving upstream because that's the direction we normally travel when we explore the Lester Prong watershed.

Little cliques of hikers have been giving their own names to their personal stomping grounds for years. For example, I've heard some folks speak of the Real Charlies Bunion, the Tourist Bunion, the Boobs, Picnic Ridge, Eagle's Nest, and NoName Ridge – all names that have no meaning outside the insiders of those groups. Because this process of naming happens so naturally, I'd bet the farm that this same thing has been going on since the beginning of time. Ancient hunter-gatherer tribes undoubtedly encountered rivers and waterfalls and gave them their own, common-sense names. If a tribe's first encounter with a watering hole resulted in killing a panther, then that watering hole might forever be Dead Panther Spring. On the other hand, if the panther got the better end of the deal, it might henceforth be known as Dead Hunter Spring. Either way, the names evolve out of common use based on real life (Panther Springs, Mill Creek, Low Gap) with an occasional flourish of creativity (Jumpoff) or humor (Charlies Bunion).

Giving permanent, official names to rivers and mountains is a relatively new phenomenon in American history which began only as outsiders in the form of explorers, scientists, and government officials encountered these remote places. These ambassadors of civilization had to standardize the names so they would know which rivers and ridges they were talking about among themselves for the purposes of navigation, boundaries, and ownership. You can't make a good map of your domain without names for the places you are mapping. In the Smokies, this process didn't happen until the 1930s as the old pioneer names were replaced by a different, official set of titles, and apparently only those groups of hikers or hunters who are appointed as advisory committees to governmental boards will ever have the chance to emblazon their place names on an official map.

So "Jumpoff" provides a vivid description of this sheer, eastern face of Mt. Kephart. It's an appropriate name, but keep in mind that "jump off" is a colorful description, not a suggestion – a noun, not a verb; declarative, not imperative.

The view from the Jumpoff is dramatic and unique. For those who think of the Smokies as a land of smooth, green mountains... okay, you are about 95% correct. But to see some of that other 5%, go to the Jumpoff and look east toward Charlies Bunion, into the area that could

126

easily be called the Land of Sharp Edges. Of course, the rocky outcrop of Charlies Bunion is a centerpiece of this section, but the ridge leading up to it as well as the parallel ridges beyond it are battered and scarred. While this is a great view in any season, a summer view will be the most visually distinctive, allowing you to see the contrasts of green foliage versus the brown-gray, rocky scars.

From the other side of the Land of Sharp Edges, just beyond Charlies Bunion, looking back at Mt. Kephart is equally impressive. How long has Mt. Kephart looked like this, like a deformed giant? Since birth? Or has its entire eastern side been scooped off and deposited downstream in more recent millennia? Walking up the watershed where the debris would have to flow, there are many tangled trees and boulders from recent landslides, but there's not half a mountain in these creeks. Whether it was a sudden catastrophe or a long, slow process, visualizing the huge piece that is missing from this mountain is mind-boggling.

While the view from the Jumpoff to the ridges of the east is best during the summer, the view from those ridges west toward the Jumpoff is best after a light dusting of snow or ice. This whitens the moss and shrubs that cover the upper half of the Jumpoff and gives it a Yosemite look, like a wall of bare granite. This is the perspective that shows how truly rugged and steep Kephart's eastern face really is.

While my three hiking partners and I had been talking for months about exploring Lester Prong all the way to the base of the Jumpoff, Greg Harrell was the first to actually do it. Of the four of us, he's the one most likely to hike off-trail by himself. He may even prefer to go by himself; although, he hasn't come right out and said so, probably because none of us have come right out and asked. It's just generally understood among us that on any given Sunday, Greg may show up at our church with tales of a Saturday hike that took him to some place that none of us had yet explored. He has topo maps at home with mysterious blue lines that he's drawn up and down and across and along dozens of obscure creeks and ridges. It's his three dimensional, Smokies "to do" list. To keep him from doing all these new trips without us, we've had to

127

pressure him into solemn pacts with us – promises that none of us will explore Eagle Rocks or the Cat Stairs or some unnamed ridge until *all* of us are able to go. But we don't have a pact for every blue line, and there are implied statutes of limitations, so he takes off without us every now and then.

Greg seems to have a special "death wish" gene that the rest of us don't have. The fact that he visited the Jumpoff area by himself suggests the presence of this genetic defect. The fact that he went in February confirms it. We've all done February hikes before, and they are usually uncomfortably fabulous, but you have to put yourself in the right frame of mind by embracing the cold weather as a point of pride rather than discomfort. However, the thing that puts Greg's initial Jumpoff trip in a special category is that much of it involved a wet, river hike – and by "wet" I mean hiking *in* the river. Not near the river. Not by the river. *In* the river, ankle to knee to waist deep. Yep, there's definitely a genetic defect lurking under the surface. If it weren't such dangerously bizarre behavior, he'd have our respect for such foolishness.

Like most of his hikes, the description of this one begins like this: "Park at Porters Creek …." Greg seems to enjoy the fact that you have to hike almost four miles to the end of Porters Creek trail before the real adventure begins. From the end of this trail there's an old path that leads even further along Porters Creek, crossing it several times, and eventually crossing Lester Prong which flows into Porters from the southwest.

Actually, there are a couple of old paths, and the one that parallels and crosses Porters Creek is the less visible of the two. In August, 2009, a seventy year old, experienced hiker parked at the Porters Creek trailhead, hiked the four miles on Porters Creek trail and intended to continue on this old path along Porters Creek. Somehow he managed to lose this path, and instead of working his way up Porters Creek, he ended up lost and on the top of Porters *Mountain*, where he camped for several days until the Search & Rescue team found him.

My partners and I have been up this route many times. In fact, it was one of the first off-trail trips that we discovered in the Smokies. While I don't know exactly how the hiker got off track and lost, I can visualize several spots where it could have happened. The most likely is at the end of the official trail, by the Porters Flats backcountry campsite, also known as Campsite #31. At this spot, the old path continues to the left, but within about a minute there's a barely-visible split. At this split, the less-obvious, less-visible path to the right leads along the creek. The more-obvious, more-visible path bears to the left and heads up the western slope of Porters Mountain. After sending you up this slope, this path quietly, calmly disappears. If you continue upslope, hoping to rediscover the trail, you'll end up in the rhododendron thickets and rocky ridge of Porters Mountain. Without a good map and compass, at this point you'll probably be lost. On the other hand, if you can figure out where you are, you can push your way along the ridgecrest to Porters Gap on the Appalachian Trail. I've done that trip once. I don't intend to do it again. We weren't lost, but we were roughed up a bit. It took over a week for my cuts and bruises to heal.

Of course, today we'd be avoiding Porters Mountain. We'd follow Porters Creek along the old, barely-visible path. Staying on this old path will lead you up the rough, slippery creekbed of Porters Creek to the Appalachian Trail on the main ridgecrest, near Dry Sluice Gap. But things get even rougher and more interesting if you hop off this path and slosh your way up Lester Prong because Lester Prong leads eventually to the Jumpoff.

So six months after Greg's initial trip, when temperatures were at a more civilized level, all four of us (Greg, Keith Oakes, Charlie Roth, and I) did the Lester Prong-Jumpoff trip. While the name Jumpoff has some glamour, the name Lester Prong doesn't. It sounds tame, even to the point of being a bit dorky. I don't want to offend anyone out there who's named Lester, but there's a reason why wrestlers and other celebrities name themselves Rock, Diesel, Bono, Sting, even Ray or Jon, but never Lester. (To avoid the appearance of conceit, let me hasten to say that I fully understand that they don't name themselves Greg, either.) It's just not a name that conjures up images of bravery and adventure. But Lester Prong is anything but tame. Yes, it's small – it would be nearly impossible to drown in it – but it wouldn't be hard to fall to your death. If I had been on that advisory committee, I'd have suggested Deathwish Prong, only because Styx Branch (you know, the river that flows through Greek hell) was already taken by a creek on the other side of Mt. Le Conte.

After hiking up Lester Prong for about half an hour, we began to see car, truck, and trailer sized tangles of debris – trees and rocks – in the creek. This is always a sign of a landslide, usually the result of a sudden, heavy rain that saturates the ground and pulls several acres of soil off the mountain side, bringing tons of rocks and trees with it. This conglomeration will ride its way downstream as a wall of mud, wood, rock, and water, eventually slogging to a halt and creating huge tangles in the river valley.

After a few hundred yards of these intermittent tangles, which got bigger as we moved further upstream, we came to a fork in the creek around 4,700' elevation, about 1,300' below the Jumpoff directly above us. The line of debris flowed from the right branch, showing that this most recent landslide had come from that direction, Greg's initial February route near Horseshoe Mountain to the north. The left branch was much steeper and had a long, thin, scoured look with only a few, loose rocks and a modest stream of water running down the middle, meaning that if we were going to follow Lester Prong as far as possible, this was the fork we would take.

This was the point where our hike changed from a feet-only affair to feet & hands because this left fork was slippery and steep. Later we calculated that the overall incline of this section was about 45° to 60°, which doesn't seem difficult on paper, but on the ground it's tough because a 45° (or worse) incline is an average. There would be ten or twenty feet of 60°+ incline followed by a few feet of maybe 10° or 20° or 40°, followed by another ten or twenty feet of steep, wet cascade, followed by a few feet of easy stepping. The result is mostly hands and feet climbing, with only a few brief reprieves. Did I mention the fact that water has been flowing over this bed of rock since time immemorial? So it tends to be a bit on the smooth, slippery side of things with very few sharp, strong hand and footholds. The result is that we spent much of our time a few yards to the side of the cascade, alternately pushing and pulling our way through a thick layer of green, wet, soft, loose moss, plus a lot of roots and branches.

130

In this kind of climbing, our most trusted allies are red spruce trees. We can trust these trees and their roots with our lives; although we try not to put ourselves in that position very often. Whether climbing up a steep, rocky bluff or through a steep thicket of shrubs and trees, it's best to keep your weight evenly distributed among your four points of contact – two hands and two feet – but occasionally it's necessary to put all your weight on just one point. I will rarely do this on a rock surface but will resort to it upon occasion if I can use a root or branch – but only healthy spruce trees. They are always strong and sturdy, which is something I can't say confidently about birch, rhododendron, mountain laurel, and the dozens of other bushes that grow on these steep slopes.

A close second is sand myrtle which is a small, leathery bush that often grows in the cracks of very acidic, rocky terrain, which is exactly what the ridges and cliffs of the Land of Sharp Edges consist of. We won't put all our weight on a single sand myrtle the way we would a spruce root, but we can use a myrtle bush to pull ourselves up with as much or more confidence than we place in the rock itself, simply because the rock is fragile, Anakeesa slate that sometimes breaks off in your hand when you pull on it. The myrtle that grows in the cracks of these walls of slate really is more trustworthy than the rock it grows on.

Rhododendron is a distant third. Apparently, its roots aren't designed to dig deep into cracks in the rock, so these plants – which seem strong and rubbery at lower elevations – are often weak and brittle on these high, rocky slopes. Only occasionally can they be trusted as a secure hand-hold. Mountain laurel – rhododendron's close cousin – is also a bit too brittle and breaks too easily. So we tend to use the laurel and rhody to help us keep our balance when we need just a little extra help in leaning the right direction. It's like holding on to a handrail as you go up a flight of stairs. You don't need it to support your entire body weight; you only need it to provide a little support to help you keep your balance.

As we worked our way up, we spent more time in the moss and bushes than we spent in the creek because the creek was now a long, winding cascade which was too steep and slippery for us to trust. Only occasionally could we get in it and climb directly on its rocky path, and even then, only on segments that were ten or twenty feet high – if any higher, a slip and slide would be long and painful, then dark and silent.

The result was a long, slow ascent as we grabbed and pulled and pushed and rested. Repeat, repeat, repeat. The next day, as I recuperated from our adventure, my legs and arms were a little sore, but the body part that suffered the most was my fingers. The *muscles* in my fingers were almost too sore for me to grip door knobs, write with a pen, and type on a keyboard. I've never seriously pondered the fact that there are muscles in our fingers, and to the best of my recollection I've never done any activity that actually made my finger muscles sore… until the grabbing and pulling of this trip. From now on I guess I'll have to put finger exercises into my workout routine; although, I have no clue what kind of exercise to do to get a good finger workout; maybe kneading bread dough or digging in sand. Is there such a thing as finger curls? It's a question personal trainers are never asked because finger muscles aren't glamour muscles, except maybe to a rock climber or a masseuse.

This was the first trip on which I wore gloves because a couple of recent, off-trail trips had resulted in some damage to my hands and wrists. I normally get some bumps and bruises, but on one of these trips I had managed two good cuts on my hand and wrist. I don't know how I got them. In fact, as I recall, Charlie and Keith asked where I got the bloody cuts, and I couldn't tell them because I hadn't noticed until they pointed them out. Although, I suppose I would have noticed sooner or later because one of them wouldn't stop bleeding. As a result, I have some good pictures of me wearing a blood-stained shirt. It looks worse than it really is, which is the way I like things to be – that is, not as bad as they seem; the fact that things appear dangerous to the outside observer means that you'll get more admiration than you deserve. The cut on my wrist didn't bleed a lot, even though it was deeper and longer. In fact, Keith called is a "laceration" which had a nice, manly ring to it, but again, it sounded worse than it really was.

So, after that trip, I began wearing gloves on some of these off-trail jaunts. Some guys wear stout, sticky gloves like NFL receivers wear, but I opted for a $13 pair of leather work gloves from Wal-Mart, and in this case that seemed somehow appropriate. Not only were these gloves less expensive, but they had a simple "going to work" appearance that I kind

132

of like because some of these hikes are a lot like work, even to the point of looking forward to quitting time when you can go home and take a shower. My hiking partners use headlamps on our night hikes, we all wear hats to protect our heads, and Charlie wears protective goggles on some of these trips, so between headlamps, hats, goggles, and gloves we look like a gang of laborers heading down into the coal mines. All that's missing are the lunch pails and a canary in a cage.

This cascade, which we now call the Jumpoff Cascade, went on and on and on. One hundred feet, two hundred feet, one football field. More climbing. Four hundred. Five hundred. Two football fields. More climbing. Seven hundred. During the climb we didn't know exactly how long this cascade extended, but we made a pretty good guess based on elevation and angle. Greg, Keith, and Charlie all had altimeters which measure elevation using barometric pressure. Their equipment all pretty much agreed that after 1,000 feet of vertical elevation gain, we came to a split in the cascade at 5,700'. We had ascended vertically 1,000 feet at a 45°+ angle, which would mean our horizontal distance was about 1,000 feet as well. Using the old Pythagorean Theorem from high school geometry class for calculating the hypotenuse of a right triangle, we came up with an estimate of about 1,400 feet. Up to this 5,700' split, this cascade – which still continued up both of these small forks at this split – was 1,400 feet long!

To grasp the magnitude of that, consider that Ramsey Cascades, one of the most popular waterfalls in the park, is about 100' high. Abrams Falls, another visitor favorite, is about 30' high. Yes, these two waterfalls have much greater volume and width than Jumpoff Cascade, which at this high elevation is generally just a heavy trickle… but 1,400 feet for cryin' out loud! And it continues several hundred feet up both of these upper forks on Mt. Kephart.

It's discoveries like this that make hiking in the backcountry really special. There are hidden, rarely-visited waterfalls and cascades all over the park: Mill Creek, Upper Ramsey, Cannon Creek, Sugar Cove, First Trib. They are everywhere, and in terms of sheer length and drama, Jumpoff Cascade dwarfs them all.

It's so long that just standing at the bottom and looking up its path gives you absolutely no idea of its real length. It twists and turns and just

133

disappears after about 200 feet. So you can't see it from the bottom. Later that day, as we stood atop the Jumpoff and looked down, we could see the general path of the creek as it zig-zagged down the slope, but there was too much distance and greenery to see the actual rock and water cascade. From above there's no visible evidence that anything extraordinary is happening in the valley below – other than a wonderfully steep slope. And the Lester Prong valley is so remote that there's no place to stand in the distance and hope to see this cascade. The only way to view it is to climb alongside it for several hours, from bottom to top, which only adds to its mystique. It's unapproachable, unattainable… and, therefore, that much more enchanting.

On the less-dramatic, more-delicate side, this slope surrounding the Jumpoff Cascade is covered in thick, wet moss with frequent outposts of Grass of Parnassus, a lovely, white wildflower that few visitors ever see. As my *Wildflowers of the Smokies* says, "Consider yourself very lucky to find this outstanding native of bogs and seepage slopes." My hiking partners and I are not exactly wildflower enthusiasts, but we do like to know what's going on around us, so we did indeed consider ourselves lucky to stumble across these small, white reminders that much of the wonder of the Smokies is at knee or ankle level.

The split in the creek at this "top" of the cascade is at 5,700 feet – about 300 vertical feet from the top of the Jumpoff. At this point we all split up, not out of design, but simply to follow our various interests. I decided to go up the left fork; although I can't really explain why. This fork had the heavier flow of water, and it seemed that it would lead to the crease where Mt. Kephart meets the AT. (It didn't.) Maybe I was hoping there would be a few gawking tourists at the top when I walked out of the woods. Greg, Keith, and Charlie followed the right fork which seemed to head straight up to the highest point of the Jumpoff, but certainly couldn't go all the way to the top, simply because the last hundred feet or so would be a nearly-vertical climb. Even a guy with a death wish gene would have enough presence of mind to think about the people who love and depend on him to keep him from trying to climb that last vertical hundred feet.

So my three partners headed right, but they spread out a bit as well. There was a rocky scar that stopped their progress across the face of Mt.

134

Kephart, so they did some backtracking and re-routing to find a path that would lead them to the top. In short, they had the same troubles that I was having – rocky cliffs that would form a barrier that had to be avoided, usually by moving laterally along the base until a gap in the cliff would allow them to move upward. It's a zig-zagging route that always holds that possibility of climbing for an hour or two, only to find yourself hemmed in by cliffs above and to both sides, meaning that the only option is to retreat and regroup.

There were several points in their climb that this seemed to be happening. Occasionally during the afternoon, I was able to look across the slope only to hear and see patch of rustling bushes on a frighteningly steep slope, but they were usually able to find a crease or a gap or a ledge or some escape route that eventually led them to the top. Of course, this involved the same tactics that we had been using for the past two hours – push through the bushes, hang on to roots and limbs, crawl up moss-covered rock, rest, repeat.

While they were engaged in their struggle, I was working my way up the left fork in much the same manner. They had stayed with their part of the cascade for several more minutes before the slope became too steep and they had to move laterally. I also stayed with my fork of the creek, but it quickly became too steep and slippery for me to actually climb in the cascade, so I moved to the brush and thickets along the right side of the left fork. As I pulled myself up through the bushes and moss, my imagination began to run away with me. The slick cascade wouldn't let me go further left. What if I came to a rocky cliff that wouldn't let me go higher and another that wouldn't let me go right? My only option would be to backtrack, but backtrack to where? The fork where we had separated? How long would that take? Where would my partners be? Would they have stumbled upon a route to the top that I might miss?

I didn't exactly visualize my own death, but I did wonder how much an NPS rescue mission costs and how low the overnight temperature would drop. I guess I'm just not cut out for off-trail hiking in unknown territory by myself. Greg Harrell has a death wish gene. Apparently, I have a sissy gene. Although, in my defense, one of my fears did materialize. I found myself hemmed in by the cascade on my left and a rocky cliff above me and to my right. So I began to backtrack,

135

not knowing exactly what I'd do if I came to a point that would allow me to move right again. I had climbed through that territory a few minutes earlier and had ended up stuck. What could I do differently? (My sissy gene was definitely exerting its control over me.)

It was then that I noticed that the other side of the cascade looked a bit more manageable, a smoother slope and maybe fewer rocky walls to maneuver around. So I worked my way down the edge of the cascade, clinging to spruce roots and sand myrtle when available but settling for other shrubs and moss when necessary, until I found a narrow ledge across the cascade. Stepping along this wet ledge wasn't my preferred option, but I was down to Plan D or E by now, so I worked my way across the flowing water, making sure I always had two hands and two feet firmly planted on the rock. The slope here was about 45°, maybe 60° in a few sections, so it wasn't technical rock climbing, the main drawbacks being that my ledge was about four inches wide, and wet, and the long, fast, bumpy tumble that I'd have to endure if I slipped. If my feet slipped off the narrow ledge, my only hope was to grab that ledge with my hands as I began my slide. If that didn't work... well, my grandchildren would one day hear stories about their Grampy, without ever actually knowing him. I'd zip down the slope for several hundred feet like a steep bobsled ride, but without the bobsled. I decided that my best option was: just don't slip. Period. That's why this was Plan D or E, not A or B.

As I slowly shuffled across the cascade, I wondered how Charlie, Keith, and Greg were faring. Earlier I had looked across the slope and seen one or two of them stuck in the shrubs of a nearly vertical slope. From where I sat I pitied them because there seemed to be no alternative for them other than backtracking downslope and trying again. At the end of the day, I was amazed when they told me that they had found their way across and up because from my vantage point it had seemed impossible. As Greg succinctly put it about some of his predicaments, "I was in a few spots that I didn't want to be in." He didn't elaborate further. He didn't have to. We all knew exactly what he meant. At this moment, as I crossed the cascade, I was in one of those spots.

As it happens, the other side of my cascade was not as smooth and easy as it had appeared, a "grass is greener on the other side" kind of thing, I suppose. The rock faces that I continued to encounter pushed me further and further away from the cascade and up the slope of the creek valley. I hated to lose contact with the cascade because I had visualized myself following it all the way to its source, but the small ridge that I was ascending was too comforting to pass up. Although I had never been on this particular ridge before, it felt very familiar. It was steep but wooded, so I knew there was enough soil to support the trees – another sign of manageable terrain. There would be less rock and more dirt than what I had been crawling on for several hours. Although I couldn't see the light at the end of the tunnel, I knew there was an end of the tunnel up ahead.

This ridge was thick with trees, mountain laurel, briers, and other obstructions, but it was a pleasant relief from the cliffs and cascade. My sissy gene liked this route better, so I followed the one main rule of getting to the top of a ridge – when in doubt, go up, some way, somehow, and you'll end up at the top. You can zig and you can zag, but all routes lead to the top. My partners and I had become well acquainted with this rule. It's one that never fails, and it didn't fail me this day. Later on, after we were all reunited at the top, Greg said that he spent a few minutes sitting among the bushes, wondering what to do next, when he heard me pushing and crashing along the ridge less than a hundred yards away. He watched me make my way toward the top. Once again, being a guy of few words, he didn't say whether this gave him comfort or more frustration at his plight.

Keith and Charlie had apparently crossed a rocky scar at a different place than Greg did which highlighted how much luck is a part of this process of picking your way around rocky scars and faces and through laurel thickets. In this kind of terrain, you tend to hike in ten or twenty foot segments. You don't usually have the luxury of looking far ahead and seeing the big picture. You just try to get from point A to point B, and point B is rarely more than a few yards away. Only after you arrive at point B can you begin to look for point C. It's exactly how I play chess and why I gave it up. I don't look more than one move ahead, which of course means that I always lose. The main difference is that in chess I *won't* look far ahead, whereas in bushwhacking I *can't*. The main similarity is that when you don't think ahead, you'll lead yourself into some situations you'd rather not be in.

Sometimes the route you take leads to the end of the tunnel, sometimes it runs you into another wall. It's a lot like rolling dice. Sometime you get lucky and sometimes you don't. Keith and Charlie managed to find a path of least resistance that evaded Greg. At one point he was in such tight quarters that he had to take his pack off and tie a rope to it so he could climb over a rocky spot and pull his pack up after him. I think that was one of those spots that he didn't want to be in. If he has a sissy gene, it was probably causing him to wonder – like I had – if there really was a route to the top and how much a S & R mission costs, and who pays for it?

About an hour after we had split up – yes, it took us about an hour to travel that final 300 feet – Keith and Charlie reached the top, a mere hundred feet from the northernmost overlook at the top of the Jumpoff. At about the same time, I pushed through the bushes at the top of my nameless ridge. As I stood on the trail at the top, it seemed too small to be the AT or the Boulevard. Could it actually be the thin trail that runs along the edge of the Jumpoff? After walking a minute or two, I passed the southernmost overlook of the Jumpoff. Somehow my ridge had topped out not near the AT as I had expected, but about 200 feet from the southern end of the Jumpoff overlook area on the top of Mt. Kephart.

I went to the middle of the Jumpoff overlook and yelled for Greg, wondering where he was. His response came back to me immediately, because he was only about 50 feet below me. (Later, as we sat at Arbys eating our celebratory meal, Greg told me that at that moment, he was just sitting and wondering what to do next. To quote him: "It was good to hear your voice." For Greg, that's a warm and fuzzy moment.) We talked for just a moment – me above and Greg below but both hidden from each other by the shrubs – then I moved north along the Jumpoff and found Charlie and Keith sitting at the spot where they had topped out. About fifteen minutes later Greg came up at their spot by aiming at their voices as they taunted him for being so slow. Because I'm the slow one in our group, this was one of those rare instances in which I arrived at our destination before he did. I should have taken advantage of the situation and joined in the taunting, but I was too tired to muster up any

138

enthusiasm for the project, so I let Keith and Charlie do all the work. After all, I didn't have much experience at the taunting end of the pecking order. I'm usually the tauntee, not the taunter.

We spent fifteen minutes at the top of the Jumpoff, basking in the view, the quiet, the cool breeze... and the sense of accomplishment. It was only at this moment that I realized how *relieved* I was to be finished. It wasn't physical relief; it was mental. This trip's stress level had been a bit higher than average, probably the result of risk mixed with angst about the unknown. I wouldn't go so far as to say we were in serious danger, but for those last few hours we all understood that the consequences of a moment of clumsiness or carelessness could have been serious. We also understood that a few people had probably done this route before, but we didn't know any of them, so we weren't 100% assured that we could reach the top before the sun set. Running out of daylight is always a nagging concern when we are off-trail because there's a very, very thin line between being off-trail in the dark and being lost, and I'm pretty sure that while you are doing it, they'd feel like the same thing. Spending the night hanging on to a spruce sapling on the upper 100' of the Jumpoff would make a great, great story... once it was over, and we were all sitting at Cobbly Nob eating cheeseburgers.

Of course, the views, the 1,400' cascade, the effort, and the angst all worked together to make this one of our most memorable Smokies trips. For a full month afterward, during quiet moments I'd find my thoughts drifting to that eastern slope of Mt. Kephart – everything from the rush of adrenaline to the delicacy of the Grass of Parnassus.

As I write this, we've all done this Lester-Jumpoff trip one or two more times, and I must admit, each time has been a challenge. I had expected that the drama of the unknown wouldn't be quite as pronounced because we now knew that it is possible to get to the top, but that wasn't quite the case. Yes, we now know it's possible to reach the top, but finding that route isn't a foregone conclusion. Even a slight deviation from a previous route can create a trajectory that puts you in a spot that you don't want to be in, which is something that has happened to us every time we've made this trip.

139

Eventually, sanity prevailed and we decided that we should take a break from the Jumpoff. While we'd had no near-death experiences, we did begin to wonder aloud if perhaps we weren't pushing our luck. How many times can a guy put his trust in sand myrtle bushes, worn slate, spruce roots, and globs of wet moss, and escape unharmed? We'd been rolling the dice and had continued to win, but eventually the laws of probability would catch up with us. So we quit while we were ahead.

But like any temptation – gambling or otherwise – a relapse isn't completely out of the question, especially in late summer when the Grass of Parnassus is in bloom and the Jumpoff's Sirens sing their song.

Chapter 9

Cat Stairs, Falcon Cliffs, and Snake Dens

$\mathbf{W}$e were reclining at the Best Lunch Spot, my favorite spot in the Smokies. *My favorite spot.* I don't think I've ever written or said that before. In the past, there's always been a hesitation or an implied disclaimer: "one of my favorite spots" or "the best spot in the Smokies, tied for first place with a thousand other spots" or something along those lines. But as I've thought about our many trips, both on-trail and off-trail, and let the highs and lows of these trips simmer and swirl beneath the surface, I think I can honestly and confidently say that the Best Lunch Spot, nestled away in the cliffs of Greenbrier Pinnacle, in the area called the Cat Stairs, is the place I would go if I had just one, final Smokies trip to make, one last place to go to spend a few hours. My favorite spot.

Even though it should go without saying, I should probably say that the Best Lunch Spot may not be "the best" spot in the Smokies. A *favorite* spot is totally subjective, like your favorite flavor of ice cream. If something is your favorite, you don't owe anyone an explanation. I like chocolate more than vanilla. End of story. If you ask me why, I won't be able to give you a rational, scientific proof. I don't *need* to give you any proof. I *can't* give you proof. All I can say is that I like chocolate more than any other. That doesn't make chocolate the best, but it does make chocolate my favorite. So… end of discussion.

There are just too many ways to define "best," too many factors to consider. Is a waterfall *better* than a panoramic view? Or, is a view *of* Mt. Le Conte better than a view *from* Mt. Le Conte? The programmer hasn't been born yet who can write the definitive algorithm to calculate the best spot in the Smokies. I'll leave that argument to people who like to argue about such things.

Oddly enough, the hike to the Best Lunch Spot is not necessarily my favorite *trip*. We've had some doozies, and I'd have to say that my single, favorite trip was our first trip up the Jumpoff, on the steep face of Mt. Kephart. It was huge and scary. I didn't fully comprehend how scary until we got to the top, and I felt the knot that was my insides loosen and relax, finally realizing that, yes, I would survive. I wouldn't spend the night on the face of the Jumpoff. There would be no S & R.

On the other hand, my favorite ongoing, annual trip is probably Rocky Crag (aka "the real bunion"). The route starting and ending at Porters Creek trailhead is the proper, fully-righteous way to do this trip, but that route seems to get a bit harder and longer each year, so I now opt for starting and ending at Newfound Gap. I love that trip – down Middle Crag, up the Pyramid, up and over Falcon Point, back to the AT.

But for sheer peace and isolation, with the world's best (yes, I said "best" and I'd be willing to argue that point) view of Le Conte, plus a couple of falcons nesting nearby, the Best Lunch Spot is like no other. There are no throngs of tourists cheering you on like there are on the Rocky Crag trip. There is no heart-stopping moment of truth like Charlies Bunion. There's no over-powering sense of accomplishment like the Jumpoff or Anakeesta Ridge. Instead, there's sunshine, shade, wind, quiet, loneliness, even comfort, all with a unique view of the massive wall of Mt. Le Conte dominating the view in one direction and Falcon Cliffs in the other. It's a nice, cozy spot with great surroundings. I wouldn't even think of going there without a small stove to make hot tea or hot chocolate.

It's about a six hour trip, but I am happy to stretch it out to seven or eight hours, so it's not a huge trip, which makes it even more endearing to me. Have I neglected to mention exactly where the Best Lunch Spot is? Yes, I guess I have.

As I was saying, on this blustery, April day we were reclining at the Best Lunch Spot, my favorite spot in the Smokies. The Best Lunch Spot is our name for a modest, rocky alcove that feels like a set of exclusive balcony seats perched in the rocks a few yards away from the Cable

Route through the Cat Stairs, about fifty or a hundred feet above the base of the cliffs. This little alcove has a gnarly, old Table Mountain Pine growing in it and a smattering of rhododendron and mountain laurel bushes sprouting in various cracks in its walls. It feels like private property, and for all practical purposes, it is. There's no reason to believe any other humans have been in this inconspicuous, little spot in the last decade, or even the last five or ten decades, or maybe ever. Yes, *ever*.

This was my 20th trip to the Cat Stairs, and we were enjoying the view and the aerial display of the pair of falcons who had returned to the cliffs of Greenbrier Pinnacle just a few years earlier, after a long, long absence from this part of the park. I am 99% sure that Greg Harrell and I were the first ones to see this nesting pair of falcons when they returned to the Cat Stairs. They weren't there in the spring and fall of 2012. In the spring of 2013, they were.

Mother Nature was in her typical April funk. It was mid-afternoon and the weather had already gone through several iterations: thunderstorms during the night, to cool and foggy just after sunrise, to clearing with a warm breeze by mid-morning, to rainy, cold, and windy – and threatening snow – by lunchtime. Just another typical April day in paradise.

In July "typical" means hot and dry, with the guarantee of thunderstorms by late afternoon. In April, "typical" means... well... I don't know what it means. Nobody does. It's the time of year when my day pack is stuffed to the gills, because I have to be prepared for weather that is warm, cold, wet, *and* dry – not because it could be *any* of these, but because it could be *all* of them. The Best Lunch Spot is just large enough to keep three or four friends and their packs dry during a spring rain, unless the wind is blowing in from the west, which on this day it sometimes did and sometimes didn't.

Our trip to this hidden, rocky spot had begun two weeks earlier when, once again, the name Cat Stairs had percolated to the surface during a conversation that Keith, Greg, and I had in the church parking lot on a chilly, early April afternoon. Winter had been long and hard (by Tennessee standards), hanging on to the end of March. More than once I had spent several days trapped at home by a quarter inch of ice or

143

several inches of snow on our shaded road. During those winter doldrums I got some paperwork done – grading papers, income taxes – but I also spent too much time staring at the thermometer, waiting for spring to arrive and learning that a watched thermometer doesn't rise any faster than a watched pot will boil. If I had a pair of ruby-red slippers, I'd have put them on and repeated, "There's no time like spring." Instead, I had to settle for listening to Copland's *Appalachian Spring*, trying to force spring to show itself. The music worked about as well as the ruby slippers would have.

In addition to the uncooperative weather, the three of us had been too busy for a dozen different reasons, and we were all losing patience with this overall state of affairs. It was time to do something manly, something that would involve bumps, bruises, sweat, dirt, and maybe some blood. So our choices seemed to be either a bar fight with a biker gang or an off-trail hike in the mountains. We opted for the mountains, partly to avoid significant bloodshed and partly because our wives wouldn't let us go to a bar – which is a clue as to how a bar fight would have turned out.

In recent years, our hiking discussions tend to narrow themselves down to a few familiar options: Cat Stairs, the side ridges of Cammerer, Rocky Crag, Styx Branch to Myrtle Point, Big Duck Hawk, Chimney Tops. A half dozen favorites may not seem like much, but the fact that each of these trips has several permutations immediately increases our options to well over a dozen different trips. Our parking lot conversation turned to the Cat Stairs for no particular reason. Most likely, one of us hadn't been there in a while and mentioned it out loud. Once on the table, no one had any reason to veto the idea – it's a perennial favorite, after all – so the idea stuck. Or, maybe someone mentioned April's profusion of low to mid-elevation wildflowers. Or, maybe we hoped the timber rattlers wouldn't yet be out on Bird Branch to the Cat Stairs, so we should go sooner rather than later. Or maybe the enemy was stinging nettle rather than rattlesnakes. Or maybe we had six hours for the trip, but not twelve, so we'd avoid dawn-to-dusk death marches like Roaring Fork or Cannon Creek. And of course, there's always the hope of seeing some significant wildlife in this isolated part of the park. Whatever the reasons, Cat Stairs prevailed.

We had come up our standard Cat Stairs route: past the Barnes graves, up the Castle branch of Bird Branch to the base of the cliffs, north along the base of the cliffs, past the Roman Column to the Cable branch of Bird Branch. From there it's just a short scramble to the Best Lunch Spot. To exit, we would descend via the Cable route back to the Barnes home site and graves, then an hour back to the car parked on the road to Ramsey Cascades. Simple.

It's good to have a standard route to know and follow, but it's even better to go through the process of exploring a wild, new area and to figure such things out for yourselves, which is what we had done over the course of several years and about a dozen trips.

How had it all begun? How did we come to this point where we had been to the Cat Stairs at least twenty times and now had familiar places – Harrell's Folly, Roman Column, Cable Route, Best Lunch Spot – that had become old favorites?

We had first encountered the Cat Stairs in the writings of Harvey Broome, one of the early leaders of the Smoky Mountains Hiking Club. The first time I read his book *Out Under the Sky of the Great Smokies* I was baffled by his frequent references to places that I'd never even heard of, much less visited: Mt. Winnesoka, Woolly Tops, Drinkwater Pool, and... Cat Stairs.

I had no idea where the Cat Stairs were, but the name immediately caught my attention. Cat... as in big cat... as in Wampus Cat... as in Mountain Lion. Every hiker I know wants desperately to believe that there are still mountain lions (aka panthers, painters, pumas, cougars, catamounts, wampus cats) in the Smokies, but deep in our hearts most of us accept the official pronouncements of the NPS: there are no mountain lions in this region of the country and haven't been for six or eight decades. In fact, in 2011 the US Fish and Wildlife Service declared the eastern cougar (aka eastern mountain lion) to be officially extinct.

Apparently, there are two ways to have a species removed from the Endangered Species list: they can make a comeback as the peregrine falcons did, or they can disappear completely. The eastern cougar's disappearing act was a combination of loss of large tracts of wild land, loss of its prime prey (deer), and sheer slaughter by humans with guns. In other words, it's essentially the same story as every extinction since woolly mammoths, saber-toothed cats, and giant sloths disappeared about 10,000 years ago.

The silver lining of this story is that the eastern mountain lion is actually a subspecies, along with the other subspecies of mountain lion: the western cougar, Florida panther, and South American cougar. So no *species* has actually been lost, and a comeback is possible if western cougars migrate east. I don't have much hope for this because there's very little wild land east of the Mississippi. On the other hand, I do know of an 800 square mile chunk of land that is punctuated by only a few roads and campgrounds. And some sections of this refuge have fewer outposts of humanity than others, this Greenbrier section of the park being one of those less-civilized places.

For those of us who still cling to the hope that two or three of these reclusive cats are still around, every year there are about five or ten reported sightings (but not clear photos) of mountain lions in the park by people who ought to know the difference between a mountain lion and a bobcat, bear, or coyote. I've seen only one mountain lion in the wild (on a motorcycle trip across an empty, marshy expanse in Minnesota – it was dusk and I saw only its silhouette), but it was easy to identify – that smooth, cat-like gait, the long tail, and the small, boxy head. I didn't even know there were mountain lions in the area, so I wasn't predisposed to imagine one. There was simply no other creature that it could possibly have been. Mistaking a bear or bobcat or large housecat for a cougar would be like mistaking a VW bug for an F-350.

The experts say the sightings in the Smokies are probably cougars that were pets (usually of the South American subspecies) which grew too big and were released by their owners. My initial reaction was disbelief: Who buys mountain lions as pets? The experts must be wrong – no one would be so egotistical or cruel as to buy a mountain lion and keep it locked in a cage, would they?

Upon just a moment's reflection... yeah, I guess they would. We slaughter a species then a few folks decide it would be cool to have a cougar, so they buy a few and put them in cages. It's sort of what we did

146

to the Native Americans, except that we called the cages Indian Territory or reservations. So considering our history... yeah, pet cougars make a certain amount of sense, even though the difference between domesticated and wild animals should be obvious to anyone with a brain or a conscience. A cougar in a cage should be illegal under the Eighth Amendment.

So cougars in the park is not the same thing as a "self-sustaining population" in the park, and it would probably be too controversial for the NPS to reintroduce these carnivores back into the Smokies. Reintroducing otter or brook trout is safe. Big cats would be a different story. The first time a local cow was killed, there would be calls for the offender to euthanized, the same way aggressive bears who have lost their fear of humans are dealt with.

I attended a talk by a well-respected expert on mountain lions who showed us maps and pictures and told of credible witnesses who had reported sightings in the park. He never came right out and declared that there are mountain lions in the Smokies, but I could tell by the twinkle in his eye that he's a believer. Or he wants to believe. I know a person of faith when I see one because I'm one, too. I want to believe that those big, dangerous cats are in the park, and where better to live than these lonely, rocky precipices known as the Cat Stairs at the west end of Greenbrier Pinnacle.

For the record, I've never seen even a footprint of a mountain lion in the Smokies, even at the Cat Stairs. Although, I personally know one witness – a knowledgeable and honest person – who claims to have seen one in the park. So, right now, I want to believe, but it's just a matter of time and a couple more witnesses until I become a true believer, truly convinced by the evidence.

We were compelled by the mystique of the name "Cat Stairs" to pay them a visit, so in April, 2009 we made our first trip there. We had been doing serious off-trail hiking for about two years, so we were getting the hang of reading the creekbeds, slopes, and ridgelines. If there was no trail, we could see where there *could be* a trail. In our wanderings we'd often find ourselves stepping over big piles of bear scat. So we and the bears were making similar decisions in maneuvering across the landscape. We took that as a sign of something good, a point of pride – thinking like a bear. It was about this time that, in the spirit of calling things what they are, we stopped calling these paths "manways" and began calling them "bearways."

A local friend of mine told me that, yes, there used to be a Cat Stairs path, but he hadn't been on it in over twenty years and couldn't remember anything specific about it. A couple of folks in the Smoky Mountains Hiking Club said that they had been on a Cat Stairs trip several years ago, and then gave me a couple of quick tips, mainly about the location of the trailhead. A volunteer in the park's Backcountry Office asked if we intended to go by way of the Barnes Cemetery, which we'd never heard of. Then our friend, Charlie Roth (Dutch Roth's grandson), told Keith and Greg about the book by Ken Wise called *Hiking Trails of the Great Smoky Mountains* that gave a written description of a route to the Cat Stairs. (Unfortunately, Ken's directions were a lot like knowing a few phrases of a foreign language in a foreign county – they are enough to get you into trouble but not enough to get you out. We couldn't quite visualize what he was describing.)

So armed with a map, compass, altimeter, GPS, plus a few hints and a copy of Wise's directions, we found the trailhead about a half mile beyond the split in Greenbrier Road. Between the four of us (Greg Harrell, Keith Oakes, Charlie Roth, and me) we were able to sometimes put our heads together, sometimes spread out across the Bird Branch watershed, sometimes get lost, sometimes get found, and eventually find our way to the path that led to the saddest spot in the Smokies, about two miles from the road: the graves of Delia, Julies, and Rosey Barnes, the young children of John Barnes.

Later we discovered that among Smokies aficionados, the Barnes Place is a well-known, well-kept secret. It's a truly touching location – a quiet reminder of human frailty in the midst of a powerful, unforgiving wilderness. There are poignant metaphors buried there as well, waiting to be unearthed by some wandering poet. We spent a few minutes at their graves, as we have done every time since then, just to pay our respects to those three little kids, and to be alone with our thoughts and prayers for our own families.

From the Saddest Place the worn path continued another couple of minutes to the crumbling chimney of the old Barnes home, and behind the chimney the "trail" continued toward the cliffs on the western end of Greenbrier Pinnacle.

About twenty minutes past the chimney we stepped off this lightly-trod path at the point where an even lighter path turns north and east around the west end of the Pinnacle. This was the point where Copeland Divide becomes Greenbrier Pinnacle, and we would follow this broad, wooded crest up to the rocky Cat Stairs. We had looked carefully for this spot, and were glad and somewhat proud at having found it. However, later it occurred to us that we could have turned upslope at any point between the Barnes' chimney and this western end – any route would lead *up*, up toward the cliffs which would begin at 4,100', about 1,000' vertical feet above us.

One disappointing detail we discovered as we hiked up this ridge on the western end of Greenbrier Pinnacle is that the phrase "Cat Stairs" on the USGS topo map is probably misplaced. The Cat Stairs spot on the map is a plain, wooded ridge with nothing unusual or extraordinary about it. No cliffs, no exposed rocks. Just dirt and trees. The topo lines are wide and smooth – none of those tightly packed lines that merge into a single mass. The steep, open cliffs that any reasonable person would call the Cat Stairs are about a half mile southeast of the topo map's location.

For an hour we walked and crawled up this ridgecrest, using branches, roots, and rocks to help pull ourselves up this steep, wooded slope. We worked our way over and around a few interesting rock outcrops, stopping for lunch and views at the very first outcrop at 4,100' – which we now call the First Stair – which was actually the best spot of the day. When we finally reached the site of the old firetower at the top of Greenbrier Pinnacle, we looked at each other and shrugged our shoulders. We had expected high, open, scary rocks providing a continuous string of unparalleled views. What we got was a couple of good views at a couple of rocky spots, and some crawling in dirt and leaves around some big, smooth boulders. What we didn't get was an adrenaline rush from maneuvering along a narrow ridgecrest. Nor did we get any 300', Yosemite-like vertical cliffs.

We weren't exactly disappointed with the Cat Stairs, but they clearly had not met our expectations. We even wondered for a few minutes if we had taken a wrong turn and missed the real Cat Stairs, even though we had hiked right through the "Cat Stairs" label on the topo map. This was one of those rare occasions in which a trip in the Smokies hadn't lived up to the hype that we had created in our own minds. Maybe all those cliff and cougar musings were just self-induced propaganda.

We finished that first trip by descending through the giant boulders of Devils Den on the slopes of Greenbrier Pinnacle about a half mile south of the Cat Stairs. As always, it was a great day in a beautiful, rugged place. We had explored new territory and had followed in the footsteps of Harvey Broome and others hikers of an earlier generation. No complaints. However... while none of us verbalized it at that time, we all were wondering the same thing: had we missed something?

In the subsequent weeks, as we began to share pictures and to reminisce, we realized that we were all thinking the same thing. The problem wasn't the Cat Stairs; the problem was us. From across the valley the bold, gray cliffs on the west face of Greenbrier Pinnacle are very prominent features, several hundred feet high and maybe a quarter mile long... and somehow in our haste to get to the top we had missed them. We needed to give the Cat Stairs another chance. Or, the Cat Stairs needed to give *us* another chance. We had failed them. So we got out our topo maps and did our homework for another trip.

One of the things we had learned in our off-trail ramblings was that creekbeds can be interesting, beautiful routes up to the top of a mountain: Bear Pen Hollow, Trout Branch, Cannon Creek, Lester Prong. (There are cascades and plunges and wet cliffs all over the park, completely trail-free and tourist-free.) We had become accustomed to following creeks up the steep sides of mountains. So we now began to see Bird Branch not simply as a creek to cross near the Barnes Place but as a possible entrance ramp to the Cat Stairs. If we were interpreting the topo lines of our map (USGS: Mount Guyot) correctly, the watershed of Bird Branch emerges from the Cat Stairs cliffs; that is, "our" Cat Stairs, not the map's. (We now ignore the USGS designation and refer to the cliffs on the western end of Greenbrier Pinnacle as the Cat Stairs.) The wiggles of the topo lines hinted that perhaps these creekbeds might cut through the cliffs and provide access to the top of Greenbrier Pinnacle. Or, if not the top of the Pinnacle, then perhaps some fun scrambling routes among the cracks and crevices of the cliffs. This is how an obsession takes root; it usually begins with a topo map.

So 2009 was the year we began our Cat Stairs fling. Some folks in our group have compared our relationship with the Cat Stair to a drug addiction that you can't quit because you can't quit. Or, the Sirens' Song, luring us to wild, rocky places. Or, a love affair; a wild, torrid affair that might get you in trouble but is impossible to walk away from. In the next five months, we went to the Cat Stairs six or eight times. We just couldn't stop going back.

Now that we knew how to get to the Barnes Place, it became our standard base camp. Every time we went to the Cat Stairs cliffs, we'd stop to visit those three headstones, then from the site of the old cabin we'd follow the path of the Barnes Place spring as it emerged from the base of an ancient oak tree and cut a deep, wide gully down to Bird Branch. At the junction of this gully with Bird Branch, there is actually a Three Branch Junction, as we've come to call it, of Barnes Tree Spring, Cable Branch, and Castle Branch. Of course, none of these names show up on any maps. They are the names we've given them because one comes from the Barnes Tree Spring, while the other two lead up to rocky ravines through the cliffs. One is the ravine that an old phone or telegraph cable once ran through up to the firetower; the other leads to a ravine with a turret that would fit well atop a castle wall – thus the names: Cable and Castle. And, yes, both these routes – and *only* these routes – cut through the cliffs and lead to the top.

One of our best discoveries was that the one, good overlook on the old, decommissioned Greenbrier Pinnacle trail is actually the top of the Cable Route. As I recall, it was Greg Harrell who was awakened one Saturday morning by the Song of the Sirens, so he jumped in his car and raced to the Cat Stairs. He scrambled up the Cable Route and followed it all the way to the top, only to find himself standing on the old Greenbrier Pinnacle trail just ten feet from the overlook. Most of us had done the Greenbrier Pinnacle trail in the early days of our off-trail ramblings. We had all discovered that this trail which led from the Ramsey Cascades trail to the old firetower on Greenbrier Pinnacle had just one really good overlook at a point a few minutes from the top. Even the old firetower site has no good views. (The main thing I remember from my only hike up the old Greenbrier Pinnacle trail is that I stepped out of the rhododendron into the clearing of the old firetower site, but I didn't pay close attention to where that opening in the rhody was. An hour later, when I was ready to leave the top, I couldn't find the opening of the trail. That was one of my first off-trail lessons: whenever you leave something or enter something or change directions, stop and think: "what is this going to look like when I am coming back this way?")

This Greenbrier Pinnacle Overlook is the one, most-memorable spot on the Greenbrier Pinnacle trail as it provides a broad, open view west across the Greenbrier valley to Mt. Le Conte. To have discovered a direct, off-trail route to this overlook was huge. We can now stand at this overlook, knowing that the rugged ravine below our feet is actually a passable route, a secret passage way to cliffs, boulders, and secret alcoves that provide shelter from a spring thunderstorm.

We also explored the Castle Route about 200 yards to the south and found that it intersects with the old Greenbrier Pinnacle trail about a tenth of a mile from the overlook. And, like the Cable Route, it provides access to numerous nooks and crannies in the cliffs. On a trip that Greg Harrell and I took during this Cat Stairs fling, we hiked up the Castle Route from Three Branch Junction and arrived at the castle turret at the wooded base of the cliffs. From there, rather than continuing up to the overlook near the top, we hiked north along the base of the cliffs less than half a mile and found ourselves standing at the northwest end of the cliffs, the point at which the cliffs simply dissolve into the dirt, trees, and shrubs of the end ridge of Greenbrier Pinnacle. We were back at our original lunch spot – the First Stair – from our very first trip. Although it had taken us a half dozen trips, we had circumnavigated the cliffs and had found three good routes to the top, plus a few other interesting side routes that were so spontaneous and convoluted that we could never intentionally replicate them.

One side trip that we can easily retrace (because it is very visible and is located midway between Cable and Castle at the base of the cliffs) leads to a Roman Column with a four foot, round boulder balanced on the top. It's the closest thing I've seen in the Smokies to those weird spires you sometimes see in Arches or Canyonlands National Parks, or a "glacial erratic" in Acadia National Park in Maine. I've scrambled up onto it a few times (it's a good falcon viewing spot). Once as I reached under the boulder to hold on tight – it was a windy day – a bat flew out from under it. I take that as another good sign – we think like bats as well as bears. Any trip on which you see more bats and piles of bear scat than people is a good trip. Using that rule of thumb, all our Cat Stairs excursions have been good trips.

There's another route which we now call Harrell's Folly. It received its name the day Greg Harrell was showing the Castle Route to a couple of friends, and he managed to take them up an obscure, side branch of the Castle Creek. When they arrived at the base of the cliffs, the castle turret wasn't there and nothing looked familiar. They were in the wrong creekbed, about 1,000' south of the Castle Branch. He received a well-deserved taunting, and this little feeder creek received a new name: Harrell's Folly. At least, that's what Keith, Charlie, and I call it. I'm not sure what Greg calls it because he doesn't talk about it much.

Even though our new, preferred route went up and into the cliffs via Bird Branch, we knew we needed to try our original Copeland Divide route again, the one in which the Cat Stairs didn't meet our expectations because we were too rushed and naïve to know how to treat them. As we passed through the Barnes Place, we heard a light patter on the remnants of winter's dead leaves. Without giving it much thought, we assumed that we were hearing the gentle start of a spring rain in the mountains, like the brass and strings of Copland's *Appalachian Spring*. But somehow the sound wasn't quite right because it seemed to precede us as we walked, but it didn't follow us. A closer inspection revealed thousands of small, brown-and-black grasshoppers scattering as we approached, then nestling under the leaves for safety. Copland's piece provides musical allusions to the dawning and dimming of the day, rain waxing and waning, soft breezes ebbing and flowing, a warming sun... the gist of springtime's simple gifts, but no sprinkle of grasshoppers on dry leaves. That's one minor omission in an otherwise perfect work.

Beyond the Barnes Place we knew the lay of the land and the access points to the cliffs. As we struggled up the west end of the Pinnacle, we were slipping and sliding on wet dirt and leaves. Two steps forward and one step back. Thank goodness for my walking stick.

I had always liked that idea of a walking stick – a simple, sturdy, wooden stick – but I liked it only in theory, not reality. It seemed to me that a stick would just get in the way, being just one more thing to carry. However, one day not long ago on Porters Creek trail at campsite #31 I found a four foot long stick leaning against a tree. It was cut and stripped and had a neat little bend near the top. It spoke to me in some mystical, non-verbal way, so I picked it up, and it fit me perfectly.

I had never given much thought to the proper length and shape of a good walking stick, but it's probably the kind of thing that gets debated around campfires, much like fly fishermen debate the pros and cons of fly rod length and flex. So, maybe there are reasons to want a short walking stick, or two sticks, or two ski poles, or adjustable poles, with rubber tips, or titanium points... but I've come to depend on my crooked, four foot, wooden stick, sometimes as a third foot, sometimes as a handrail. I don't use it like ski or trekking poles. I use it more like a canoe paddle or gondolier's pole. When going uphill, I often plant it a few inches behind me and push on it like a gondolier on the canals of Venice. When going down, I'm able to save my aching knees at the end of the day by planting it in front of me and easing myself down. And of course, I love the fact that it was free and simple. As Thoreau said, "That man is richest whose pleasures are the cheapest." He may very well have had walking sticks in mind because he was a first-class, obsessive walker... and a cheapskate, like me.

And it helped me on our ascent up to the First Stair. The dirt was slippery but deep. I could plant my stick firmly in the soil and maintain my footing with a minimum of backsliding. I'm tempted to say that I couldn't have hiked up the ridge without it, but the fact that I didn't use it the first time combined with the fact that my three hiking partners on

154

this trip didn't use a hiking stick means that I probably could have made the trip without the stick. But it helped.

When we arrived at the First Stair we scrambled out on the rocks and enjoyed the open air and the view – just as we had on our first trip. But for the next hour instead of hurrying on to the top as we'd done on our maiden voyage, we took every opportunity to bear to the right toward the cliffs which were below us and to our right. These right-handed tangents were the key to enjoying this section of the Cat Stairs. We found rocky alcoves and ledges and chutes and dead-ends and drop-offs. And, of course, open air and views. The cliffs were exactly where they had always been, but this time we took the time to find them and to enjoy them, and they rewarded us for our effort.

If there's one thing I've learned from my time outdoors, it is this... There's no guarantee that things will work out well or as planned, but if you'll put yourself in a position for good things to happen, it's pleasantly surprising how often they do. As a poker player once told me, "Luck favors the backbone, not the wishbone." I'm not sure how that applies to poker, but it fits outdoor life perfectly. Good things happen to those who put themselves in places where good things ought to happen. All of our trips to the Cat Stairs had confirmed this basic principle of outdoor life.

Thinking back, our only real mistake on our first trip had been tunnel vision. We thought our goal was to make it to the top of Greenbrier Pinnacle via the Cat Stairs route. We should have known that our goal was to enjoy the Cat Stairs, which just happened to lead to the top of Greenbrier Pinnacle. As in tasting fine wine or eating a good cheeseburger, the journey is as important as the destination – another basic principle of life.

Of course, this route did eventually take us to an intersection with the old Greenbrier Pinnacle trail, just a few yards from the overlook at the top of Cable Route. From the overlook we could see patches of white clinging to the steep slopes and rocky niches across the face of the mountain below us. I think of these serviceberry trees as the advance guard of spring. They are among the first trees to bloom, and their wispy white flowers stand out against the browns and grays of early spring. In the old days these trees were harbingers of the church *services* (thus

155

their name) that would soon resume as the circuit-riding preachers emerged from their winter hibernation. The serviceberry in my yard had bloomed well over a month ago, so it had taken spring five or six weeks to climb the 3,000' in elevation from my home to this overlook, roughly 500' per week.

After a few handfuls of M&Ms and Cliff Bars, we dove into the rhododendron and down the Cable Route, bearing alternately right and then left to find the path of least resistance around large, slick rocks and slides. Within an hour we were relaxing in the Best Lunch Spot, our private balcony in the rocks, providing grandstand views of the Greenbrier valley and Mt. Le Conte to the west and the cliffs to the north.

So every spring we visit the west end of Greenbrier Pinnacle, hoping to catch a glimpse of the falcons or some other rare creature, but so far there's been no sign of wampus cats. Normally, in addition to the falcons, all we see are vultures, hawks, ravens, chickadees, salamanders, grasshoppers, and piles of bear scat.

And an occasional snake.

When skeptics ask me about off-trail hiking, they usually bring up the topic of snakes, usually in the form of "Aren't you afraid of running into a snake?" My answer is usually somewhat evasive. I tell them I don't even think about it because if I did, I'd probably talk myself out of going. If I'm feeling especially bold, I might say, "Fear of death doesn't keep us from dying. It keeps us from living." Although, I could also honestly add that I never see venomous snakes... until the first time I saw one...

As the day progressed, the cold and drizzle finally gave way to spring. Mother Nature had decided to let April be more like May and less like March: sun, rising temperatures, blue sky with a touch of haze. The change was sudden and dramatic, which we appreciated... as did the snakes.

Our trip back down Cable Branch was delightful, partly because we were working *with* gravity, not against it, but mainly because of the

156

seasonal wildflowers: the whites of stonecrop and sweet white trillium formed a clean background for the purple-blue of wild geraniums and violets. Against this carpet of color were the many rocks and logs, which I used to think of as merely minor obstacles to overcome, but I now think of as ideal snake habitat. I was picking my way slowly over and between the rocks and logs, alternately using my walking stick and my free hand to keep my balance and preserve my aching knees. As we approached the 3,000' elevation and were preparing to bear north toward the Barnes Place, I leaned toward a log simply to put my hand on it to maintain my balance. As I shifted my weight toward it, I looked at the spot where my hand would touch, only to see that it was already occupied – by a coiled rattlesnake, two feet away.

You know all the stuff you've heard about rattlesnakes warning with their rattle before they strike? Not on a mild day in April, apparently. I don't know if he was still sluggish from the cool temperatures, or maybe I had approached him so suddenly that he didn't have time to become agitated and give a warning, or both, or neither. All I can say is that he seemed unconcerned to the point of boredom. I'm pretty certain that even a bored rattlesnake would strike if pushed or grabbed by a careless human, but I didn't test that theory. I used my walking stick to nudge him gently away, to see where he'd go. He slithered under a nearby rock and finally buzzed his rattle, not as a warning but as a parting expletive.

That was my closest encounter with a venomous snake. For the rest of the day, every stick or root was, for a moment, a rattlesnake. Now when people ask about snakes, I allow as how, yes, there are a few. Depending on the elevation, temperature, terrain, and season, I look for snakes. If the ground is broken and holey, I'm on high alert. On trails and unbroken surfaces, I don't think about them at all. The problem, of course, is that off-trail hiking is about 10% unbroken surfaces and 90% snake dens. So the odds are in the snakes' favor.

A week later, Keith and I were again on Cable Branch, and he nearly stepped on a timber rattler coiled on a rock. I'd love to describe his gyrations in avoiding it, but words fail. He was a blur of flailing legs and arms, while falling backwards and squealing like a schoolgirl. So, that was two rattlesnake encounters in eight days, which is enough to get your attention… and keep it… for the rest of the spring and summer… and several years thereafter.

A few weeks later we were talking to the Greenbrier ranger and mentioned our rattlesnake encounters. The ranger's tone was so casual and nonchalant that it almost hurt our feelings: "Yeah, Greenbrier is full of 'em. I mean, just *look* at it." As he said those words he looked out into the woods and swept his arm in one of those "one day all this will be yours" sorts of gestures. Keith and I just stood there staring blankly into the distant woods and rocks and rhododendron.

In other words, any guy with half a brain should be able to just look at the broken terrain and know that the Greenbrier backcountry is just one big snake den, something that took us about six months and two rattlesnakes, plus being told plainly by a ranger, to figure out. Sure, obvious.

Now, when I go to the Cat Stairs, I look for wildlife: bears, bats, mountain lions, peregrine falcons… and, yes, timber rattlers. It's the perfect habitat for all of them. I mean, just look at it!

Chapter 10

The Three Sisters

The first time I laid eyes on Charlies Bunion, many years ago, I was shocked. My reaction was typical of anyone who has spent time in the Southern Appalachians: "What is this doing here?"

Charlies Bunion is a high, exposed, rocky outcrop – something that is rare in the Southern Appalachians where almost every square inch is covered with dirt, moss, ferns, flowers, shrubs, and trees. The result is only an occasional open view. After all, these mountains are called Smoky, not Rocky, meaning that the trees are plentiful and go all the way to the very top of every mountain. (In fact, they'd go beyond the top if they could. Tree line at this latitude would be about 8,000 feet above sea level.) From the air, the Southern Appalachian Mountains look as soft as a bear's butt.

In the unique case of Charlies Bunion, this rock was exposed in the 1920s through the combined efforts of nature and humans. The human part came in the form of a wildfire that started on the heavily lumbered North Carolina side of the Smokies, then moved up and over the main ridgecrest and into the upper Porters Creek watershed in Tennessee. This removed most of the plant life that held the soil in place. A couple of years later, nature, in the form of a heavy rain, finished the job by washing away the remaining soil, creating three bare side ridges which start among the upper tributaries of Porters Creek and climb quickly to the main ridgecrest.

Everyone's first exposure to these side ridges comes as they walk the four miles on the AT from Newfound Gap, past the Boulevard and Ice Water Spring, to Charlies Bunion. In the last half mile leading to the Bunion, there are several views of this steep, barren side ridge as it starts among the hardwoods and (dead) hemlocks along Lester Prong, gathers a narrow forest of spruce trees as it rises above 4,000', changes to sand myrtle, moss, and bare rock during its final 500', and culminates in the rocky peak of Charlies Bunion. A hiker who doesn't bother to observe

159

Charlies Bunion as she approaches it on the AT may never see the ridge that leads up from the valley to the Bunion simply because the ridge is so steep that it's almost impossible to see it from atop the Bunion. Most folks who visit the Bunion are completely unaware that there's a side ridge leading up to it from the valley below. They think it's just a bump on the main ridge, not realizing that almost every peak on the AT is actually a mountaintop with slopes or ridges splaying out to the sides.

Once at the Bunion, there are excellent views west to Mt. Kephart and the Boulevard, north into the Porters Creek valley from Mt. Le Conte to Greenbrier Pinnacle, and east to Porters Mountain and beyond. For views south into the Bradley Fork watershed in North Carolina one needs merely to scramble to the very top of the Bunion, which – surprisingly – visitors rarely do, probably because the short path to the top is neither obvious nor dramatic.

The other two "sisters" of this story lie to the east, between the Bunion and Porters Mountain. Neither of these ridges has an official name, and to the casual visitor they look like a couple of inconspicuous pieces in a very big puzzle. These two ridges – which my friends and I call Rocky Crag and Middle Crag – do not dominate the skyline. They aren't massive, and while the Rocky Crag ridge has several distinctive spots, the Middle Crag can be easily overlooked as being merely a pile of rocks – a really, really steep and rugged pile of rocks.

One of our occasional bushwhacking partners, Jenny Bennett, who had been doing this much longer than we have, told us the Smoky Mountains Hiking Club used to call our Rocky Crag the "Real Bunion" and today's Charlies Bunion was called the "Tourist Bunion." I wish I knew how far back in time those names go, but she didn't know. She learned about them in the 1980s.

There's an old black and white picture by George Masa of our Rocky Crag labeled "Charlies Bunion," and the old Smokies hiker, Harvey Broome, seems to have climbed our Rocky Crag and called it Charlies Bunion, although his descriptions are a bit vague. The fact that the USGS quad maps have the label "Charlies Bunion" right on top of our Rocky Crag also suggests that the Rocky Crag is the real Charlies Bunion. On the other hand, we've run across several obvious errors on those USGS quad maps (e.g., Arch Rock and Indian Gap), so they aren't infallible. We've also seen a picture of Charlie Connor (the Charlie that the Bunion is named after) standing on the "tourist bunion." The picture is labeled Charlies Bunion. So, if the hikers who talk about the tourist and real Bunions were relying solely on the USGS maps, they may be right, or they may be barking up the wrong tree. Like us, they probably found it necessary to create names for these various ridges, simply to grease the wheels of conversation within their group because it's hard to carry on a discussion about objects and places that have no names.

As a group, these Three Sisters are nearly invisible from the Appalachian Trail. There are no significant elevation changes in the trail, no prominent peaks to grab your attention ... unless you are below them on the Tennessee side of the main crest. From the bottom of these ridges, looking up, there are three very distinct "peaks" as these side ridges join the main ridge. As far as I can tell, this is the only line of sight that provides a clear view of these Three Sisters. From any other spot in the park, they are easily overlooked. So, if you ever want to visit the Three Sisters, don't bother asking a ranger about them because I'm about the only one who calls them by that name. In fact, the name didn't even occur to us until after we had been tromping around the bases of these ridges for well over a year. We were sitting in a heath thicket at the base of the Charlies Bunion ridge and noticed that from below, three ridges and their peaks were clearly visible... but only from below. The Three Sisters were born.

The fact that these three ridges are below the main, state line ridge, have no official names, and no official trails, means that even avid hikers tend to overlook them. They just don't stand out from the crowd, which is fine with us. That's why our trips up and down these ridges are always solitary experiences. The other reason for this solitude is more compelling: you could die on some of these ridges.

My hiking partners and I had been exploring this Porters Creek section of the park for over a year: Dry Sluice manway, Porters Mountain, Boulevard Prong, Cannon Creek, Horseshoe Mountain. All great, tough trips. If these had been the only trips we ever did, we could still retire knowing that we'd had a lot of fun seeing some great sights: heath balds, steep creekbeds, hidden cascades, impressive landslide scars, plus a lot of just-plain-hard buswhacking through rhododendron hells, greenbrier vines, and blowdowns. We could have retired with a sense of accomplishment. Like many folks, we had skirted the edge of the Three Sisters many times by hiking on the AT to Charlies Bunion and beyond. And, again like most folks, we had no clue that a visit to the Bunion via the AT was just scratching the surface.

But, luckily, we kept going because Greg Harrell loves topo maps, and he pays attention. Between his poring over these maps and his many trips up Porters Creek manway, he was the one who noticed these side ridges. Up until that moment, our off-trailing had focused on finding old, decommissioned trails on old maps. Greg and the Three Sisters were the ones who broke us loose from those dotted lines on old maps. I've occasionally wondered, but still don't know, how many other aspiring off-trailers start on old trails and paths but eventually realize that every ridge and every river is a potential route worthy of exploration. It took us a year or two to figure that out.

In the span of just a few weeks, he climbed all three ridges and returned with tales of his exploits. His eagerness to explore by himself combined with his propensity for hyperbole puts him in the same class as Jim Bridger and Jeremiah Johnson. You have to follow his tracks, partly for the adventure and partly to separate fact from fiction. Bridger's unbelievable stories led to government expeditions to Yellowstone. Greg's tall tales resulted in our series of trips to the Three Sisters.

On a bright, warm May afternoon, Keith Oakes, Charlie Roth, Greg Harrell, and I parked at the Porters Creek trailhead and walked about four miles to the Porters Flat campsite. This four mile walk is also known as "paying our dues." It's the foreplay leading up to the real thing, which is sort of a shame. This Porters Creek trail is a good trail. It is known as one of the best spring wildflower hikes in the Smokies, it parallels a beautiful river, and it even has a decent waterfall (Fern

Branch). It's unfortunate that we don't slow down to appreciate its beauty... but we don't. Not anymore. I'm sorry to say that it has become simply an entrance ramp onto the main road, like a foyer in a cathedral. In some sense, I feel like we've lost something important... a sense of perspective maybe. We feel like we've moved on to a deeper level of intimacy with the park, which is good, but I miss those days when even a simple hike on a popular trail was a treat. Is it like a love relationship in which you move beyond the early days of dating and enter the comfort of commitment and familiarity? You are happy to have moved to a deeper level, but you occasionally miss the freshness and innocence of those early days. Or maybe we're just addicts who need stronger and stronger doses to maintain the buzz, something new to keep things exciting.

Fortunately, I occasionally fish on Porters Creek, and being a lazy fisherman who dawdles and piddles more than actually fishes, I do take time to absorb the simple beauty of this quiet place. But not today.

At the campsite we found the lightly worn path leading through green rhododendron thickets and along the edges of Porters Creek. This path, variously known as Dry Sluice manway (because of where it ends) or Porters Creek manway (because of where it begins), provides quick, steep access to the AT from Porters Creek. It's one of the few paths in the park that is marked by rock cairns strategically placed precisely at the places where they need to be. If the trail crosses the creek or simply becomes hard to find, just stop and look and you'll see a cairn up ahead showing you the way. It's a fun hike, but today we'd stay on it for only about thirty minutes. Before long, there's a split in the creek: Porters Creek to the left, Lester Prong to the right. We followed Lester.

There are three main tributaries that flow down from the main ridgecrest into Lester Prong and divide the ridges of the Three Sisters. On this day in May we turned south up the first tributary. Like many of the sites on this trip, it has no official name. Greg calls it the Rocky Crag Tributary. I call it the First Tributary – capital letters optional – because it's the first of three tributaries. Apparently, Greg has a bit more of a creative flair than I do, but you'd never know it by looking at him. Although, I'll take credit for the name "Three Sisters," but even that name came from laziness rather than creativity. It's just easier to say

"Three Sisters" than "the three side ridges between Mt. Kephart and Porters Mountain."

There's a nice, 60' cascade on this first tributary. It's not the most impressive spot in the park, and we've discovered that the creeks in the park are full of these hidden gems, but every one of them feels like a special gift that belongs only to us. That's part of the joy of off-trail hiking in obscure places – you have a sense of ownership because you are the only ones there... and it often feels like you are the only ones who have *ever* been there.

Climbing up these cascades is interesting. Sometimes there are just enough horizontal hand and foot holds to scramble slowly and carefully up the cascade – sometimes in the water, sometimes along the dry edges. Other times the creekbed is just too steep and slick, requiring a side trip through the rhododendron. The side trip becomes an extended detour whenever rocky cliffs along the sides of the cascade push us far out of our intended route. Instead of traveling parallel with the creek, we are pushed away perpendicularly until the rock wall shrinks back into the dirt and shrubs, giving us a chance to move upward once again and then back to the creek.

These detour-inducing rocky faces are very common along the edges of cascades, which makes sense. If you think about it, a cascade is a steep, watery slide caused by water running over a steep, rocky face. This rocky face isn't usually just a few feet across. It is usually dozens or hundreds of feet wide, the watery cascade being only a small, visible part of it. The rest of this rock face is covered up with dirt and flora. So hiking around the watery part of this wide, rocky face will usually run you into the dry part of this rocky face. Sometimes there are cleavages and bushes that enable you to worm your way up to the top, sometimes not... thus the lengthy detour. And of course, it should go without saying that the central feature of these detours is rhododendron, as always.

Just past the top of the 60' cascade, we turned left out of the creek and began our ascent up the side of the Rocky Crag's ridge. There's not a lot to say about this part of the trip, other than this: it's a relentless crawl through rosebay rhododendron, greenbrier vines, and occasional birch and spruce trees. It's hard and dirty, but not dangerous because the angle of ascent is a fairly steady 45° – the phrase "fairly steady" being the key.

We've been on slopes that were about 45° *on average*, but they consisted of several yards of flat horizontal walking, interspersed with several yards of nearly vertical climbing. They are like giant stair steps. Those vertical moments can be difficult and a bit scary, depending on how long a fall would be. On the other hand, a *steady* 45° is a totally different experience. At 45° you are probably not in danger of falling down the slope. A misstep would result in a harmless slide of just a few of feet. In addition, 45° is gentle enough to allow the long-run accumulation of soil and the growth of shrubs and trees. The thick tangle of bushes and trees can be a bit annoying to negotiate, but it does guarantee that there will be plenty of branches to hold on to, or to stop your tumble if you make a mistake.

So our route up the side of this ridge was hard but uneventful, but all that changed once we reached the actual crest of this ridge. We were now on the spine of the ridge that would take us, several hours later, to the Rocky Crag (aka "the real bunion"), the easternmost of the Three Sisters.

The Smokies are full of these narrow side ridges, the best of which are in this Porters Creek and Le Conte area. The highly acidic, fragile Anakeesta slate that stretches from the Chimneys, across Mt. Le Conte, to the Three Sisters creates the narrowest, rockiest ridges in the park. Eighty years of soil accumulation and plant growth have softened the edges of these ridges a bit, but only a bit.

These dozens of obscure, unnamed side ridges have become my favorite feature of the park. They are always beautiful and sometimes scary, which makes them doubly appealing. Every time we hike on one, there's a "top of the world" feel, even though there are many ridges and peaks surrounding us, so there's a sense of being right in the middle of everything you want to be in the middle of. The best way for the typical hiker to get a taste of these ridges is to hike/climb/crawl from the first Chimney to the second at the end of the Chimney Tops trail. A milder taste is the brief Rocky Spur side trail near the top of the Rainbow Falls trail.

I'll always have a soft spot in my heart for Porters Mountain – a particularly large side ridge – because it was here that I fell in love with those trail-less, rocky ridges. The crest of Porters begins as a hardwood forest, but as the elevation increases that forest becomes punctuated with narrow, open spots – called "heath balds" in the park literature. Some heath balds – Brushy Mountain, for example – are broad and gently sloping, while the heath balds of Porters Mountain and the Three Sisters are narrow. Walking out of the forest and into a heath ridge is like steeping out of a cool, dark building and into a warm, sunny day. Both are good, but the sudden explosion of sun and sky is breathtaking, as are the views.

On the spine of the ridge leading to the Rocky Crag, we soon began to encounter exposed lines and jumbles of jagged rock – sometimes flat, sometimes angled up to make footing difficult, always decorated with a thick mat of low-growing sand myrtle.

And this is where things get interesting, especially if one has a fear of heights which, apparently, I do.

I've always known that I don't do well on high, open spots. Standing on the edge of an overlook, I can feel myself being pulled forward, even to the point of getting a bit light-headed. It's not a spinning, blackout kind of thing; more of a weak legs and lose your balance syndrome. I can cross bridges, look out windows, climb trees and ladders, and work on my roof – I've even rappelled down a vertical cliff a time or two without a problem, but climbing up or down a rocky face or just standing at the top with nothing but air around me can make my heart race and my legs buckle.

I guess that's why I had my one and only Smoky Mountain Meltdown on this ridge.

There are two challenging spots on this ridge, both being obvious knobs or teeth that protrude from the backbone of the ridge. The lower one looks, from certain angles, like a pyramid while the upper one looks like a rounded knob. In fact, I think it looks like a "bunion," and we've occasionally wondered aloud if maybe this knob is the one, true Charlies Bunion. To keep things simple, we call the first, lower peak the Pyramid because that's what it looks like, and we call the upper bunion Falcon

Point because we've had numerous falcon encounters there, including finding the skull of a duck.

Getting to the top of both of these knobs involves walking along a narrow, rocky ridge and climbing up a few, modest 60° rock faces. In and of themselves, the climbs are not deadly because they are usually only ten or twenty feet long, and there are almost always good hand and foot holds. For me, the real problem is the open air that surrounds them.

I was able to climb up the lower Pyramid with some anxiety, but not enough to force a retreat. I managed to stay focused on the rock in front of me rather than the air around me, and I did just fine. However, somewhere in the process I succumbed to the temptation to look around at the views in the distance, and I noticed all the empty airspace around me, and the high, rocky ridge leading to Falcon Point, and all the air around it, and that got me spooked.

The upper, rocky knob (Falcon Point) that soon confronted us was not extremely dangerous. It is at least ten feet wide with several ascents of only ten or twenty feet at much less than a 90° angle. There are plenty of rock hand holds mingled with clumps of sand myrtle bushes growing in the cracks in the rocks, so there are adequate opportunities to grab in case of emergency.

On the other hand, from below, Falcon Point *looks* horrible, which can lead to a negative case of mind over matter – that is, the climb is physically possible, but your mind can convince you otherwise. It's over fifty feet high, and the sides drop off almost vertically for several hundred feet, and the rock is not hard, sturdy sandstone or granite; it is fragile Anakeesta slate. Sand myrtle bushes and this breakable slate provide sturdy handholds 99% of the time, but at moments when the only thing I can see around me is empty airspace, I tend to focus on that 1% failure rate. My pessimism eclipses my courage: the glass isn't 99% full; it's 1% empty.

A hard-core rock climber would have pitied me for being so nervous, but serious rock climbers are made from different material than I am (plus, they have ropes and harnesses to rely on). I have no safety harnesses and a touch of agoraphobia which flares up whenever there is nothing but air to my right and left... and this was one of those moments. As I think back on it, maybe my fear is of widths, not heights.

167

Anyway, this bluff was at least ten feet wide, so if I would just stay in the middle, I couldn't possibly fall off the side to my death. "Don't be clumsy. Stay in the middle. Test every hand hold." I knew that if I just stayed away from the edges, then any moment of clumsiness would lead only to a couple of bumps and bruises, maybe a broken bone, and a few moments of hyperventilation.

We have developed a proverb for these kinds of occasions, and it goes something like this: "It's okay to be stupid, and it's okay to be clumsy. Just don't do both at the same time." We developed this maxim as we encountered some spots in the mountains that can be a bit precarious: waterfalls, slippery boulders, narrow ridges, rocky bluffs, a left turn in Gatlinburg. In other words, try not to be clumsy, but if you must, don't let it happen when you are somewhere that you shouldn't be.

This proverb comes into play in all sorts of places in the outdoors. Simply jumping from one river rock to another is a prime example. Such a seemingly simple act is a cracked head just waiting to happen because jumping from one wet rock to another is dumb. If you slip, your stupidity and clumsiness have converged to get you hurt. Being clumsy *or* stupid is okay. Being clumsy *and* stupid simultaneously can end in a concussion or a puddle of blood.

The last time that happened to me, I took a picture of my bruised, bloody face and sent it to me wife with the caption: "Rock, 1. Me, 0." I was jumping from one river rock to another. I knew the jump was about a foot longer than I was capable of, but I thought, "What's the worst that could happen? I'll get my foot wet." I was wrong. The worst that could happen was that my foot could reach the rock but slip back down into the water so quickly that I wouldn't get my hands on the rock to save myself. Instead, I kept my balance by smashing my face into the rock. Truth be told, I enjoyed telling the story for the week that it took my black eye to heal.

So as the four of us approached the rock face, Greg, Charlie, and Keith began their climb. I lagged behind, watched them climb, looked at the empty air around me, and chickened out. My heebie jeebies got the best of me. I sat at the base of the rock face, disgusted with my lack of testosterone, while they climbed over the top. Fortunately, with a little advice from the others, I was able to find an alternate route through the trees and bushes along the base of the knob, which was a stroke of luck because some of these ridges are so steep and rocky that the only alternate route is to give up and go home by backtracking down the rocks that we had just come up.

Ironically, if I had known ahead of time about the alternate route around the knob, I might have been able to climb over. I had somehow become obsessed by the possibility of not being able to climb over and not being able to find a route around the knob. The anxiety of backtracking got the best of me, partly because I didn't want to be the guy who ruined the trip for everyone, but mainly because it's often harder to go down a steep rock face than to go up. In other words, I was in a spot where "between a rock and a hard place" stops being a figure of speech and becomes a literal description of your predicament. Knowing of the alternate route would have provided some peace of mind.

I was able to crawl up the easier, back side of the knob, so all four of us had a great lunch at what has become one of our favorite spots in the park. The fact that we were in view of a few tourists a quarter mile away on Charlies Bunion made our time on the upper knob even better; although, my enthusiasm was a bit subdued because I knew that I hadn't earned the right to be the object of admiration by adoring tourists. I was an intruder who had slipped in through the back door.

The next few weeks were hard for me, knowing that I had proven my little boyhood, not my manhood. I suppose living with failure is something we all have to contend with, and you'd think I'd be used to it by now because I've had plenty of practice, but I'm not one of those who gains satisfaction from knowing that I "did my best." On that day, I had done my best and come up a few inches short on the courage scale. Worse yet, there were witnesses.

A couple of months later, I tried again. This second time I simply talked myself through it. I reminded myself not to be clumsy, but with specific instructions. "You have two hands, two feet, and two knees. Make sure that at least four of those have a good, solid hold. When it's time to move one of them, test the new hold and move slowly and deliberately. Never put all your weight on just one or two of those body parts. Three is the minimum." Greg, Keith, and Charlie say, "Don't trust

169

just one thing." I say, "Don't trust just two things." Same principle, just more cautious math.

So that's what I did, and I climbed right up that upper knob. No problem. It was almost easy, but of course, "easy" was never the issue. Fear of empty air was the issue. Since that day, I've realized that most of the time these rock faces have sturdy hand and foot holds. The difficulty of the actual climbing isn't usually the problem. Slips and falls are rare. However, if a fall did happen, the consequences could be severe. It's fear of those unlikely consequences that's the issue. If you can get over that mental hurdle, the actual climbing is manageable.

But all that empty air magnifies the possibility of those consequences. I can climb up a rocky face, knowing that my fall backwards might only be ten or twelve feet and that I'd have to fall *sideways* several feet to tumble down the 200 foot drop to my left or right. I can remind myself of the physical impossibility of such a feat – gravity pulls us down, not sideways – but all that empty airspace simply overwhelms all those rational arguments about gravity and probability. Fear of heights or widths or air or whatever can't always be overcome by rational arguments.

So instead of thinking about gravity and probabilities, I now just focus on that square yard of rock in front of my face. My mantra is something like this: "Look straight in front of you, not back, not down, not left, not right. Focus on the rock and your one next move. Move only one body part and move it deliberately, slowly. Never trust just two things."

That seems to be the trick. It's not bravery. It's not even positive thinking. It's just focusing on what needs to be done next. That, and only that. Then, simply repeat that sequence until, a few minutes later, you are at the top.

This might be one of those rare occasions from which we can learn a lesson for life: in lieu of bravery or brilliance, just focus on the task at hand, your one next move. That, and only that.

Our day ended at the top of the Rocky Crag, a pleasant, scenic spot about an hour beyond my defeated nemesis, Falcon Point. The top of Rocky Crag is easily accessible from the AT. Just walk about a quarter mile past Charlies Bunion and look for the worn path on the left leading up a grassy, shrubby slope. It's a short, steep hike to the rocky outcrop. From there you can look west to Charlies Bunion or north toward Brushy Mountain and Greenbrier Pinnacle. And as you look north, look down. The prominent knob about two hundred yards below is Falcon Point. It's one of the best spots in the Smokies – isolated, beautiful, and just risky enough to be interesting, but not deadly, unless you do something stupid and clumsy at the same time.

The roughest of the Three Sisters is the westernmost ridge – the one that leads up to Charlies Bunion and the gaggle of tourists that hang around it on pretty days. Greg Harrell had done this trip once before, and he had assured us that it had several intimidating spots. He has been known to exaggerate upon occasion, but mainly if the story being told uses me as its whipping post. I wouldn't call him an outright liar, but he does tell his stories with an excess of enthusiasm. He tends to use facts to construct the foundation of his tales, but then throws them aside once he gains some momentum. Nevertheless, when it comes to trail descriptions, he's usually accurate and objective, with only occasional flights of fancy. So I was nervous, once again.

On a foggy, October morning the four of us parked at Newfound Gap and made a quick, four mile walk on the AT to Charlies Bunion. We stopped for a minute to pay our respects and to take a quick look at the ridge we would be ascending a few hours later. Standing at the top of Charlies Bunion I got light-headed just looking down, trying to see the narrow ridgecrest. I could see the lower reaches of the ridge, covered with a spruce forest, and I could see a bit higher as the spruce gave way to an open, rocky ridge, but I couldn't see the last few hundred feet below my feet. For a better view, I would need to crawl down over the precipice, which I chose not to do. So I spent most of the rest of the day wondering about the uppermost sections of that ridge, which is a good way to be in a full-blown funk by the time you reach the scary stuff.

After spending a few minutes at the Bunion, we continued east on the AT to the Rocky Crag. From there we pushed our way down the tunnel of rhododendron and laurel to Falcon Point, down its lower side (where I'd had my meltdown the previous spring), and on to the Pyramid. From this ridge we had great side views of the Charlies Bunion ridge, a quarter mile away. We could see quite clearly several spots that could give us trouble. We've learned from past trips that merely seeing a ridge or cliff or landslide scar from a distance gives no clue about the real degree of difficulty. The degree of difficulty and danger can only be determined up close. Only when you actually touch the rock and look up can you begin to see hand and foot holds, cracks, paths, and shrubs. It was at this moment that I began reminding myself: "It's not always as bad as it looks." Although, deep in my heart I knew that sometimes it *is* as bad as it looks, and occasionally it's worse.

A bit past the Pyramid, we dropped left off the ridgecrest and pushed our way through the shrubs and trees to the First Tributary, down the 60' cascade, and into Lester Prong. After spending a few minutes walking up Lester, we turned south on the Third Tributary and began our climb up the side of the ridge that would take us to Charlies Bunion.

I've just described a trip down the Rocky Crag ridge, one of my favorite Smokies locations, in a quick couple of paragraphs. It deserves better – a long, eloquent eulogy reciting its glories. Instead, I've treated it as if it were an entrance ramp on a highway. If I ever come to see this Rocky Crag part of the trip as a mere inconvenience, it'll be time for me to retire my hiking boots and slip quietly into old age – puttering around in my rose garden, mumbling to myself and chasing the neighborhood kids out of my yard.

By early afternoon we reached the lower portions of the Charlies Bunion ridgecrest, and the vegetation changed immediately from a dark, shady forest to an open, heath bald full of low-growing, sun-loving shrubs of the heath family. The deep, forest soil had given way to a thin, rocky spine. This change in vegetation was a clear sign that we had entered a different ecological community.

Smoky Mountains literature talks about the various forest communities within the park: northern hardwood forests above 4,500', cove hardwood and closed oak forests below 4,500', open oak and pine forest on dry, exposed slopes below 4,500', etc. Amazingly, I can walk right through several of these zones without noticing, so I envy those botanists and ecologists who are so thoroughly familiar with the species

172

and relationships between them that they can sense the changes happening as easily as the rest of us notice the onset of a thunderstorm. When I watch a baseball game, I think I know what's going on, but when I hear a well-versed fan discussing pitching strategies, hit & runs, and managers' options, I realize that I don't know baseball as well as I think I do. Watching a baseball game or walking in the woods must be a pleasantly familiar experience to someone who really knows their stuff. Knowledge brings a deeper level of appreciation, so that when a baseball player watches a game or a botanist walks through a forest, they are seeing things that I have no clue about. I envy them both.

Maybe that's why I love heath balds. Even I can notice them because they are so obvious. One minute you're in a shady forest; next, you're in bushes and sunlight. And the vegetation is pretty consistent, which helps: catawba rhododendron, mountain laurel, carolina rhododendron, blueberries, stunted red spruce and table mountain pines... and rocks. And if those rocks are highly acidic Anakeesta slate rather than sandstone, then you'll find yourself wading calf-deep in sand myrtle, that tough little plant that seems to grow right out of the rock itself, which is not far from the truth.

So we climbed right into a heath clearing on the ridgecrest and sat for a while, enjoying the warmth of the sun by sitting on exposed rocks surrounded by plants of the heath family. At the state line ridgecrest above us we could see the jagged peak of Charlies Bunion. Between us and the Bunion we saw first a thick spruce forest covering the ridge, then the exposed rock of the last 500 feet.

It was here that we noticed that from below, these three ridges looked like three peaks. Until this moment, even though we had been splashing around in Lester Prong for a year, we had thought of these three ridges as landforms that sloped *down* from the state line crest. Walking along the AT, you could look down their spines as they fall away into the Lester Prong valley. Now, for the first time, I began to see these ridges as things that go *up* – up to their peaks on the state line crest. At that moment, in my mind they became the Three Sisters, peaks that I had never before thought of as *peaks* at all. It's no exaggeration to say that this was an "I once was blind, but now I see" sort of thing – not exactly a religious conversion, but definitely a paradigm shift and another lesson in life: things look different depending on where you are standing.

As usual, there was a slightly worn path along the crest of this ridge, running over rocks and through beds of sand myrtle. These paths are bearways, the evidence being the occasional piles of scat so robust and disgusting that they could only have come out of a bear. We've never encountered a bear on these ridge hikes, probably because we grunt and thrash our way through the underbrush, so these shy, powerful creatures have plenty of warning of our intrusion into their domain. The chances are slim that we'll ever see one up here, but it's obvious that they haunt these ridges, which only serves to enhance the charm of these trips.

It took us about an hour to push and weave our way into and then out of the spruce forest. At that point, the real adventure began. This was the reason we had come and the reason we were nervous: the rocks. I was reminded of the Sirens of Greek mythology who sang their song to lure ships and their crews to their deaths on rocky shores. I don't know exactly what the temptation was, maybe an enchanting song, more likely the sound of women's voices to sailors who had been at sea for weeks, but for us on this ridge it was the rocks themselves; their songs were calling us upward.

We knew this could be done because Greg had done it several months earlier, by himself, which is something I probably wouldn't – no, *couldn't* – do. By myself on a risky trip, my imagination often gets the best of me. It's not the legitimate fear of getting injured with no one to help. It's more primordial than that. It's a kind of loneliness, a need for human contact. There's something primal about having a partner to share the risk that helps me proceed with confidence. An S & R team has a much better chance of finding a *pair* of hikers than in finding a solitary hiker because a pair is more likely to avoid panic and to make good decisions. A solitary hiker will panic and become irrational, even to the point of running away from his rescuers when they arrive on the scene. Even a hiker with a dog is more likely to stay calm and rational than a hiker alone. There's actually a subfield of psychology called *lost person behavior* which examines human behavior in lonely, stressful situations. So, even though I've never been truly, fully lost in the woods,

174

I can recognize the importance of human contact in maintaining confidence in the face of a challenge. It's deeper than simple peer pressure. It's more like... *comfort*. It's something I've felt and believe, even though I don't completely understand it.

There were several significant, rock walls to climb, yet each one was surmountable. Each one had several routes that could not be taken, but one or two that could, which created a dilemma. The route with the best hand and foot holds would often be along an edge with a long, long drop below. On the other hand, the route closer to the center where the fall might only be ten or twenty feet would often have the weaker hand and foot holds. So the *chance* of falling on the edge route would be less, but the *consequences* of a fall would be enormous. The chance of falling on the middle route would be higher, but the consequences would be somewhere between moderate and substantial, but not enormous. Early in the trip, I had decided that whenever I had a choice, I would take the route less likely to kill me. It seemed like the obvious choice at the time, but the fact that the climbing was harder, less certain, made me second guess myself several times. It's one of those times that you must choose the least bad option. The problem was that I couldn't really figure out which option was most bad and which was least.

I still don't have any words of wisdom here. Sometimes I'd take the edge route because the climbing was sturdier. A couple of times I took the middle route because a slip wouldn't result in death, but the climbing itself was slippery. I never felt comfortable with either option, mainly because I never felt comfortable, period.

So the four of us worked our way slowly up the rock faces, picking our handholds carefully: "Look straight in front of you. Move slowly. Test every rock. Never trust just two things."

Greg's estimation had been accurate: this ridge was much worse than the Rocky Crag. Much. Several rock faces were higher and steeper. The handholds were excellent, which seemed little comfort to me because there was too much air, everywhere.

I watched Greg, then Charlie, then Keith work their way carefully up the rock. Then I followed, bringing up the rear just like always. As I tightened my gloves and straps, it occurred to me that this Charlies Bunion trip had given us a new experience: fear of watching someone

175

else get hurt. Not only was I nervous for me; I was nervous for them, too. It was a moment of mental confusion bordering on embarrassment: spending the entire day playfully taunting and insulting each other, then worrying about each other's safety. That's just not our standard operating procedure. I had no mental category to place this in. So, of course, I said not a word of it to anyone, but I thought about it a lot.

Somehow we all persevered and made it to the top. I can't deny that male ego and peer pressure played a part, but for me the thing that enabled me to reach the top was a simple lack of alternatives. There was no bailout route, no plan B. Backtracking was out of the question because on these steep, rocky walls going down is harder than going up because when your nose is hugging the rock face, you can't see your feet. You know there must be footholds down there somewhere because you came up this way an hour ago, but you don't know where those footholds are now.

The drama finally ended not with some sort of grand finale, no fireworks, no cheers. Instead, I simply pulled myself over that last ledge where my three partners and a few tourists sat, watching. My first words were a simple oath: "I'll never do that again." Although my batting average for keeping my oaths is well below 1.000, I fully intend to keep this one, and so far, I have. Whenever Greg or Keith suggests another trip up the Bunion, I'm able to concentrate really hard and make their voices sound like Charlie Brown's teacher. "Whah, Whah, Whah." After all, I've an oath to keep.

So all that remained was the middle of the three ridges, which we call Middle Crag.

Greg Harrell had been the first of our group to scramble up these Three Sisters. He had done Middle Crag and Charlies Bunion in a single day several months prior to our Charlies Bunion trip. He had gone up the Middle Crag ridge and down Charlies Bunion. I have no idea how he did them both in one day, no idea how he did them by himself, and no idea how he went *down* the Bunion ridge. As far as I'm concerned, that's something that only a super-hero or the village idiot would do.

After his initial trip, we four had made a pact that none of us would go up Middle Crag until all of us could do it together. The pact lasted exactly one year, then I broke it, lowering my oath-keeping batting average even further. Actually, Greg, Charlie, and I broke it, abandoning Keith like an outcast at the edge of a leper colony. We all felt bad, for about ten minutes, and then decided that we were letting October slip through our fingers, it had been exactly one year since we made our pact while sitting on Charlies Bunion, and the statute of limitations had run out. We'd spent the entire year trying to find a day when all four of us could go, and we'd come up short. After fifty-two weeks of trying, we began to see that we'd have to settle for 3 out of 4. So as Keith sat near the 30 yard line watching Alabama roll over Tennessee (as usual), the rest of us did the Middle Crag. I worry about Keith sometimes. My expectations for him are already pretty low, but he sometimes still manages to not meet them.

Our standard route for exploring the Porters-Lester watershed was, at that time, to park at the Porters Creek trailhead, hike up the trail and manway, up the ridge of the day, then after a few minutes on the AT we'd descend via the Dry Sluice manway and back to Porters Creek trail and the car. This route is roughly ten miles and generally takes about ten to twelve hours. The hardest part for me is the descent down Dry Sluice (Porters Creek) manway. At the end of a long day, this steep, slick path brutalizes my legs, knees and toes. In this respect, I'm like the canary in the mineshaft. My aches and pains are a warning to the younger guys that their day is coming. Charlie, who is almost my age, doesn't whine about the manway as much as I do, but he fully understands my plight. His knees aren't quite as old as mine, but they've had their share of abuse. So, to appease me, we took an easier route.

We all believe that the fully righteous way to do these ridges is to approach them from below after a long hike from the Porters Creek trailhead. Paying these heavy dues really does make the climax of the trip more rewarding. But there's also value in trying something new every now and then, and if this new route is also easier, well... the rest of them won't have to listen to my whining about my knees. So everybody wins.

177

We started this trip at Newfound Gap and walked four miles on the AT to Charlies Bunion. Having started early to avoid the October traffic, we had the rock to ourselves. We weren't entirely sure what our route down into the Lester watershed would be, but we knew that at the end of the day we'd top out on the rocks of the Middle Crag and walk four miles on the AT back to Newfound Gap.

We had discussed the possibility of starting at Porters Creek trailhead and ending at Newfound Gap, but that would require a significant hitchhike back to Porters at the beginning or the end of the day. We aren't opposed to trying to catch a ride, but we've had varying success when we've tried it in recent years. Actually, I have some fond memories from my younger, backpacking days of hitching a ride at the end of a few days on the AT. Most of my trips back then included sections of the Appalachian Trail simply because reverence for the AT is deeply ingrained in every hiker east of the Mississippi, and I was no exception. I didn't intentionally set out to hike the AT every time; it just happened, partly because the highest and best peaks are on the AT (with a few notable exceptions), and partly because eastern hikers are drawn to the AT in a subliminal, almost mystical way. Why? Because it's there. Because it's the AT.

The problem with hiking the AT is that there's rarely a loop involved. It's all one-way, so hitching a ride became a standard part of most hiking trips: carry a sleeping bag and cooking equipment, sleep in shelters or under the stars, take lots of pictures, hitch a ride back to the car. Standard Rules of Engagement.

Sometimes we'd be picked up by a kindred spirit – a backpacker who knew what it feels like to come out of the woods needing to get back to his car. Other times we'd be picked up by a good ol' boy in a pickup truck who knows what it's like to need a ride when your truck is stuck in deep mud far from the blacktop. Occasionally we'd get a ride from an old man and his wife in their truck. The old folks were actually my favorites because it was usually obvious that the old guy had been young once and seemed to get some pleasure out of helping some young kids to do what he had once done. Or, maybe he was just returning a favor that someone had done for him fifty years ago. I'm confident about this because those are my motivations and memories when I pick up a gaggle of backpackers in need of a lift. Just hearing them talk is like a visit to the past for me. Their energy and enthusiasm are refreshing.

As we drive I want to tell them to enjoy these youthful years because they will end all too soon, but then I realize that they *are* enjoying these years without any lecture from me. Instead, we chat for a few minutes, they tell me where they've been and where they are going, and I just smile and nod and live vicariously through them. It also gives me hope for the future: there are still a few adolescents who prefer being outdoors to shopping, TV, and video games. They also seem refreshingly uninterested in growing up and making money. I suppose this could be interpreted as irresponsibility, but as John Gierach once said, "Life is short and responsibility is over-rated." So I gladly give the kids a ride to help them along on their journey.

So hitchhiking is always an option, but on this particular trip it wasn't a very good one because it would entail three different roads, the last of which is a dirt road, several miles long and dead ending at the Porters Creek trailhead. It would be out of the way for most folks because it's... well... out of the way, which is the whole point.

The fact that we chose not to hitchhike bothered me some. We seemed to be opting for convenience over adventure, which is perfectly understandable, but it's not the way I want to live the last few decades of my life. On the other hand, I'd already chosen convenience over adventure when I convinced the guys to end our trip at Newfound Gap instead of descending the knee-pounding manway. So, for whatever reasons, we chose the easy way – we'd start and end at our own car, parked at Newfound Gap.

This could have been one more thing for me to feel guilty about, but guilt doesn't hang with me quite as heavily as it used to because as I've grown older I've learned there are two ways to a guilt-free life: either don't do anything wrong or don't feel guilty when you do. Like most humans, I live somewhere between those two extremes, probably a bit more toward the "don't feel guilty" end. So, today I would hike guilt free. My aching knees would see to that.

As we sat on Charlies Bunion looking east, we saw a narrow, but obvious, line of shrubs and small trees in the valley between us and the

Middle Crag ridgeline. This was neither unusual nor unexpected, but it was a pleasant surprise that this sliver of forest between these two ridges went all the way to the top of the main crest, ending near the edge of the AT. This was not only the most obvious route down; except for the Rocky Crag ridge, it was the *only* route down. We began to see that we could simply step off the trail, over the edge, and down this steep but wooded ravine.

The freedom to simply step off the trail whenever we choose has been another highlight of off-trail hiking. There have been several times when we've stepped into the mountains with a destination in mind – Cat Stairs, Anakeesta Ridge, Big Duck Hawk Ridge – but with no clear plan for how we'd return. We were confident that as the afternoon shadows began to lengthen, we'd sit on a rock, eat some chocolate and Fig Newtons, and discuss the various creeks or ridges that we could use as an exit. This trip would follow that pattern except that we knew our exit route – up Middle Crag ridge and then west on the AT to Newfound Gap. The blank spot in the itinerary was getting down from the trail to the bottom of the Middle Crag ridge. The fact that a key component of our trip was unknown was no cause for concern.

I don't actually know when we made this shift from fully-planned to partially-planned trips. It just happened – incrementally, invisibly, inadvertently. In retrospect, it was a significant paradigm shift, so it's odd that we didn't notice it until long after it happened. It's much like global warming or that old illustration about a frog in a pot of boiling water – you wake up one day and realize that something important has changed, and has been changing for a long time, right under your nose.

So we stepped confidently off the trail and down into the steep, slippery ravine, sometimes on two feet, sometimes crab-walking on all fours, sometimes applying the brakes with a strategic butt scoot. The trees were mostly yellow birch, the most common pioneer tree of old landslide scars. I first noticed this pattern on the lower mile of Alum Cave trail, the route of a magnificent thunderstorm and landslide in September, 1951 and several more thereafter. From Arch Rock all the way down to the trailhead, yellow birches line the banks of Alum Cave Creek, all of them virtually identical in height and diameter. Since then,

I've seen the same phenomenon on Anakeesta Ridge, the Jumpoff, Big Duck Hawk, and numerous other landslide scars.

As we worked our way down the slope, the birches all seemed old but not ancient. I guessed maybe fifty years old; although, I really have no empirical basis for that guess other than they looked somewhere between young and old. Fifty seemed like a nice round number. Then I remembered where I was and that this area had been denuded in the late 1920s. Assuming that it hadn't been denuded again sometime later, we were walking through what happens about 85 years after a landslide. There were a few spots of bare rock, but most of it had been covered up with thick, spongy moss, followed by a layer of soil on which shrubs and birches were growing. This was raw, unadulterated plant succession in which bare rock turns to forest. If this was eighty-five years worth of progress, then this rock-to-forest process happens much faster than I would have guessed. Although, a moment's thought reminds me that the *rock* doesn't actually change into dirt; the rock gets *covered* with dirt, on which the forest grows. So the rock doesn't have to take millennia to erode into soil. All that's required is that the leaves from the surrounding forest find their way into this ravine. Apparently, leaves seek a low point just like water, a process that undoubtedly began the very next autumn after the 1920s fire and rain.

Of course, from the look of things, the steep, rocky slopes to our sides, which are covered mostly in carolina rhododendron and sand myrtle, may never turn to forest simply because the soil doesn't build up there in sufficient quantities to support anything larger than these tough little bushes. Rather than some day achieving a climax forest, those rocky walls may get only as far as a climax heath thicket. It's a beautifully vivid picture of ecological niches – each species selecting a spot that it likes best and settling down for the long haul. Birches in the thin soil of the ravine. Rhododendron and sand myrtle on the steeper rock walls. An occasional red spruce tree in a level spot with thick soil. Exactly as Mother Nature had drawn up the plans.

This trip down the ravine was comfortably familiar, but it was an interesting adventure down a new piece of land. Like many high, narrow valleys in the park, the lower we descended, the wetter the route became. I don't know the hydraulics involved in bringing water to the surface in terrain like this, so I tend to fall back on the same explanations that people have used for thousands of years: magic. As far as I'm concerned the water appears by magic, turning the dry ravine into a creek, which makes the walking slippery and messy. It's surprisingly easy to get wet and dirty when the running water is only half an inch deep just by being careless. Sliding down a moist rock while using your hands for support means that your legs, butt, and hands get wet. Somehow, before long your arms, shirt, and face are wet, too. Again, magic.

We decided that this route down the Second Tributary was steeper and slicker than the Dry Sluice manway, not nearly as bare and rocky as the (more recent) scar on Anakeesta Ridge, and almost as steep and slick as the lower elevations of the Jumpoff. In other words, there was nothing in our experience that was exactly like it but many things that were somewhat like it. It was unique enough to be fun but not unique enough to be unnerving. Once again, we'd read the landscape, found a route that looked manageable and interesting, then stepped off the trail and found that we were right (which doesn't always happen).

At this rate of descent, we lost elevation quickly and soon found ourselves midway between the AT and the mouth of this modest tributary to Lester Prong. So at about 4,700' elevation, we turned right and made our way up the slope of the Middle Crag ridge. It was time to head back up to the AT on the main crest via the middle of the Three Sisters.

Before long we were on the wooded crest of this side ridge, and in familiar territory. Although, I had never been here before, the topography had a nice, familiar feel to it – a lot of soil supporting mountain laurel, catawba rhododendron, and red spruce trees with occasional rocky obstacles to be avoided or climbed. We spent most of the next hour in tangles of laurel and rhododendron under a canopy of mature spruce trees, with occasional rocky, open heath balds and rocky openings providing views of the Charlies Bunion ridge to the west, Rocky Crag ridge to the east, Greenbrier Pinnacle to the north, and the rocky, shrubby top of Middle Crag ridge above us to the south. We were in the middle of our favorite playground in the Smokies.

The main question remaining to be answered was: how difficult would this Middle Crag ridge be? Greg Harrell had been on it once about a year earlier, and his best recollection of the ridges of these Three Sisters was that Charlies Bunion was the most difficult, Rocky Crag was the least, and Middle Crag was in-between. However, the missing piece of information was "where in-between?" If Middle Crag was near the Rocky Crag end of the difficulty spectrum then today would be risky enough to be interesting, but not dangerous. If, on the other hand, it was near the Charlies Bunion end, then today would be a trip that would end with another oath: "I'll never do that again."

To be honest, from our earlier perch on Charlies Bunion, the Middle Crag looked like it could be just as challenging as the Bunion ridge had been. There were several sections of steep, exposed rock with precipitous drops along the sides. And to be honest again, that fact had been weighing heavily on me all day. The prospect of another Charlies Bunion day hadn't exactly ruined my day, but it had clearly captured my attention, much the way almost stepping on a rattlesnake will hang with you for the rest of the day. You can't simply talk yourself out of thinking about it.

So I thought about it. A lot.

To make a long story short... it was on the Rocky Crag end of the spectrum. A couple of places where I needed to focus on the rock rather than the surrounding air, but not too bad. Numerous places where you could die if you fell three or four feet sideways, but gravity doesn't work that way. While there were some risks, I can confidently say that Middle Crag ridge looks worse than it is. From Charlies Bunion it looks like a ridge well-suited for someone with a death-wish, which is perfect because there were half a dozen tourists on Charlies Bunion watching our every move. To them, we looked like three daring souls who were going where others dared not tread. Technically, that's somewhat true, but as I said, it wasn't as bad as it looked, but our audience didn't know that. I'm not a particularly daring soul, and I had no trouble ascending the ridge and scrambling up the rocks, so pretty much anyone who can do a couple of pull-ups and a few push-ups could do this trip, unless being surrounded by open air gives them a light head and weak knees.

My favorite part of this ridge was the final twenty minutes. The flora was thick myrtle and rhododendron with a clearly-defined, open route along the ridge, with several open, rocky prominences providing views down to where we had just traveled, and in all other directions as well. As we stood on these jagged rocks, the shrubs were below us, at ankle or knee level. Again, more views, more air, but lots of shrubs to provide a sense of security.

The top of this Middle Crag ridge is less obvious than the other two sisters. It's simply a spot among the rocks and bushes where, if you continue on, you'll find yourself going downhill a few dozen yards into North Carolina to reconnect with the AT. So instead of going down, we pushed our way through more bushes along the top edge of the rocky, bushy bowl between Charlies Bunion and the Middle Crag. This ten minute excursion was a fine end to the journey, providing several more jagged rocks to lean on as we peered down into the bowl filled mostly with species of the heath family that would put on a magnificent show from late May through June. So, instead of vowing to "never do that again," I ended the day with a different vow: "I'll be back in the spring."

This was a vow that was made not out of fear or compulsion but in a moment of mental clarity resulting from another good day in the mountains. And it's one that I've kept, almost every spring, since that first series of trips to the Three Sisters.

Chapter 11

A Road Runs Through It

The old wagon path across the Smokies used to run pretty much where US 441 runs today, except that it crossed the main ridgecrest a mile west, at today's Indian Gap. In the mid-1800s Arnold Guyot, the Swiss geographer who made a career out of exploring and mapping the Appalachian Mountains from New England to North Carolina, *found a new gap* that was 230 feet lower than Indian Gap and called it Newfound Gap. Low Gap would have been a good name, but there are Low Gaps scattered all over the Southern Appalachians, and we didn't need another one. When the road was improved for automobiles in the late 1920s, it was re-routed through Newfound Gap.

Newfound Gap is a very popular spot right in the middle of the park, but when it comes right down to it, Newfound Gap is merely a parking lot, full of cars and tourists. It's a nice spot with good views, but it is by no means the best spot in the Smokies. It's a perfect illustration of the fact that *popular* doesn't mean "fabulous" or "extraordinary." It means "crowded," a detail worth remembering the next time someone tells you about a popular road, trail, or attraction. They intend their words as a recommendation, but they would be better taken as a warning – "don't go there unless absolutely necessary."

Nevertheless, Newfound Gap does have several redeeming qualities. One is the sign that says "Tennessee - North Carolina State Line." Probably every kid who visits the Smokies has her picture taken there, with one foot in each state. If my math is correct, it's exactly half as exciting as standing on the Four Corners in the southwestern US, and much more crowded, but on a clear day the view is endless.

Another neat thing about Newfound Gap is the large rock platform where President Roosevelt dedicated the park in 1940, six years late. This platform is called the Rockefeller Memorial because the Rockefeller family gave $5 million toward the creation of the park. That's quite a gift, but perhaps not as much of a sacrifice as the matching $5 million given by the people of Tennessee and North Carolina, so this rock platform could be called the People's Memorial without distorting the truth one iota. Politics and class warfare aside, it's fun for the kids to climb around on, or for adults to stand where FDR once stood. I suppose it could be a bit dangerous for a reckless kid, but I climbed around on it when I was a kid, and I let my kids climb on it when they were young. We all lived to tell the tale. Nevertheless, it's best to keep kids on a short leash, especially middle school boys whose sense of adventure has outpaced their physical coordination.

Another significant feature is the Appalachian Trail, which crosses the road at this point. Springer Mountain in Georgia is about 200 miles to the southwest, and Mount Katahdin in Maine is about 2,000 miles to the northeast. If you've never set foot on the AT, this is your easiest chance. Walking southwest on the AT for about a mile, you'll arrive at an inconspicuous, little notch in the main crest called Indian Gap.

Indian Gap is the top end of Road Prong trail, which is significant because Road Prong is the route of the old road – called Indian Gap Road – that crossed over the crest of the Smokies. Road Prong trail was the top three miles of the overmountain road until it was relocated to Newfound Gap about ninety years ago. To walk on the Road Prong trail is to tread the path of bears, Native Americans, pioneers, cattle, hogs, Confederate and Union soldiers, moonshiners, and ninety years' worth of hikers.

The West Prong of the Little Pigeon River begins at the point where the old road and the new road split, at the bottom end of Road Prong trail. It is here that two creeks converge – Walker Camp Prong and Road Prong – to form the West Prong of the Little Pigeon. The old road follows Road Prong up to the crest while today's road follows Walker Camp Prong.

On the Road Prong route, starting at the parking lot at the Chimney Tops trailhead, you quickly cross two streams, the first being Walker Camp Prong and the second being Road Prong. From either footbridge you can look downstream and see where these converge, forming the West Prong, which is the river you see as you drive down out of the park, through Gatlinburg and Pigeon Forge. Its full name is the West Prong of the Little Pigeon River, which eventually converges with the

186

Middle Prong which flows out of the Greenbrier section of the park. Together they form the Little Pigeon River. Don't confuse these with the West and Middle Prongs of the Little River which converge and flow through Townsend as the Little River. And don't confuse any of these with the Pigeon River which flows along I-40 on the east end of the park. Got it? Little Pigeon. Little. Pigeon. Three different river systems whose waters don't mingle until they reach the Tennessee River.

Before the Road Prong trail was an officially-maintained trail, it was a pioneer wagon road. Before that it would have been an Indian footpath, and before it was an Indian footpath, it would have been an animal trail. I'm certain of that because, well, that's the way these things work: animals, people, wagons, cars. Many of the roads you and I take for granted were blazed by deer, bears, and buffalo.

If a bear traveled from Tennessee to North Carolina via Road Prong to Indian Gap rather than following Walker Camp Prong to Newfound Gap, there's a reason, and it probably had something to do with the fact that a bear lives by the same code that football coaches of yore followed: run it up the middle because the shortest distance between two points is a straight line. Road Prong is shorter and more direct than today's Newfound Gap Road, so it's perfect for a bear, or anyone else who doesn't mind some steady, direct walking.

The usual explanation for rerouting the road from Road Prong to its present path hinges on the fact that Newfound Gap is about 230 feet lower than Indian Gap, but a quick look at the map shows that opting for Newfound Gap required a lot of extra paving and numerous twists and turns as the new road wiggles its way up the slope of the main ridgecrest. There was undoubtedly more to choosing the present route than simply saving 230' in elevation at the top because saving that 230' required three extra miles of road building.

Road Prong's direct assault on the main ridgecrest gains about 1,780 feet in 3.3 miles to reach Indian Gap. That's very manageable for a hiker. In fact, it is almost exactly the 500' per mile elevation change that most trails in the park exhibit. Scenery-wise, a road along Road Prong would be a pleasant, 3.3 mile route up a narrow river valley, but there would be no breath-taking panoramas that a tourist could enjoy through the windshield. On the other hand, today's road paralleling

Walker Camp Prong takes over 6 miles to climb about 1,500 feet to Newfound Gap. That's a lot more winding, twisting pavement, which means less strain on our transmissions because it's an incline of only 250' per mile. And the views are fabulous in those last few miles of road.

In the 1920s and 30s, the National Park Service under the direction of Stephen Mather made dramatic views a priority in their road building, and that philosophy shows itself extravagantly on Newfound Gap Road. The drive and the views of that last few miles up to Newfound Gap are as good as any in the entire national park system. While Road Prong is the kind of route a black bear or Running Bear or Bear Bryant would choose, the Newfound Gap route is tailor-made for artists and poets.

I think of the Road Prong trail as consisting of three segments: the easy, wildflower mile; the riverside mile; and the hurricane Opal mile. The first mile of this old roadbed is commonly known as "the easy part of the trail to the Chimney Tops." In fact, this first mile is technically the Chimney Tops trail, with the Road Prong trail officially starting at the one mile point. (According to a few old maps and books, this first mile is the first mile of the Road Prong trail. However, today the NPS says that this is now the Chimney Tops trail. One mile up this trail, the Road Prong trail begins by splitting off to the left.) This is probably one of the most heavily walked miles in the park because lots of people hike to the Chimney Tops, and even more people *try* to hike to the Chimneys but give up somewhere in the middle of the second mile. This first mile is a fine wildflower walk during the months of April and May, culminating in a magnificent display of fringed phacelia.

After about a mile, the "hard part of the Chimney Tops trail" turns right while the Road Prong trail bears left. This open area where these two trails split is known as Beech Flats. Whenever you see a flat area in the Smokies you can safely assume that it was once a home site or a lumber camp or a CCC camp, or all three. In this case, Beech Flats was the site of a lumber company cabin and an old, Civil War era cemetery. The cemetery is overgrown with rhododendron now, the only marker

188

remaining being a three foot tall, wedge-shaped rock on the right side of the trail. (I've heard this rock described as "arrowhead shaped," but I'd say it's the shape of a piece of pie or a wedge of cheese. Its pointed end is down on the ground and its top end is rounded. This rock is standing on the right side of the trail, about one minute before you reach the trail junction of Chimney Tops and Road Prong.) There's apparently not a lot of documentation about this cemetery, but from what I've read (assuming what I've read is correct) there are several dozen Confederate soldiers buried here, all Cherokee Indians, resting under a thicket of rosebay rhododendron.

The second mile up Road Prong is a river walk, a noisy walk during all but the driest seasons of the year. The trail and the river stay close to each other, occasionally crossing and bumping into each other, occasionally separating briefly, but always staying within shouting distance. And because this river valley is rather steep, the walking is a bit difficult, and the river is noisy, with many chutes, falls, and plunges. In this respect, Road Prong trail is very typical of many riverside trails in the park – the river is the main character in the story, leading you higher and higher, up toward the ridgecrest. Then, once it is confident that you are capable of finishing the hike on your own, the river becomes a creek, then a rivulet, then a trickle, then it simply disappears, leaving you alone with your thoughts and the occasional scolding chickadee or singing winter wren.

About halfway through this second mile is another flat area called Indian Grave Flats. This is the burial site of a single Cherokee Indian who was killed by Union soldiers who had forced him to serve as their guide. When he refused to go any further, they shot him and left him to die. Confederate soldiers found him and buried him somewhere in this flat area. If I were a novelist, I'd write stories centered on these mountains and the tragic events along Road Prong. Walking this neglected roadway can be a strand in the rope that ties us to the past. It's unfortunate that so much of that past involves death, war, theft, and murder. So being tied to the past is perhaps overrated. Nevertheless, just as an individual's choices have tangible consequences, the events and processes of the past have created the world that we live in today, so we might as well try to make sense of where we've been so we'll have a clearer picture of where we are now. Besides, the future will probably hold about as much death, war, theft, and murder as the past, so spending time in the past may not be such a bad idea.

Winter had finally, fully tightened its grip on East Tennessee. It was late December, the temperature had barely risen above freezing for a week, and I had developed an acute case of cabin fever. I tried tying flies for the spring fishing season, but spring still seemed so far away that I just couldn't stick with it. I tried walking on our road a few times, which helped some, but there was not enough adventure to outweigh the painfully cold air. When I walk on my road, I pass a house with a pair of dogs who take their job of barking at strangers very seriously, but on this particularly cold night they didn't bark. In fact, they didn't show themselves at all. They were probably nestled in their dog house trying to stay warm. I guess there are times when even dogs don't want to get up and go to work. I know how they feel.

When Saturday morning rolled around, I decided on the spur of the moment to go to the mountains. For most of us, life holds very few "spur of the moment" moments, so when the opportunity presents itself, it's best to hop in the truck and go, even if you don't know exactly where you're going. That's the kind of thing that can happen when I don't have anything better to do, and often when I do. I call it a "somebody left the gate open" moment. As I entered the mountains, I realized my truck was taking me to Road Prong.

As I hiked the Road Prong trail, I was infatuated by the river and wondered if it might be fun to hike *in* the river – in warmer weather, of course. Over the years, I've spent a lot of time in Smokies rivers with a fly rod in my hand, chasing trout. I've also done a few off-trail hikes that have ended up in the river – Mill Creek, Ramsey Prong, Raven Fork. Those hikes are a lot of fun if you don't mind wet feet and cold legs. Some folks call Road Prong the most beautiful river in the park, and although I'm reluctant to make that kind of verbal commitment, I think I understand. The beauty of a spot is directly and strongly proportional to the amount of effort expended to get there. Paying dues in the form of sweat and time is as much a part of the magic of a place as the beauty of the place itself.

On this trail there are also some dues to be paid in the form of wet feet because there are several spots on the Road Prong trail where the river and trail merge into one. You find yourself sloshing and rock hopping, trying to stay dry and wondering if you've accidentally wandered off the trail. You haven't. Instead, the river has wandered onto the trail.

On my December hike I had to do something I rarely do – I quit because I came to a point in the trail/creek where I could go no farther. The water wasn't dangerous, but rain the previous night had made it calf deep in one stretch, and the rhododendron and icy rocks would not let me hike on the riverbank. It was hike in the creek or don't hike at all, and because wet feet on a cold winter day, with a three mile hike back to the car, is something I try to avoid, I chose not to hike at all. I turned around without making it to the top of the trail at Indian Gap. It wouldn't have been dangerous, but it would have been uncomfortable, and some days I'm just not in the mood. I've noticed those days tend to cluster in December, January, and February.

Harvey Broome once wrote that "there's something about the [mountain] water that brings you back." He was talking about the old, mountain dwellers who left their new homes and jobs in the city because they couldn't bear the taste of city water, but he could just as well have been speaking of the attraction of these rivers. Their movement, texture, and noise create a temptation too powerful to resist. Two weeks later, I tried again. I drove to Newfound Gap, parked my truck and walked a little over a mile up a snowy Clingmans Dome Road to the small parking area at Indian Gap. The weather had warmed up nicely to a balmy twenty-five degrees, so I was determined to keep my feet dry. In fact, I wore my fishing waders and boots which looked a bit strange, but there was no one else on the road or the trail, so my fashion faux pas went undetected.

Starting at the top of the crest meant that there was no creek yet, so the first five or ten minutes of my hike were extremely quiet, almost lonely. If there's no wind, a winter day in the Smokies is deathly quiet. There's no obvious animal noise, except for an occasional chickadee or

191

junco; although, somewhere there are mammals of various sizes snooping around the many nooks and crannies of the park, looking for someone just one or two links below them on the food chain. An inch or two of snow muffles the sound of those random creaks and thumps that a forest will occasionally make for no apparent reason. The main sources of winter noise in the Smokies are wind and water, so if they are absent, a walk in the woods resembles a sensory deprivation experiment.

Of course, even in the Smokies the quiet doesn't last for long, and this hike was no exception. I was soon joined by the headwaters of Road Prong which provided familiar background music which grew louder – a crescendo – as I moved further downhill.

This upper mile of the Road Prong trail between Mount Mingus and Sugarland Mountain has a unique character, partly from the spruce and fir trees, but mainly because of the wreckage. There are several swaths of destruction in this section where trees have been dragged down and piled together by wind and water. This has happened several times in the Smokies when a heavy rain has caused mud and rock slides, quickly denuding the mountain side: Charlies Bunion, Chimney Tops, Mt. Le Conte, Anakeesta Ridge, and here in the Road Prong valley between Mt. Mingus and Sugarland Mountain. Much of the wreckage here on Road Prong was the result of Hurricane Opal in 1995. (Some published trail descriptions place Hurricane Opal in 1989, but they seem to be confusing Opal with Hugo.)

The dead trees are piled up in several small feeder creeks to both the right and left, and there are several places where you walk *under* a tangle of trees suspended above the trail like a natural arch. I enjoy a good mountain thunderstorm, and I've been in a few that have made me a bit nervous, mainly from the lightning strikes, but being here to witness this event would have been certain death at the hands of water, rock, mud, and wood. It's a good reminder that the peace and solitude that we seek in the wilderness is a bit melodramatized. Emerson was right to shift our view of nature from conquest to appreciation – he used words like *sublime, beauty, reverence, virtue, exhilaration,* and *enchantment* – but we mustn't forget that for every exhilarating view and sublime moment there's a corresponding example of power, destruction, or death. That's the lesson this top mile of the Road Prong trail teaches us.

The continuation of the old Indian Gap Road over the main ridgecrest and down into North Carolina was called Oconaluftee Turnpike or Luftee Pike (aka Thomas Turnpike, named after Will Thomas, an adopted, white Cherokee who oversaw a civil war era improvement of this old wagon road). It was established as a wagon road in the 1830s but, like the Road Prong route, would have been first an animal trail and then an Indian path many years before being widened into a wagon road. Not only do great minds think alike, so do foot travelers such as bears, Native Americans, and pioneers. Because there's no maintained trail following this old route, finding it is a bit more difficult than finding the Road Prong route. The old Luftee Pike starts roughly at Indian Gap and follows the Clingmans Dome Road a few dozen yards to the east before dropping over the edge into North Carolina on a lightly worn path.

This old route is still visible as a path that meanders among the trees and brush for about five minutes before disappearing into a nasty tangle of blowdowns and rhododendron. On the other side of this tangle, it cuts east across the face of the main crest and through a small notch in Thomas Divide before curving southeast to Luftee Gap, which is a substantial parking area and overlook on a sharp, 90° bend in today's Newfound Gap Road. While today's road follows the crest of Thomas Divide, the old Luftee Pike roadbed drops down into the valley of a small creek called Beech Flats Prong which begins just below the Luftee Gap parking overlook.

On a warm day in late August I joined a group of seventeen other hikers of the Smoky Mountains Hiking Club led by one of the club's patriarchs, Al Watson. He had spent a few days scouting out the route of this old turnpike and led us on this path on the slope just north of Beech Flats Prong. We spent our few hours on the slope paralleling the creek until we arrived at a sharp S curve in today's road, a little over a mile below Luftee Gap. Just as the old path on the Tennessee side had followed the Road Prong valley, this North Carolina portion of the

193

overmountain road had followed the Beech Flats Prong valley until it merges with Kephart Prong to form the Oconaluftee River. I'm a little embarrassed to say that I don't remember much about Beech Flats Prong. It's probably a fine, little creek, but because this was an off-trail hike, I spent more time focused on the immediate issue of staying on the correct path while climbing over and around blown-down trees. When hiking, there's a sort of Maslow's hierarchy of needs at work in which off-trail hiking doesn't allow time and energy for day-dreaming, noble thoughts, and attentiveness to beauty. Instead, you focus on the immediate task of pushing through bushes or over tree trunks and not getting lost, all within a 20' radius. Trail hiking, on the other hand, relieves you of those basic necessities and allows the mind to dwell on virtues such as truth, goodness, and beauty. All of which is just a fancy way of saying I didn't pay attention to the creek.

Today's Newfound Gap road, which performs a giant S switchback to climb to the crest of Thomas Divide, is the result of a relocation during the early 1960s. When the 1800s Road Prong and Luftee Pike was replaced with Newfound Gap Road in the 1930s, the new North Carolina portion followed the Luftee Pike road rather closely. Just as the 1800s Luftee Pike paralleled Beech Flats Prong (on the slopes just north of this creek), the 1930s Newfound Gap Road paralleled Beech Flats Prong on the slopes of Thomas Divide just south of the creek. Today the abandoned, pre-1960s road is called the Beech Flats Quiet Walkway, starting midway between mile markers 19 and 20 on Newfound Gap Road in North Carolina. In the early 1960s this portion of Newfound Gap Road was abandoned in favor of today's route along the crest of Thomas Divide, which provides more panoramic views than the old, Beech Flats Prong route.

Today's road on this North Carolina side is remarkably straight for several miles as it follows Thomas Divide south toward Cherokee. The road has broad, exposed, grassy shoulders and expansive views. Along the road you can see, in season, everything from dandelions to violets to yellow lady's slippers. Toward the western horizon, Clingmans Dome stands high above the valley of Deep Creek flowing south toward Bryson City and Fontana Lake.

194

At the end of our August hike, I decided to hike back up the Beech Flats Quiet Walkway (the old pre-1960s roadbed of Newfound Gap Road) to my truck at Newfound Gap. The fact that this was late August was significant because it was still warm enough for stinging nettle to be growing in profusion along this quiet walkway. While this annoying nettle tends to grow profusely in shaded creekbeds, it's also well-suited for growing directly through abandoned asphalt. So, the serenity of this quiet walkway was interrupted by the whining and muttering I do whenever I'm waist deep in a sea of this unfriendly plant.

After an uneventful hour of walking on old asphalt that had deteriorated almost to dirt, I neared Newfound Gap and saw a black bear eating berries in a thicket of bushes beside the path. We heard each other at about the same moment, we both looked up, made eye contact for one brief moment, and the bear shot down the mountainside. It fit what all the books say: black bears are more afraid of you than you are of them. Generally, I'm not too concerned about bears. Nevertheless, walking up on one at close range does require a modest degree of fortitude and forethought. If she had stood her ground, I would have backed away slowly while talking in gentle tones, reminding her that she's supposed to be afraid of me, and if she had charged I would have stood my ground, partly because that's what the experts tell us to do, but mainly because I'd be too scared to run. But the bear ran away, which means my "stand my ground" strategy has never been fully tested, which is actually a little disappointing. I'd love to have a bear encounter story full of dirt, dust, bravery, and blood, even though the more likely outcome would be dirt, dust, fear, and urine.

As I began walking again, I saw a second, smaller bear feeding among the bushes. A much smaller bear – a cub. The first bear had been the mother. You know how you should never mess with a cub because a mother bear will defend her cub at all costs against all dangers? Not this one. Mama took off like a coward to let her little one fend for itself. Of course, while standing there hoping the cub would run, I didn't know that yet. For all I knew the mother was sneaking up behind me at this very moment, or deciding that she needed to come back and save her cub who was too stupid to run. Personally, I thought she should be mad at her cub, not me, but I knew there was a good chance she wouldn't see it that way. Whether out of stupidity or stubbornness, I've found bears to be immune to sound logic.

So, the cub wouldn't move, and the longer we both stood there, the more likely it seemed that the mother would return to set the record straight. I shouted at the cub. No response. I threw a rock at him, but didn't want the mother to see me. Would she make the connection that throwing a rock was an attack on her baby, or was her brain too primitive to make the human-rock-cub connection? I suspect bears aren't capable of analytical, cause & effect thinking, simply because so many humans haven't mastered it, but this was not the time to conduct further research. I backed away but continued to throw an occasional rock, then immediately dropped my hands to my side so the mother – wherever she was – would not know that I was pestering her baby. Maybe she'd think rocks were falling from the heavens.

As with most bear incidents, this one ended with no drama and no pictures. The cub finally got the message and ran, the mother didn't return to maul me, and I continued my walk while singing loudly and badly, just in case bears have a sense of music and rhythm that would be offended by my songs.

It occurred to me later that probably more bears than humans use this abandoned road. I had seen these bears on an old, asphalt road – a route probably blazed by bears and later adopted by humans for their own purposes. But now, just as old homesteads were being overtaken by forests in the coves below, and old chimneys were turning into piles of rocks, and the words on old tombstones were being erased by rain and ice, the pre-1960s Newfound Gap Road was reverting to its original owners – the bears. Time was flowing backwards as a paved roadway was becoming a bearway again, wild and nettle-filled. These two bears would perhaps live their entire lives in the Beech Flats Prong watershed between Indian and Newfound Gaps. The cub would live to see the forest get a little thicker and the abandoned asphalt a little softer.

It feels to me as if some sort of circle is closing – not the circle of life exactly – more like the past catching up with and overtaking the present, like a clock running backwards. Abe Lincoln reminded us that "the future arrives one day at a time," but not here in the Smokies, on these abandoned farms and roads, where it is the *past* that is arriving, day by day, season by season. Nettle grows, bears multiply, and asphalt turns to dirt. We reconnect with the past simply by walking in the woods because here among these hallowed hills the past has returned to reclaim its birthright, slowly but surely.

In most places around the world, the flow of history seems to be from wild to tame, from forest to pavement, from farms to strip malls, from bears to cars. Developers everywhere can point to their latest brick-mortar-pavement creations and proclaim, "All this was once forest." And yet, sometime soon, probably in the spring before the stinging nettle emerges, I'll bring my granddaughters here and pass the torch. I'll tell them about the cub who wouldn't run away, and I'll point to the spot where he stood and, with a sweep of my arm, proudly proclaim: "All this was once asphalt... but never again."

Chapter 12

Alone on the Chimneys

I can understand why the Chimneys have been a favorite destination for several generations of hikers. Harvey Broome wrote glowingly of his frequent trips up their rocky tops. Jim Thompson and Dutch Roth took dramatic pictures of them that are still used in Smokies publications today. Michael Frome began his classic Smokies history, *Strangers in High Places*, with a story of his hike up to them. Because a good destination is a key ingredient of a great hike, the Chimneys should be on everyone's "to do" list. So it's odd that they were on my "don't do" list for twenty years, mainly because the parking lot is always full and the trail is always crowded. Okay, not *always*...

I take a little bit too much pride in the fact that I spend most of my Smoky Mountains time in places that most people not only rarely visit but have never even heard of: Cat Stairs, Anakeesta Ridge, Groundhog Ridge, Rich Butt, Styx Branch, Harrell's Folly. Some of those names are the official titles that show up on maps; others are unofficial names that only I or my hiking partners use. I've pretty much written off places like Laurel Falls or Clingmans Dome because a local guy who values solitude shouldn't waste his time at the crowded, touristy spots with full parking lots and littered trails. So I rarely go to the hot spots because they are full of people who don't know any better. Yes, it's an attitude that reeks of conceit, and my only defense is that I have a few scars and bruises to prove that I've paid my dues, which ought to buy a guy the right to a few ounces of vanity.

So, for twenty years I had included the Chimneys as one of those places that wasn't worth the trouble. That changed on a Friday evening in May a few years ago.

I was trying to think of a place to take several college students on a quick trip into the park. They all were somewhat familiar with the park, so they knew how good it can be, and they also knew that any outdoor excursion can be disrupted by traffic, bad weather, poison ivy, or a host

198

of other random events. Whether things went well or not, they might not blame me. On the other hand, this was our first trip together, and as the teacher I was in charge of pulling it together, so I felt the pressure to perform that we've all felt whenever you are in charge of something that has elements that are totally out of your control. If the trip went poorly, they'd probably be gracious, but we'd all know who to blame: me, because I was the grown-up. Among the innumerable drawbacks of old age, the inflated and unjustified expectation (by others) of competence and wisdom is near the top of the list. I've never done anything to show the younger generations that I'm wise and competent, and I resent their jumping to such unwarranted conclusions. But they do.

We already had plans to hike to Mt. Le Conte, Porters Creek, and Mt. Cammerer, and I needed one more destination. The Chimneys seemed like a good prospect, but I couldn't bear the thought of joining the crowds, not to mention the fact that we'd have to leave Jefferson City around 6 or 7 am to get a parking spot at the Chimneys trailhead.

Somewhere in the discussion the idea emerged that we could go in the evening rather than the morning. From the moment the conversation turned in that direction, it had my full attention simply because it flies in the face of the prevailing wisdom. Whenever you read any NPS literature about visiting the park, the most common advice given for avoiding the crowds is to "go early" in the day. Arise well before the sun and get on the trail while everyone else is sitting down to their first cup of coffee. It's a strategy that works well enough, but I've never fully embraced it because I tend to be a nonconformist who doesn't take advice well, I'm not exactly a morning glory, and traffic can be messy even at 7 am. So the idea of arriving *late* resonates with me on several levels.

At the risk of over-generalizing, the best strategy for avoiding crowds in the Smokies is to "go late." Most people are creatures of habit. They'll eat lunch exactly at noon, even if it means standing in a line that stretches out the restaurant door. Coming fifteen minutes early or an hour later would virtually eliminate the waiting time, but very few people are willing to deviate from the norm so they spend inordinate amounts of time standing in lines or stuck in traffic. Likewise, Smokies visitors are so predictable you can set your watch by them. The picnic areas are full at noon and 5 pm. The most popular trails are full in the morning and nearly empty by 4 pm. So a plan to avoid the crowds which starts with the phrase "sleep late" should have caught on by now, but creatures of habit tend to develop an immunity to good ideas.

So, we'd make a late hike to the top, hang around long enough to watch the sun set, then scramble carefully down to the trail by the light of flashlights, headlamps, and the moon. Yes, we'd hike for about an hour in the dark, but no one seemed intimidated by that prospect. So within a matter of minutes a workable plan emerged: Leave Jefferson City around 3 pm, be on the trail by 5 pm, be at the top by 6:30. That would give us a couple of hours to explore and relax before the sun set.

On the next Friday we put our plan into motion, and it worked perfectly. Even the weather – the second most volatile factor in the mix, traffic being first – cooperated, but only at the last second. The day had been cloudy and rainy, and I had resigned myself to the fact that this would be a wet hike. I don't mind seeing the Smokies in all her moods – wet, dry, angry, happy, whatever – so my chief concern was convincing the students that weather is part of the experience and that a thunderstorm in the Smokies is exciting. I reminded them that the first few pages in their textbook were about a hike to the Chimneys and the first sentence was: "It was raining in the Smokies." Fortunately, the students (three girls) all had an adventurous streak and seemed perfectly happy to hike in the rain.

The most important ingredient of a great hike is a substantial payoff, usually a great view or something interesting like cliffs or a waterfall or wildflowers. For this trip it would be a combination of a view and cliffs. The view would be of the south side of Mt. Le Conte, Peregrine Peak, Fort Harry cliffs, and nearly the entire length of the Sugarlands valley and the road below.

Folks who don't get out much assume that to get a great view you have to hike or drive to the highest spot available, such as Clingmans Dome or Mt. Le Conte, but that's not necessarily true. There are many, many great views from mid-elevation locations in which you are surrounded by impressive peaks, forests, and valleys. You find an open spot surrounded by air – such as the Chimney Tops – and enjoy the 360° view. Because the views don't stretch to the distant horizon, you find

200

yourself focusing on nearby ridges, watersheds, and peaks. You listen to the sound of wind dancing from ridge to ridge or the constant rushing of rivers down below. In some ways, it's like going to a concert at an old, small concert hall rather than a stadium that seats 100,000. The concert hall is intimate and personal, and on the drive home you find yourself asking each other, "Were those gargoyles on the walls?" Or, "The acoustics were perfect."

The Chimneys are a concert hall where a soaring raven will catch your attention, and you'll find yourself spending five or ten minutes simply watching the bird fly. Once you lose sight of him as he drifts further away, you experience an overwhelming sense of envy. At that moment you'd like nothing better than to be a bird, even settling for the fate of a vulture that spends its life eating rotting animals. Even though it sounds like a punishment out of Dante's *Inferno*, dining on carrion seems a fair price to pay for the ability to float effortlessly at mountaintop level.

But it's the cliffs that make the Chimneys the Chimneys. They are a pair of rocky, exposed peaks connected by a narrow, rocky ridge about one hundred yards long and mingled with various shrubs of the heath family. The whole thing sticks out like a couple of sore thumbs, about 1,300' above the valley floor. It's a scene that is actually fairly common in this section of the park, but most of these somewhat dangerous landforms are inaccessible to the casual hiker and invisible to the car-bound visitor. In this respect, the Chimneys are an exception – they are visible from the road and accessible via a two mile, steeper-than-average hike.

The second ingredient of a great hike is good hiking partners. A "good hiking partner" is defined not by a list of essential characteristics but by the absence of one significant trait. Your partners can by young or old, fast or slow, Republican or Democrat, religious or pagan, funny or dull, but the one thing they absolutely cannot, *must* not, be is a whiner. A whiner will suck the life out of a day in the mountains because he is convinced that he's the center of the cosmos, and humankind – most immediately in the person of you, his hiking partner – is duty bound to attend to his needs, which are many. Of course, you don't grasp this, so the whiner will spend the day seeking to educate you concerning the laws of the universe and your place in it. If it's raining, he'll be sure to tell you about it, as if you hadn't noticed. If he is cold and wet he'll inform you, as if it was your job to do something about it. To misquote a Proverb: Better to dwell in the corner of a housetop than to hike with a whiner. In short, a whiner needs a babysitter, not a hiking partner.

There were no whiners among us. The three girls were all outdoorsy types, but you'd never know it by their names: Madison, Alexis, and Amber. Now that I've written them down, they look a bit, well, trendy – the kind of names you'd see in Hollywood. They should all have big bows in their hair and Vera Bradley packs. But they don't fit that stereotype. They were rugged and ready.

There was a light drizzle, which seemed perfectly fine with everyone. There was no sign of grim resignation, no sense of obligation. Everyone was game for whatever Mother Nature decided to throw at us. Clouds and rain? No problem; after all, this is the Smokies in May. Frustration with rain and clouds would be asking the mountains to stop being the mountains. You take whatever the mountains give, with grace and stoic dignity. And I quickly learned that "stoic dignity" is not simply a synonym for "male ego." Or, if it is, then girls can have a male ego, too. These girls are the best evidence I've seen that one's name does not determine one's destiny – President Barack Hussein Obama being a close second.

I didn't have the courage to take the shortest route through Pigeon Forge, so we took the slightly longer drive through Cosby and into Gatlinburg with only a minimal amount of aggravation. Because the weekend traffic was still a few hours away, we managed to dodge the cars and pedestrians of Gatlinburg without incident. This was one of those rare occasions in life in which our plans were actually unfolding as intended. I knew that I'd have to someday pay for this fleeting moment of good fortune, but I didn't let that ruin my day. One of the few things I've learned over the years is not to get the blues in advance.

As we passed the Sugarlands area, the rain continued to fall, and I reminded everyone once again that "It was raining in the Smokies." And again, they let me know that they were all in. Still no whiners.

A few minutes later we passed the Chimneys Picnic area on the banks of the West Prong of the Little Pigeon River. In a previous life this was the Chimneys Campground, but now it's full of picnic tables and a couple of bathrooms, plus a nice, civilized nature trail – the Cove Hardwoods Nature Trail that starts and ends near the beginning of the picnic loop road. My wife and I try to make an annual visit to this nature trail, preferably between mid-April and mid-May, for the prolific-bordering-on-profligate display of wildflowers: hepatica, spring beauties, trilliums, violets, stonecrop, bishops cap, jack in the pulpit – all the stars are there, with the main characters changing each week.

Soon after the Chimneys picnic area, the silhouette of the two Chimneys came into view, and within a few minutes we arrived at the Chimneys parking area. It was a quarter full and emptying fast, partly because of the bad weather but mainly because we had waited until late in the day to begin our adventure. Everyone who hikes the Chimneys shows up early in the morning to get a parking spot and finishes by 3 or 4 pm. By 5:00 the parking lots at most trailheads in the park will be virtually empty, so anyone willing to hike in the late afternoon and walk back at dusk or in the dark is virtually guaranteed to have to solitary experience. It's a strategy that works almost everywhere in the park except Cades Cove, the one popular place that is *most* crowded in the evening.

The first mile of the Chimney Tops trail is either the Chimneys trail, or the Chimney Tops trail, or the Road Prong trail, depending on what map or book or sign you are looking at. The trail parallels the creek called Road Prong because this path used to be the route of the old road up to the main crest at Indian Gap and down into North Carolina. In the 1920s the road was rerouted to its present course through Newfound Gap, so a walk along Road Prong is a walk along a route that has been used for millennia by wild animals, Indians, pioneers, farmers, and finally hikers. I try to dwell on those kinds of details when I hike a trail like this, to absorb the local history through mental osmosis. Unfortunately, I've never been very good at meditation because I have what I would call an active mind and others would call a short attention span, so I usually end up just looking at the ground to keep from twisting an ankle. In spite of my best efforts at self-improvement, I guess I'm just a tangible kind of guy who's drawn to what's here rather than what used to be here. But what used to be here is interesting and worth noticing.

So, the first mile of this hike parallels a pleasant, shady creek tucked deeply between Mt. Mingus to the east and the Chimneys to the west. The mild thunder of the creek, rosebay rhododendron, and a light drizzle were our companions as we moseyed our way up this easy half of this afternoon's hike. I'll spare you the details because, well, there aren't many details. We walked, talked, and time passed quickly.

The second mile is the actual Chimneys trail which pulls away from Road Prong trail and creek. It had been twenty years since I'd walked this second mile of trail, and my memory of a long, steep, relentless climb was a bit exaggerated.

Just as we had started up the steep part of this second mile, we encountered a couple coming down the trail – a man and a woman on the young end of middle age. I sometimes like to ask, "Are we there yet?" just to see what kind of response I'll get because I've noticed over the years that this is one of the few situations in which women are more likely to lie than men. And that was exactly what happened. The woman smiled and in a very comforting, enthusiastic, motherly tone, she replied, "Oh, yes! Just a little further!" Bless her lying heart. We had a long, uphill slog ahead of us, but I just smiled and thanked her. The guy who was with her, a few steps behind, made eye contact with me and shook his head, then whispered, "It's a long way, man. A long way." The woman lying and the guy telling the truth. Just another one of life's little surprises.

Keith Oakes had joined us because it had been too many years since he'd done this hike, as it had for me. He followed his usual pattern of speeding quickly from point A to point B. Madison hung with him, while Alexis and Amber hung back with me. Or I hung with them. Either way, we hiked together. Yes, I had to stop a few times to catch my breath, but my worst expectations weren't realized. Except for the rain. I had expected rain, and that's what we got – just a light drizzle, but enough to keep our rain jackets on. "It was raining in the Smokies," as usual.

Everyone's spirits were pretty high, especially as we began to level off as we reached the ridgecrest which leads from Sugarland Mountain to the Chimneys. And our spirits soared even higher as the clouds began to part – as if on cue from the Director – just as we reached the first Chimney. Once again my most consistently accurate rule for happiness had been fulfilled: Lower your expectations. I had expected the worst (rain and clouds and no views), and on a normal day, that's exactly what you'll get, but on rare occasions life delivers a nice surprise which you of course accept with gratitude, but without being fooled into raising your expectations for the next time. After all, every silver lining has a cloud.

We all accepted the parting clouds humbly, and perhaps a bit skeptically, knowing they could close in around us at any minute. But they didn't. Instead, the clouds simply went away, vanishing into thin air. The sky became a bright, freshly-washed blue. The wind blew. The wet rocks dried quickly. The sun blazed in the west, and we even had a brief rainbow at eye level as the last of the clouds melted away in the east. I vowed right then to invite these three girls on all our trips because one of them – I never figured out which – was obviously a good luck charm. Keith and I never get this kind of treatment. We get briers, snakes, fog, slippery rocks, yellow jackets, and stinging nettle. Today, with these three young ladies, we got a rainbow.

The scramble up to the top of the first Chimney is a bit spooky, but the jagged rock creates nice hand and footholds up a moderate incline. If you are the type that gets a bit light-headed when surrounded by nothing but air, then you go up using your feet and hands. If you aren't, then two feet and good balance is all that's necessary. I've heard rock climbers describe one of the levels of ascent as "the kind your dog could climb." Yes, this was the type an adventurous dog could walk up with only an occasional pause or slip.

So we all scrambled up to the top, being sure not to stumble into the one crevice that folks are warned to avoid. It's actually a hole that leads about twenty feet down and across to a "window" on the west side of the chimney. It's the kind of place I call a "death is optional" site. If a guy wanted to jump to his death, this place would suffice. On the other hand, if you don't want to die, you won't. This window hole is five or

205

six feet across and has just enough good hand and footholds to make a climb down into it (and back out) quite manageable for a human (but not your dog). But there isn't an abundance of holds, so you have to pay attention, find the holds, and use them slowly and deliberately. An added benefit of this hole is that any breeze blowing through it is cool and refreshing; I suppose because this small tunnel is dark and shady. So it's a pleasant, five minute side excursion that has one more benefit – it looks a lot worse than it really is. So if there are spectators, they'll be impressed with your bravado, even though there's really not much bravado involved. Several of us worked our way down into the tunnel, one at a time, even though there were no gawking tourists to impress.

And of course, the missing tourists were the reason we were here late in the day. Not only were the clouds parting and disappearing, so were the tourists. It was just the five of us, lounging around the top of the first chimney, enjoying the fact that the last of the tourists were leaving as much as we were enjoying the views and the setting sun.

After a few minutes of basking in the expanse and the loneliness, it was time for a little bravado. The second chimney was beckoning.

I've read trail guides that talk about a "narrow ridge" in the Smokies, by which they mean wooded, sloping sides with a rounded top about twenty or thirty feet wide. Usually, it would be perfectly possible to walk down the side with only a modest amount of sliding. Such ridges (e.g., the Boulevard or Sugarland Mountain) look narrow and steep from a distance, but up close they are just trails on wooded ridges with an occasional open, rocky vista. They are great trails on great ridges, but they aren't scary narrow.

The "narrow ridge" between the two chimneys is scary narrow. It's about one hundred yards long and about ten feet wide, consisting of refrigerator-sized chunks of broken rock mixed with sand myrtle and an occasional stretch of solid ground. And there's a steep slope on the sides – they drop almost vertically for a hundred or more feet. Death isn't likely, but it is possible. About once every ten or twenty years I'll hear a report of someone falling and dying at the Chimneys.

Most of this connecting ridge is almost, but not quite, as bad as it looks, and in just a couple of places it is as bad as it looks. There's a path worn along this ridge, especially in places where it's possible to hop off the rocks and on to solid ground. There are one or two spots where you have to squeeze around or crawl down a rocky spot that probably shouldn't be squeezed or crawled. As long as you don't slip, you'll be fine. As long as you don't slip. It's sort of a weak link in the chain principle. Just one weak link can create a problem, even if all the other links are fine. There are a couple of sketchy spots in this otherwise manageable ridge.

One of those spots is at the very beginning – at the first drop over the top of the first chimney, and that's probably a good thing. It's like a "Do Not Cross" piece of yellow police tape stretched across the start of the ridge. It convinces people quickly and compellingly that the first chimney is far enough.

Keith and I decided to give it a try, knowing that plenty of people have done this over the years, with only an occasional fatality. So the odds were stacked heavily in our favor.

As with most of the rock scrambling that we've done in the park – Anakeesta Ridge, Rich Butt, Big Duck Hawk, Charlies Bunion – the key is to be slow and deliberate. At least, that's the key for me. I tend to be a bit more slow and deliberate than Keith and my other hiking partners, partly because I'm older and partly because I'm a sissy when it comes to heights and widths. Open air and steep sides make me dizzy, even in places that aren't especially deadly, so I have to focus on the rock in front me rather than the air around me.

Fortunately, there's a lot of shrubbery growing in the cracks and thin soil on the steep slopes of the Chimneys and their connecting ridge. They wouldn't help much if a guy were to fall off. It would just mean that when the body was recovered, it would have a lot of scratches on it. Nevertheless, the shrubs help my mental status by providing a sense of security. I know it's mostly a *false* sense of security, but somehow that part of my brain that controls the vertigo and fear gets tricked into thinking everything is okay.

So we walked and hopped and crawled and climbed our way from the first to the second chimney, with Keith doing a bit more of the walking and hopping and me relying more on the crawling. Apparently, I have more reasons to live than he does.

The second chimney is lower than the first chimney, with a nice, open area for standing and walking. Once you are there, it feels safer than the first chimney simply because the top is more open and level. And being lower, it's a great spot for pictures of the first chimney and the ridge leading back to it.

In most respects, the first chimney seems to be the better chimney. It's higher and more peaked, and it has the small tunnel to play in. But in one important way, the second, lower chimney is superior: it's an impressively lonely spot. Although there may be people sitting on the first chimney looking down on you, the ridge between creates a physical and mental barrier. You feel separated from – and maybe a bit superior to – the folks who are sitting on the higher chimney. It's one of those times that elevation – pure feet above sea level – doesn't mean much because the higher peak is easier to get to.

After exploring the edges of the second chimney (there are a few old paths that lead to some interesting spots down the slopes), the sun began to get serious about sinking below the horizon, so I got serious about heading back to the first chimney. I'm fine with night hiking, and I'm fine with scrambling on rocky ridges, but I'm not enthusiastic about combining the two. So, the challenge would be to convince Keith that we should go back to the first chimney while it was still light. The discussion went something like this:

Me: "I guess it's time to head back."
Keith: "Yeah."

Clearly, my powers of persuasion are compelling, so we hiked back to the rest of the group on the first chimney while it was still light.

There was one more significant detail to our trip, and it began showing itself about 45 minutes before the sun set. I hadn't checked the calendar carefully, but from watching the moon the previous week, I knew that we'd have a full moon, or close to it. As it turns out, we were one day shy of a full moon, which was perfect because the difference between a full moon and being one day shy of a full moon is virtually indistinguishable to the naked eye. So for all practical purposes, we had a full moon.

The fact that we were still one day away from the true full moon meant that the moon rose about an hour before sunset rather than right at sunset. So in the west we had a dramatic, glowing, orange sky. In the east, just above Mt. Mingus, we had a nearly-full moon rising quietly into the darkening sky. I was reminded of the creation story of the ancient, Hebrew scriptures: "And God made two great lights; the greater light to rule the day, and the lesser light to rule the night…. And God set them in the firmament of the heaven to give light upon the earth, and to rule over the day and over the night, and to divide the light from the darkness. And God saw that it was good." Only a hard-hearted cynic would disagree with God on this one. Truly, it was good.

Moments like this remind me that I couldn't be an atheist simply because I don't have enough faith in Blind Chance – that all we see is a lucky accident, including our ability to see and think and experience awe in the first place. Granted, the idea of a super-natural realm full of spirit beings, not to mention an omnipotent Creator, sounds preposterous. On the other hand, the alternative is the belief that, given enough time, anything can happen by sheer chance – the old "monkeys typing the encyclopedia" thing. So, both options require faith: God vs. Chance. To paraphrase Winston Churchill's comment on democracy: Belief in God is the worst explanation for the origin of the universe, except for all the other explanations.

It occurred to me later that we should have brought something to celebrate with – champagne, hot chocolate, smores, something out of the ordinary for this out of the ordinary moment. Happily, that means we'll have to do this trip again and get the details right. Since I'm one of the few, remaining Americans who is not a coffee drinker, I'm voting for hot chocolate heated over the fire of a small backpacking stove.

After it had become fully dark, with only the moon ruling over the sky, we headed back down to the trail. Scrambling down the rocky slope of the first chimney in the dark could have been a bit spooky, but the fact that most of us had climbed up and down it more than once this afternoon gave us a sense of confidence that made the descent easy, even fun in the way risky acts can sometimes be. All of us had head lamps to light our way, except me. I'm not a big fan of head lamps for night hiking. While most people use a headlamp, I prefer a small flashlight. But because I used both hands to help me in the dark descent, I had to hold my flashlight in my mouth, which wasn't comfortable or convenient. I made sure that my partners didn't see me. It was easy. I simply lingered at the back of the pack, which is my standard operating procedure, so no one suspected a thing.

Most folks think it's sheer lunacy that we would dare to hike at night, but I think it's lunacy that they would think it's sheer lunacy. It's just not a big deal: we walked, sometimes we talked, all the way back to the car by the light of the moon and our lights. End of story. There's simply nothing dramatic to report – other than the fact that it was a beautiful, clear, cool night in May, and a nearly-full moon was rising higher in the east. The only thing lunar was the moon itself.

I won't say that we *deserved* the meteorological and astronomical blessings of the day, but I will say that we had gone the extra mile to put ourselves in this position. When exploring the outdoors, that's about the best you can do – make your plans, be creative, take risks, but reasonable ones; in short, just get out and do it. Put yourself in the right place at the right time, and hope Nature will reward you for your effort, and more often than not, she does. But when she doesn't, you accept your fate stoically, telling yourself that you are an experienced outdoors-lover who can handle a little adversity without whining. And you won't be disappointed because you know that outdoor life is usually better than civilized life, but in one way they are exactly alike: things don't always turn out perfectly, so you adapt and keep moving, making the best of the hand you're dealt.

But today we'd been dealt a really, really good hand; things had worked out perfectly. While at the beginning of our hike, "It was raining in the Smokies," by the end of the day, "The full moon was shining on the Smokies."

And we were there to see it, alone on the Chimneys.

Chapter 13

The Simple Gifts of Styx Branch

Sometimes November just hangs around for two or three extra weeks, all the way up to Christmas, giving us a few, delicious weeks of crisp, blue skies and mild temps for cutting one more rick of firewood, raking the last of the leaves, or taking a glorious stroll in the mountains. While cutting wood and raking leaves are pleasant enough activities, they are both "work" by any reasonable definition, so I opted for the mountains, which can be work, but only in the very best sense of the word. And besides, I'd been acting like a well-adjusted grown-up for several weeks in a row, and I'd had just about all I could stand.

One benefit of a November hike – especially if it happens in mid-December – is the deep, deep blue sky. I imagine folks who live in the Rockies are used to those crisp, blue skies because there's not much humidity to muddy up the atmosphere and the views, but here in the East we have to wait for fall and winter for our sky to change from white to blue. Every westerner should spend a week in the Appalachians every spring or summer to see what real humidity looks like and to gain a renewed appreciation for their own crisp, blue, western skies.

An added benefit of a cold weather hike is that if you can spend the day on a south-facing slope, you can add ten or even twenty degrees to the temperature... as long as you stay in the sunshine. For example, much of Alum Cave trail is on the south-facing slope of Mt. Le Conte, but there's also a lot of deep shade. So you can stroll pleasantly along in the warmth of the sun on an ice-free trail, only to walk into the shade of a spruce grove or rhododendron thicket and find yourself slipping and sliding on an icy patch ten or a hundred feet long. If you do this enough, you get used to it and take it for granted. But then the day comes when a friend of yours is looking at the pictures of your December Le Conte hike, and they innocently ask why you are wearing spikes on your boots but only a T shirt with no jacket. The incongruity of spikes and a T shirt has never occurred to you, but it really is an odd combination that makes sense only to those who hike on south-facing slopes in the late fall. (Of course, you'll explain to your friend that the top of Le Conte is cold and windy and your jacket is in your day pack. You'll definitely need it when you get to the top.) I've never seen a hiking trails book that includes information about north-facing vs. south-facing trails, but it should be part of every trail description.

So as our schedules opened up in mid-December, Greg Harrell and I decided to do an off-trail hike/climb/crawl/wade/slide (I never know exactly what to call our typical off-trail trip – the word "hike" doesn't quite cover all the things we actually do) up Styx Branch on the south-facing slope of Mt. Le Conte. We love the name Styx because it gives the impression of a dangerous, deadly, one-way journey filled with dragons, demons, fire, weeping, and gnashing of teeth, with perhaps a little bit of utter, outer darkness thrown in just for fun. To make things even better, the general area where Styx Branch flows is called Huggins Hell. Names like that are like a flashing neon sign begging us to visit.

For purposes of full disclosure, I might as well admit up front that the names Styx and Hell are creative hyperbole generated by an over-active imagination, or something like that. The story goes that a guy named Huggins got lost in the thick rhododendron hell in this Styx Branch watershed. One version of the story says he emerged three days later, exhausted and near-death. The other version says he never emerged and was never found. I just can't bring myself to believe any of it. The only person who could truly get lost up there is a delicate city-slicker who has no idea what he's doing. If Huggins was a local resident who got lost, all he needed to do was find a ravine with some trickling water, and follow it down to the main river, which led to the homes and farms of Sugarlands and eventually to Gatlinburg. The whole process of getting from the rhododendron-infested slopes of Le Conte to Sugarlands would take a few hours, half a day at most. I suppose Huggins could have slipped on a rock and broken his leg or neck, in which case he died not because he was lost but because he was clumsy.

I suspect Huggins was actually a moonshiner with one or two stills up on the web of small creeks that form the Styx watershed. He probably dreamed up the story of getting irretrievably lost to scare nosy neighbors and government tax agents. I've done the same kind of thing when someone asks me about one of my favorite trout streams. I'll reply that, yes, there are a few small trout in the river... if you can get past all the copperheads, rattlesnakes, bears, nettle, hornets, and rabid raccoons. Among moonshiners and fishermen who have secrets to keep and only a half-hearted commitment to the truth, stretching reality a bit around the edges is part of the job description. Among politicians I find lying to be detestable; among fishermen I think it's... charming. Although, in our defense, there are probably all sorts of stinging and biting plants and animals out there. This is rural East Tennessee after all. If we were scientists, we'd call these possibly-true-but-maybe-not stories "hypotheses," which adds an air of respectability to our tales. This means that fishermen (and Mr. Huggins) aren't actually liars, just storytellers who specialize in possibilities rather than actualities. If Styx Branch were a little bigger and full of trout, I'd guess that Huggins was a moonshiner *and* a trout fisher, which would double his motivation for creative story-telling.

So Greg and I parked at the Alum Cave trailhead and walked quickly along the first 1.5 miles of Alum Cave trail. This first section of the trail is heavily shaded by rhododendron, so the snow from previous snowfalls was still on the trail. I put my micro-spikes on my boots, so I was able to walk on the layer of ice and snow with complete confidence, even reckless abandon, keeping in mind that Harrell's reckless abandon resembles a guy speeding down an interstate highway at 120mph while texting and drinking a cup of coffee, while my reckless abandon is a guy driving down the interstate at 30mph while looking around at the scenery. Both are hazards to themselves and others, but in different ways.

I've tried several different versions of various gadgets and gizmos for providing traction on ice and snow, and in my opinion these micro-spikes that consist of half-inch spikes held on the boot sole by chains on the bottom and thick rubber around the top are the best choice. Anything that has the spikes attached directly to rubber won't last long. The spikes will pull out of the rubber when you use them on steep inclines, such as hiking trails. Something that works on your icy driveway at home probably won't work for long on a rough, steep trail. Likewise, those things with coils of wire or bare chains attached to the sole of your boot won't provide solid traction on significant inclines. Again, there's a big difference between walking on level ice and walking on slanted ice. For trails in the mountains, get something with small but real spikes. Any rubber should be around the top of your boot. Everything on the bottom of your boot should be metal – spikes and chains. Unless you do seriously steep scrambling or climbing up icy rocks and cliffs, these micro-spikes are perfect for hiking on icy trails.

About a hundred yards past Arch Rock the trail makes a sharp left turn on a small foot bridge over a small stream – Styx Branch. This is the spot where Greg and I left the trail and began picking our way up the creek, stepping carefully on the rocks and gravel beds of this modest stream. Later in the winter these river rocks would be covered in ice and snow, so we would leave our spikes on, but we were still in mid-December and the heavy snows and deep freezes of January and February hadn't filled in all the wet nooks and crannies with ice. So I removed my spikes and never put them on again until the end of the day when we hiked back to the car from the top of Mt. Le Conte via Alum Cave trail.

Styx Branch is a typical Smokies, high-elevation stream. It is small (there are probably no trout in it, but if there are, they would be tiny brook trout) and lined with rhododendron thickets. Like many small creeks, this first part of our hike was one-half water, one-half rock, and three-halves rhododendron.

There are also a lot of yellow birches lining the river because these are the "pioneer" trees that tend to establish themselves in a riverbed soon after a flood or landslide scours the river of all surrounding vegetation. Before I began serious off-trail hiking, I knew nothing about this process. Now I see it all the time. In fact, I tend to be drawn to these places of rocky scars, scoured creekbeds, and massive debris fields consisting of tangled, splintered tree trunks – Styx Branch, Trout Branch, Lester Prong, Alum Cave Creek. To get a glimpse of this, learn to identify yellow birch and look for groves of them along creeks.

After just a few minutes of hiking and rock-hopping, the Styx Branch valley began to open up and became an open avenue that was steep and rocky, but easy to maneuver. The rhododendron was not squeezing and filling in every unoccupied square inch of ground, which was a nice change of pace. There's probably some sort of topographical or botanical or historical reason why some valleys and slopes are full of rhody and other are not, but I've never been able to figure out why. But I'll gladly accept the breathing room as an unexpected, simple gift, a brief respite from the usual onslaught.

Less than an hour after we left the trail, we came to our main decision point of the day at 4,700' – left or right? Either route leads to its own wonderland, so there's no wrong choice here. We went right simply because... well, I don't know why. I guess one of us said, "Let's go right" and the other one said, "Okay." No debate. No drama. It was one of those "Whatever, Dude" moments when there are no agendas to push and no egos to defend, which is quite rare when you have two guys with a decision to make.

As we worked our way up to 48...49... 5000' there were several small tributaries feeding into Styx's main flow. Most of these small tributaries flow down from the right, so we tend to bear left at these junctions as we hug the east side of the ridge that splits the Right Branch from the Left Branch of Styx. These creek junctions can be frustrating because each one is a "fork in the road" where you have to decide whether to go left or right, and the right choice is not always obvious. On the other hand, these junctions can be liberating for exactly the same reason. After all, if your goal is to explore the wilderness, then there are no wrong choices, and "getting lost" is just another way of saying that you've explored new territory.

In fact, it's quite common on these off-trail treks for us to wander in places where we've never been, but we are rarely, if ever, *lost*. A lot of people think being lost means that you don't know where you are or you are not where you think you are, but that's only about 50% of the story. You are only truly, deeply, profoundly, 100% lost if you don't know *where to go next*. There are times that we've been in the depths of the mountains, isolated from the nearest trail or road, and we don't know exactly where we are, but that doesn't matter because we know that if we'll stay in this valley or on that ridge, we'll end up at a recognizable destination – Myrtle Point or the Appalachian Trail or campsite #31 or

215

the car. Whether in the Smokies or Yellowstone or Knoxville, it's nice to know where you are, but it's *essential* to know where to go next. If you don't know where to go to get to your destination or back to the car, then yes, you are lost. That rarely happens to us in the Smokies, mainly because we have a general idea of the lay of the land and its most prominent features, but also because every creekbed is like a path that leads back down to some familiar place. There is potential danger from slipping on a wet rock or stepping on a rattlesnake or tumbling down a steep, wet cascade, but getting truly lost is the least of our worries.

The main feature of the upper reaches of this east branch of Styx is the Climbing Wall – a long, steep cliff/cascade that is simply a scar where at some time in the past a heavy rain created a quick flush of water which scoured soil, rocks, shrubs, and trees from the cascading creekbed, exposing the bare rock that we now call the Climbing Wall. And, of course, to ascend the Climbing Wall, you climb... using hands and feet and a modest dose of good judgment. As is the case with many of these exposed rock cascades, there are some places you can go and some places that you can't. But the complicating factor is that just because you *can* climb up a section of the cliff doesn't necessarily mean that you *should*. Knowing the difference between *can* and *should* is the key, which makes climbing a wet, rocky cascade in the Smokies exactly like daily life – just because you can doesn't mean you should – one of those times when frolicking in the wilderness is a perfect metaphor for living a happy, meaningful life.

A lot of us in 21st century America need a refresher course in Can vs. Should because we apparently didn't learn it the first time around. Phones that enable us to successfully, efficiently ignore the people around us would be at the very top of my "Can But Shouldn't" list, right above weaponized anthrax, texting while driving, strip mining, racial segregation, suicide bombers, imperialism, the Electoral College, and backcountry user fees in the Smokies. I'll admit that sometimes it's nice to be able to ignore the people around us, but even a good thing can be taken too far. Just a few years ago, when I'd walk into the classroom at the school where I teach, the students would be laughing and talking with each other. Now most of them are sitting quietly, staring down at their phones, in their own little worlds. The few students who don't have smart phones or whose batteries are dead are usually just sitting quietly, alone in a room full of distracted people, being treated the way the people of Jesus' day treated lepers and prostitutes. I used to wonder why each generation of old folks would whine and complain about the direction that society is taking. Now I get it. I've joined that long, long tradition of folks who wonder where we're headed and what we're doing in this handbasket.

Unfortunately, very few of these folks will ever spend any quality time in the great outdoors because there are no electrical outlets there, so if they are going to learn the difference between *can* and *should*, they'll have to learn it somewhere else, but I can't imagine where – certainly not on TV or the mall or their phones, unless they accidentally stumble upon a "great moral lessons" website and unintentionally read some words from Jesus or Gandhi or Socrates or Buddha while they wait for their video game to load.

On the other hand, there's still hope. At some point during the Civil War the generals finally figured out that they *could* march their troops across the open field as they had in the Revolutionary War, but they *shouldn't* because rifles were more accurate at long range than the old muskets had been. Mixing hundred year old thinking with modern technology didn't work. It took a while, but the generals finally learned how to deal responsibly with the new technology by digging trenches and keeping their heads down. Maybe we'll figure out how to deal with the dilemmas that our modern technology has created for us, whether it be smartphones, drones, fracking, or WMDs.

So we each scrambled up the steep, rocky slope, each of us using his own judgment of what route would qualify as a *should*. Sometimes we had the same definitions and sometimes we didn't, but we both survived. And, as we had hoped, all this happened under the bright glare of the sun. Our jackets and long sleeves were in our packs where they belonged. The sky was as deep a blue as I have ever seen. In the shade the temperatures were a little above freezing. In the sun on the exposed rock, we wore T shirts.

One of the significant features of this type of trip up an exposed scar or cliff is that it sometimes is so steep that you need to stay focused on the rock and only the rock. Move hand and grasp. Next, move foot

217

and plant firmly. Next, move the other hand and grasp. Next, move the other foot.... These rocky climbs are not vertical, but they are at least 45° and often 60°, and they are sometimes long. It has never happened to me, but I suspect a long, sliding, tumble can cause just as much damage (and more pain while it is happening) as a vertical fall. You don't dwell on this fact, but it does form the background noise in your brain as you look for your next solid handhold. We wouldn't claim to be in the same club as Alex Honnold ascending Half Dome. (He's in a class all by himself: *Homo sapiens philolithic verticalis)*. But we are in a club consisting of only a few dozen avid, Smokies off-trailers who love a pretty day and a great view, but who also love an occasional challenge to our lungs, legs, and nerves.

Whenever we'd find a nice, level spot, we would turn around and look at the ridges and valleys behind us – in this case, it was Parton Peaks, NoName Ridge, Anakeesta Ridge… a wilderness playground on the rugged, southern side of Mt. Le Conte. And up above us was the main body of Mt. Le Conte herself, our ultimate destination. We still had over 1,000' of vertical elevation before we'd reach Myrtle Point, which would be hard but entertaining. "Work" in the best sense of the word. More rocky scars. More views. More sunshine and blue sky. More discerning *can't* vs. *can* vs. *should*.

On this day, I really struggled. Probably a combination of fighting a cold all week, eating too many sweets and hamburgers the past six months, and too many birthdays. As Greg sat on the rocky scar about 100' above me, I said, "I'll be there in about 45 minutes." He thought I was joking. I hoped I was joking. Forty minutes later I dragged myself alongside him and sat for a few minutes. He casually asked, "Did you bring your flashlight?" He was as subtle as possible, but we both knew the underlying message.

So I searched through my day pack: granola bars, micro-spikes, camera, MP3 player....

Greg asked, "What's that?"
"It's an MP3 player, but it's also a digital voice recorder."
"You use it to record your deep thoughts on these trips?"
"Yep."

218

"Don't use it much, do you?"
"Never."

… rain jacket, toilet paper… and flashlight. On these trips I always bring a flashlight because I seem to struggle more often than I used to. My mojo on any given day is the wild card that determines whether our off-trail hike will be an efficient adventure that ends before sunset or a long, tiring slog that ends with our hiking back to the car in the dark. In recent years, a flashlight is as necessary as food, water, and toilet paper. I hate being the weak link in the chain, but I'm sort of getting used to it.

In fact, because I was feeling old and rickety, and had been for several months, this trip was the first time I had the thought: Will this be the last time I make this trip? Or, if it's not, when will my last trip happen, and will I know it's my last trip while I'm on it, or will I only realize it years later? Those are sad, sad questions that never occurred to me until the last couple of years. I'm beginning to realize that maybe I'm mortal after all and might not live forever.

I remember the last time I saw my mother or my Uncle Merle. They were old and sick, and we all knew their end was near, but I never considered the fact that they were having these thoughts about me: Will this be the last time I ever see Greg? And, they had undoubtedly been thinking those kinds of thoughts about a lot of things: Is this the last time I'll see my grandkids? Is this the last time I'll spend a weekend in our cottage at Middle Bass? Is this my last Christmas? My last trip to the mountains?

That's a dark cloud that casts a gloomy shadow, and while I don't live under that shadow on a permanent basis, I do catch a glimpse of it every now and then… like today, on Styx Branch. If this was my last Styx trip, do I want to know it now, or do I want to realize five years from now that our mid-December trip five years earlier was my last time on Styx? At the Climbing Wall I almost told Greg that I had gone as far as I could, and I'd head back to the car while he went on to Myrtle Point. I was feeling that bad. But I was afraid that if I did that, then I'd never come back and do this trip again. This would become my final, aborted trip to Styx, and I just couldn't bear the thought of that.

I guess that means I'll know when I've done my last Styx trip – it will be the time I try it and can't finish it because I'm just not physically able any more. Yes, that's the way it will be. This wasn't my last trip because I'll try it again and again until I can only get half way up and have to turn back, and then I'll know. It will be a somber moment, but at least I'll know when it happens, and I'll be walking back by myself, so I'll have time to think about it, to recognize what has just happened, and to come to terms with it.

I just noticed that as I wrote those last few sentences, the music that was playing on my computer was Ashokan Farewell. You probably don't recognize the name, but if you are old enough you'll remember the Ken Burns PBS program *The Civil War*, and you'll remember the segment called "Honorable Manhood" in which Sullivan Ballou writes a letter to his wife, speaking of love and duty and prophesying his death at the Battle of Bull Run ("Dear Sarah,… my love for you is deathless… how great a debt we owe to those who went before us… my love of country comes over me like a strong wind… when my last breath escapes me on the battlefield, it will whisper your name.…"), and you'll remember the haunting violin music that played as the narrator read Ballou's letter. That's Ashokan Farewell, and that's the song that was playing as I wrote the previous paragraph, so perhaps I was under its haunting spell, and now that the song is over, I've come back to my senses. So, to mis-quote the combatants in *Gladiator*: "Someday I'll make my last trip to Styx… but not yet. Not yet."

After the Climbing Wall we were still in the scoured rock of the scar, but the incline was about 45°, maybe less, so we were able to revert to feet-only as we searched for rough spots to plant our feet as we zig-zagged our way up the fragile, broken Anakeesta rock face. We stopped often, to let me catch my breath but also to turn around and appreciate the sky and the open view that every landslide scar affords. It's the kind of moment of magnificence that will – if you have any sense of gratitude for life's simple gifts – bring tears to your eyes.

Eventually, the scar began to give way to soil, grass, and a young, fir forest which produces that "Christmas tree smell" that anyone who has ever had a real Christmas tree would recognize. There aren't many things that we encounter in the wilderness that remind us of our other,

220

civilized life – which is exactly as we'd like it to b⌐
the woods to escape the trappings of that other life
flying high overhead and the occasional, loud mo⌐
Gap Road, the most common artifact of civilizati⌐
the raw wilderness is something I would neve⌐
balloons. Maybe once every dozen trips we'll find a u⌐
from a birthday party or a football game hung on a branch or lying at the
edge of a creekbed. (If you ever release a helium-filled balloon, stop and
consider the fact that you are engaging in long distance littering, some of
which end up in the Smokies.) So, the Christmas tree smell is the one,
conspicuous exception to these occasional reminders of civilization. It's
a pleasant reminder of a pleasant part of our civilized life. Thankfully,
this smell of balsam was our only reminder of civilization on this trip.
No loud motorcycles, no party balloons.

After threading our way through the fragrant, fir forest, we arrived
at Myrtle Point about an hour before sunset. Or, I should say, I arrived
about an hour before sunset. Harrell arrived about an hour and a half
before sunset. It was cold and windy, so we donned our winter apparel
for the first time since the Climbing Wall several hours earlier. I had
never really thought of it this way before, but Myrtle Point is the
epicenter of our Smokies playground. From it we can see from
Greenbrier Pinnacle to the Appalachian Trail to Charlies Bunion to Mt.
Kephart to the Chimneys to Peregrine Peak, a huge bowl of ridges and
valleys, places that have become almost sacred in their meaning to our
lives. It's undoubtedly places like this that gave birth to the phrase
"mountain top experience."

As we sat on the open rocks of Myrtle Point, we had the same
conversation we always have when we sit here, based on an eclectic
blend of Henry David Thoreau, the Shakers, and John Muir, with a dash
of Sheryl Crow and a guy I met at a Waffle House: To live simply is to
live well; that man is richest whose pleasures are the simplest; it's not
getting what you want, it's wanting what you've got; luck favors the
backbone, not the wishbone; if you'll put yourself in a position for good
things to happen, you'll be pleasantly surprised how often they do.

Instead of sitting at home, wishing for a good day, we had risked
going to the mountains on a cold, December morning. And, once again,

.vored backbone. Something good had happened, as it often does .e wilderness, even in the cold days of December.

As I think about it, the theme of that conversation at Myrtle Point has become a prominent theme in my life, now more than ever. Most of life's best gifts to us are *simple* gifts, and one of the keys to happiness is to learn to be satisfied with life's simple, wholesome pleasures, like spending time with friends and family, or an azure sky in December, or layers of blue ridges piling up to the horizon, or green ridges turning a warm gold from the light of the setting sun, or sitting alone in the evening on the Chimney Tops, or self-baptizing in Drinkwater Pool, or boiling water for hot tea in a cozy nook in the Cat Stairs, or seeing nothing but tree-tops while crouched atop Mill Creek Cascade, or watching a native brook trout take your Elk Hair Caddis in the musical waters of Raven Fork, or rebuilding a collapsed cairn on Porters Creek manway, or hearing the call of a peregrine falcon at the Pyramid, or ... well... a hundred other simple pleasures that the Smokies afford us.

Thankfully, these are things that require an investment of time and energy, but not money. They are gifts that we all can afford because they are gifts that are simple, gifts that are free.

Epilogue

More Stuff You Might Want to Know

My original plan for this Epilogue was to add more details about precise elevations, GPS coordinates, etc. However, Greg Harrell is working on a book that will give a lot of specific information about most of these routes, plus others not mentioned here. So, I'll let him fill in the gaps. (He delights in the joy of details to a degree unfathomable to normal human beings.) However, I have posted more information on my blog at *www.greghoover.blogspot.com*. Search "Paths Less Traveled." I've provided an abbreviated version of that information below.

Getting Started

Your first off-trail jaunt should be on a trail. Yes, there are actually quite a few old trails in the park that are no longer officially maintained, but they are still clearly defined by the footsteps of that 1% who still know about them. These are trails that are easy to find and easy to follow because they are very obvious – once you know where they are. But you can't discover them by looking at the park's maps and literature because the NPS won't divulge these secrets easily. You have to ask the right people in the right way – rangers, Backcountry Office employees, knowledgeable friends, Google, GoSmokies.

Here are a few to get you started: Kalanu Prong (near the start of the road to Ramsey Cascades), Greenbrier Pinnacle (a decommissioned trail off Ramsey Cascades trail), Thunderhead Prong (at the end of the road to Tremont), Rhododendron Creek (near Greenbrier ranger station).

If you try any old paths like this, you should probably do it in the summer, after there's been enough foot traffic to maintain the path. Definitely don't do these in the late fall or winter when there's a carpet of leaves or snow on the forest floor which will hide the path.

When you are ready to go 100% pathless, rock-hop up Trout Branch to the train wreck and beyond. You can't possibly get lost.

223

Significant Omissions

One unforgivable omission in this book is Mt. Cammerer on the eastern tip of the park. It's a wonderland, and the lookout tower at the top is old and iconic, but I simply ran out of space. Without going into detail, I'll just say this: The Groundhog Ridge manway begins on Hwy 32 beyond the town of Cosby, about 4.7 miles past the Cosby post office. The rest is up to you.

Other omissions, both forgivable and unforgivable:
- Parton Peaks: hop off Alum Cave trail at Arch Rock, and scramble up to the ridge above Arch Rock, and follow the ridge up. (If you are using the standard, USGS topo map, Arch Rock is shown in the wrong location.)
- Anakeesta Ridge is also accessible from the *north* via Alum Cave Creek (via Alum Cave trail, but the split in the creek is a bit hidden from the trail). There's a magnificent set of scars (we call it "Anakeesta Canyon;" at 35.6327, 83.4197 you are pretty much in the center of this canyon) that can take you to the top of Anakeesta Ridge.
- NoName Ridge: follow Alum Cave Creek; there's a Y shaped scar at 35.6354, 83.4262 which we use as the entrance and exit ramp.
- Roaring Fork, on the *north* side of Mt. Le Conte: Hike up Trillium Gap trail to Grotto Falls. At Grotto Falls, scramble around to the top of the falls and follow the creek (Roaring Fork) to the top of Mt. Le Conte. This is a big trip with lots of elevation gain and a long hike down Trillium Gap trail at the end of the day.
- There's an interesting, steep "bowl" on Sugarland Mountain – just west of the Chimneys and directly south of the Chimneys Picnic area. I've only been on it once, but we called it the Jumpoff's Little Sister because it was steep and very Jumpoff-ish in some places. Start at the Chimneys picnic area and head south into the bowl, then top out on the Sugarland Mountain

224

trail. Honestly, I don't know why this part of the park doesn't get more attention from us off-trailers. It deserves a closer look.

Jumpoff & Sharp Edges

I mentioned in my Jumpoff story that there was no place one could stand and see the full Jumpoff Cascade, which is true. However, there is a spot a hundred or so yards down from the 4,700' split from which one can see the lower half of the cascade, and it is impressive. Getting to this spot requires climbing up the point of a side ridge on Horseshoe Mountain, and either climbing a tree or tightrope walking along a blowdown that reaches out into thin air. On a recent trip to this viewing spot, we walked along the airborne blowdown and were looking south toward the cascade, but the sun was right behind Mt. Kephart and was blinding us. As we shielded our eyes and tried to stand in the shadows of nearby trees, Ken Wise finally was able to focus in on the full extent of the view – the lower half of the Cascade came into focus. His jaw dropped, and all he could do was to stand there and mumble, "Oh my gosh, Oh my gosh." Then finally he shouted, "Oh my gosh! Can you guys see that? Oh my gosh!" Ken has seen a lot of Smoky Mountain terrain. He's not easily impressed. There, near the base of the Jumpoff, he was impressed to the point of pointing and babbling. It was awesome!

Barnes & Cat Stairs

From the Barnes home site: Behind the chimney a path goes north to a spot on Copeland Divide where you can make a sharp right turn and follow this ridge up above the Cat Stairs to the top of Greenbrier Pinnacle. The GPS location of this sharp right turn is 35.7259, 83.3619.

As you could perhaps tell by the story, we rarely hike this Copeland Divide route anymore. We always go to the Barnes site, then drop down into Bird Branch (follow the flow of water emanating from the oak tree spring) and follow one of its branches up to the cliffs.

225

Three Sisters

For most of our favorite spots in the park, we have a "standard" off-trail route, and the Three Sisters is no exception. This chapter, however, didn't describe our standard route that we've adopted, partly because it didn't fit well in the story and partly because we can't agree on the route. Greg Harrell would say his standard route starts and ends at the Porters Creek trailhead. I, on the other hand, prefer an easier route which starts and ends at Newfound Gap. More info is on my blog.

The Chimneys (plus the Third Chimney)

"Alone on the Chimneys" describes a great plan for visiting the Chimneys without the crowds, but it doesn't describe any off-trail routes. There are several, some of which begin at the Chimneys Picnic area, but our standard Chimneys off-trail route starts at the tunnel just down the road from the Chimneys trailhead. More details, including a route to a Third Chimney and its 3' rock cairn, are on my blog.

Styx Branch

The route that I describe in the Styx chapter requires that you bear right at the fork in Styx at 4,700', then left at 4,850' and left at 5,050'. This is my favorite route, but you can go left at 4,700'; any creek or ravine will lead to the top... eventually.

Post Script

As I am putting the final touches on this book, in fact, as I am typing these final words in the last days of November, 2016, about 11,000 acres in the Smokies (i.e., 2% of the park's total land mass) and much of Gatlinburg have burned. Local residents will undoubtedly speak of the Fire of 2016 for generations. It is tragic and unprecedented in this region.

After several months of extreme drought, wildfires were popping up throughout East Tennessee, including several in the Smokies, one of which was the Chimneys 2 Fire which was first reported on November 23. According to the latest, tentative reports, sudden, strong winds on November 28 expanded this small, smoldering fire on the northeast slopes of the Chimneys and blew embers down the Sugarlands valley and into Gatlinburg. Several people died in the flames. Many homes and businesses and jobs were lost. Lives were changed.

The heart of the national park is closed to visitors, so I haven't yet witnessed the damage. Thankfully, last night and today have been wet. Our local area has received several inches of rain in the past 24 hours – the first significant rain since a couple of quick thunderstorms in August. The rain may have saved the rest of Gatlinburg and the Smokies, but more rain is needed; fires are still smoldering.

Perhaps some of the stories in this book will be descriptions of what the park was like *before* the fire. I'll leave it to later books and blogs, maybe by me, maybe my others, to provide the *after* picture. The most likely change is that the shrubs (and maybe trees) on the Chimneys will have burned away, perhaps not permanently but certainly for the near future. Also, the Third Chimney that I mentioned earlier in this Epilogue may become a reality because of this fire. It and the ridge leading down to it may now be bare rock like the two Chimney Tops and the ridge that connects them.

Thankfully, ecosystems and people are surprisingly resilient. Out of the ashes, the Smokies and its people will rise again.

Final Words and Acknowledgements:

I write an occasional Smokies column called "Rivers and Ridges" in our small, local newspaper, the Jefferson County (Tennessee) *Standard Banner*. I post all my articles (plus a little extra information) on my blog: *www.greghoover.blogspot.com*. Some of these articles are found in one form or another in this book, but there are also stories in those articles that don't appear in this book, and vice versa. I also have written another book, *Hallowed Hills, Holy Waters*, that has both blogged and non-blogged stories.

You can find me at the social networking site called GoSmokies (http://gosmokies.knoxnews.com). My email is gphoover@outlook.com.

Finally, a few words of thanks. First, to Dale Gentry of the *Standard Banner* for giving me the chance to write in his paper and for giving me permission to include some of that material in this book. Also, thanks to my hiking partners – Greg Harrell, Keith Oakes, and Charlie Roth – for the fine times we've shared together and for unwittingly providing the material for these stories. Also, thanks to members and friends from the Smoky Mountains Hiking Club: Ed Fleming, Ken Wise, the Page sisters (the "other" three sisters), and the others with whom I've shared bearways, rhododendron hells, landslide scars, and greenbrier tangles. Finally, thanks to my dear, patient wife, Phyllis, for her love and forbearance. I hike and fish with her blessing because she is a kind soul who understands how much I need the outdoors, and she surely enjoys the peace and quiet while I'm gone.

About the Author

Greg Hoover has lived in Jefferson City, Tennessee since 1987. He teaches Sociology at Carson-Newman University but retirement is imminent. He received his BA from Atlanta Christian College and PhD from the University of Georgia. He and his wife, Phyllis, have two grown kids, Melissa (with son-in-law, John) and Seth, and two grand-daughters, Megan and Julia, who call him "Grampy."

Photo Credits

Front Cover:
- The Jumpoff of Mount Kephart with a dusting of snow, by Greg Harrell

Back Cover:
- Best View of Le Conte from Cat Stairs, by Greg Hoover
- View of Falcon Cliffs (and my feet) from the Best Lunch Spot, by Greg Hoover